FIRE UNDER THE SEA

FIRE UNDER THE SEA

THE DISCOVERY OF THE MOST EXTRAORDINARY ENVIRONMENT ON EARTH—VOLCANIC HOT SPRINGS ON THE OCEAN FLOOR

Joseph Cone

WILLIAM MORROW AND COMPANY, INC.

New York

It is the policy of William Morrow and Company, Inc., and its imprints and affiliates, recognizing the importance of preserving what has been written, to print the books we publish on acid-free paper, and we exert our best efforts to that end.

Library of Congress Cataloging-in-Publication Data

Cone, Joseph.
    Fire under the sea : the discovery of the most extraordinary environment on earth—volcanic hot springs on the ocean floor / Joseph Cone.
      p. cm.
    ISBN 0-688-09834-7
    1. Hydrothermal vents.   I. Title.
GB1198.C66   1991
551.2′3—dc20   90-15574
                                                        CIP

Printed in the United States of America

First Edition

1   2   3   4   5   6   7   8   9   10

BOOK DESIGN BY PAUL CHEVANNES

MAP BY AMY CHARRON

In memory of my parents,
Marie Cefarelli Cone and Joseph M. Cone

Acknowledgments

No book of this sort gets written alone. Many people helped me, and I am grateful to them.

The book would not have been written at all if it had not been for the encouragement and support of the administration and staff of Oregon Sea Grant at Oregon State University. I particularly want to express my thanks to William Q. Wick, Sea Grant director during the time the book was written, James Larison, director of communications, and Sandy Ridlington, managing editor. Their continuing interest, even indulgence, through the years of this project made seeing it through possible.

For my agent, Robert Lescher, I have a special gratitude. His kindness to me and his belief in this book were more than I dared hope for.

I am deeply indebted to Maria Guarnaschelli, my editor at William Morrow, in particular for her insight and enthusiasm.

Friendly thanks also to two editors at the *Oregonian* newspaper, Jack Hart and Richard Hill, who worked closely with me on feature stories for the newspaper that later became parts of chapters.

Most of the book's contents are the result of interviews with many scientists whose professional lives have been dedicated, to one degree or another, to the study of the seafloor hot springs. A list of scientists interviewed for the book appears separately. Here I want to acknowledge individually those who took the time to review the manuscript and suggest corrections. Naturally, any errors that remain are mine.

The scientists with the NOAA Vents Program in Newport, Oregon, were my closest sources and advisers. Steve Hammond, program director, encouraged the book from the beginning. Bob Embley and Chris Fox were also especially generous with their time and information.

I am indebted to many scientists at Oregon State University for their reviews, starting with the university's president, John Byrne, and its vice-president for graduate studies, research, and international programs, George Keller—both of them well-known oceanographers. Faculty of the College of Oceanography who reviewed chapters were Bob Duncan, Jack Dymond, LaVerne Kulm, Carlos Lopez, and Charlie Miller. Thanks also to Bob Collier, Lew Hogan, and Paul Komar for their contributions of information.

Other members of the scientific community who reviewed the manuscript, and for whose comments I am indebted, were Bob Ballard, Robert Becker, Colleen Cavanaugh, Jack Corliss, Brent Dalrymple, John Delaney, Jody Deming, John Edmond, Jim Franklin, Mark Holmes, Donald Hussong, Holger Jannasch, Ian Jonasson, Clive Lister, Meredith Jones, Bruce Malfait, Janet Morton, Bill Normark, Len Ramp, Maria Restrepo, George Somero, Verena Tunnicliffe, Jerry van Andel, and Fred Vine.

Scientist and historian William Glen graciously shared insights gained from his special perspective.

Ralph Hollis, *Alvin* pilot, and former ambassador James Malone also reviewed portions of the manuscript.

Several writers who specialize in science writing also critiqued sections of the manuscript, and I gained from them many helpful suggestions. Two of these writers went considerably beyond marginal comments, offering advice and encouragement at crucial times. I thank my good friends Dick Bell and Glen Gibbons for this. I also appreciate the others who reviewed parts of the manuscript: colleagues Andy Duncan, Dan Guthrie, and Carol Savonen of Oregon State University, Richard Strickland of Washington Sea Grant, and David Perlman of the *San Francisco Chronicle*.

I thank Ned Ostenso, former director of the National Sea Grant Office, for his help getting me to sea, and Bill Merrill for being his unique, encouraging, multifarious self.

As anyone who has lived a long creative project knows, some qualities of the immediate environment make all the difference between merely surviving the event and growing from the opportunity. For her patience and for her good humor through many nights and weekends of my thinking and writing, I gladly thank my wife, Tylar.

—Joseph Cone

CONTENTS

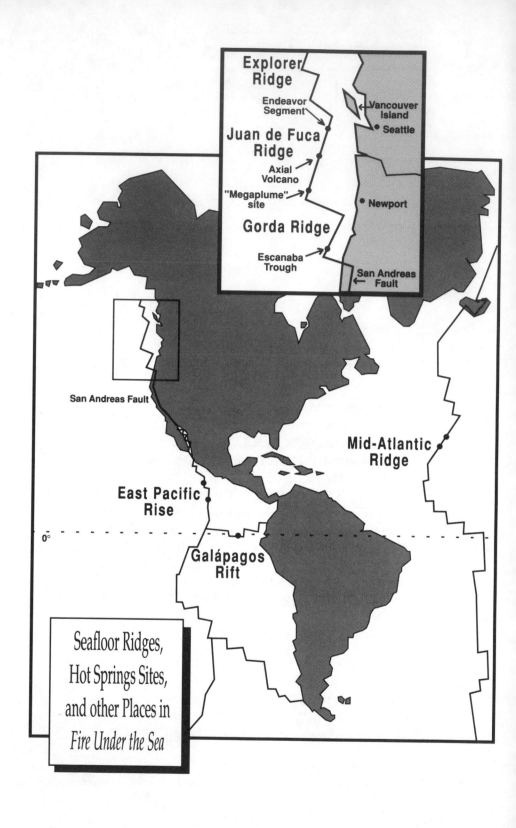

Explorer
Ridge

Endeavor
Segment

Vancouver
Island

Seattle

Juan de Fuca
Ridge

Axial
Volcano

"Megaplume"
site

Newport

Gorda Ridge

Escanaba
Trough

San Andreas
Fault

San Andreas Fault

Mid-Atlantic
Ridge

East Pacific
Rise

0°

Galápagos
Rift

Seafloor Ridges,
Hot Springs Sites,
and other Places in
Fire Under the Sea

Chronology

1920s: Alfred Wegener revises his theory of continental drift in *The Origin of Continents and Oceans*. The idea that the continents have moved across the surface of the earth through geological time achieves wide discussion but is rejected by most scientists. The idea goes underground until the 1950s while other scientists develop the tools and the insights that can refine it and make it acceptable.

1950s: Bruce Heezen, Marie Tharp, and Maurice Ewing of Columbia University are mainly responsible for the first detailed map diagrams of the ocean ridge system, which is revealed with the use of echo sounders. The ridge system is a chain of underwater volcanic mountains which extends more than 30,000 miles around the globe. Though out of sight, it is the dominant feature on the surface of the planet.

1960: In seeking to explain the features of the ocean ridges, Harry Hess of Princeton University proposes that the seafloor is slowly spreading away from them, driven by currents of heat inside the earth. Hess's spreading seafloor would carry the continents on their backs, thereby giving a mechanism to continental drift.

1961: Alan Cox, Richard Doell, and Brent Dalrymple of the U.S. Geological Survey publish the first time scale based on the change in magnetic field orientation observed in rocks from different periods of geologic time. This work has little apparent relation to oceanographic concerns, and few oceanographers notice.

1963: Fred Vine at Cambridge University conceives of a connection between seafloor spreading and the magnetic reversals noted by Cox, Doell, and Dalrymple. Vine proposes that previously unexplained variations in the magnetic signals of seafloor rocks can be explained as the signature of different geological epochs—epochs of normal and reverse magnetism. He suggests that the pattern of reversals is linked to the spreading apart of the seafloor. Vine's initial essay receives little attention.

1965: Vine and J. Tuzo Wilson of the University of Toronto refine Vine's earlier proposal in a new essay focusing on a small ridge off the northwest coast of the United States, which Wilson names the Juan de Fuca Ridge. Other scientists take notice of the idea and begin to put it to the test.

1966: Compelling new evidence collected from the floor of the Pacific Ocean convinces many scientists that seafloor spreading as described by Vine and Wilson is a reality. Wilson champions the idea that the recognition of seafloor spreading represents a revolution in earth sciences, comparable in significance to the earlier revolution of Copernicus and Galileo.

late 1960s: The new scientific worldview of plate tectonics quickly develops out of the concept of seafloor spreading. The new view envisions the surface of the earth as composed of a small number of rigid plates, moving slowly relative to each other. The plates are created by lava welling up at seafloor spreading ridges; they are destroyed at seafloor trenches. Where they collide, earthquakes are common.

early 1970s: Clive Lister of the University of Washington and Jack Corliss of Oregon State University independently publish papers predicting the occurrence of hot springs at ridges where the seafloor is spreading.

1975: American and French scientists dive on the Mid-Atlantic Ridge to see firsthand a seafloor spreading center. Robert Ballard of the Woods Hole Oceanographic Institution is largely responsible for the successful scientific use of the submersible *Alvin*. No hot springs are observed. Following this expedition, another is proposed to test whether hot springs will be found. Circumstantial evidence indicates they may occur on the Galapagos Rift off Ecuador.

1977: The first seafloor hot springs are discovered at the Galapagos Rift in an expedition led by Corliss and Ballard. Not only are fundamental insights gained about geological and chemical processes in the ocean on this cruise, but the scientists observe animal communities living in the seafloor vents that are totally unexpected and unique on earth.

1978–79: More dives along the East Pacific Rise reveal the existence of superheated hot springs and the complex mineral deposits (polymetallic sulfides) which they produce. William Normark becomes the leader of the U.S. Geological Survey's efforts to find such deposits on the ridges off the northwestern United States, the Gorda Ridge and Juan de Fuca. John Baross of Oregon State confirms that chemosynthesis, not photosynthesis, is the foundation for life at the hot springs.

1980: Jack Corliss, John Baross, and Sarah Hoffman publish a scientific paper which argues that life on earth began at the seafloor hot springs.

1981: Revelations continue as Alexander Malahoff of the National Oceanic and Atmospheric Administration (NOAA) leads a series of dives on the Galapagos Rift which discovers massive deposits of sulfides. The Reagan administration takes notice and begins planning to exploit such deposits under U.S. jurisdiction.

1983: Ronald Reagan proclaims the U.S. Exclusive Economic Zone, asserting sovereignty over the seabed to 200 miles offshore. James Watt proposes mineral exploration of the Gorda Ridge. The proposal is met with environmental concern in Oregon and California and apparent indifference by the mining industry. Further research is funded to assess the mineral potential of the Gorda.

1984: First *Alvin* dives made on Gorda and Juan de Fuca ridges by NOAA researchers, led by Malahoff. No minerals are found on the

Gorda, but hot springs and minerals are observed on the Juan de Fuca, which lies outside the U.S. EEZ. NOAA establishes a program dedicated to studying the effects of hot springs venting on the ocean.

1985: First listing of hot springs animals reveals that the majority are previously unknown to science and represent new biological species, genera, and families. Meredith Jones of the Smithsonian Institution proposes that the strange tube worms are even more unlike any other organisms; he classifies them as a new phylum.

1986: Massive sulfides are discovered on the Gorda Ridge, and quantities may be huge. But the deposits lie under two miles of water. The mining industry still shows little interest in mining the Gorda, and the government abandons its leasing plan.

1988: Concentrated gold deposits are recovered from the caldera of Axial Volcano, on the Juan de Fuca. Attention of scientists moves from understanding surface features of the hot springs systems to understanding them in three dimensions and over time. A connection between seafloor ridge volcanic eruptions and climate change is proposed.

1989: Robert Ballard uses the remotely operated submersible *Jason* to explore hot springs in the Mediterranean. Ballard envisions a new era of oceanic "telepresence," of exploring the seafloor with cameras and robots rather than with humans in submersibles.

1990: A new decade of research begins with provocative developments. U.S. academic research on ridges becomes focused by an ambitious interdisciplinary program begun under the auspices of the U.S. National Science Foundation. A new French and American research expedition is planned for the Mid-Atlantic Ridge. A study suggests that mass extinctions of life in the oceans during geologic time are associated with increased hot springs activity.

CHAPTER ONE

TOWARD
AN UNKNOWN REGION

Steve Hammond sat in the dining room of the research ship *Atlantis II*, thinking about diving to the bottom of the ocean in a tiny submarine. In an hour he would be going to a location where no one had ever been before. It had started him thinking early this morning.

He sat alone. Wisps of steam rose off his coffee as he watched the first sunlight touch the Pacific. He thought about his life, about his work, about how all the time he had been a marine geologist in a way led up to this moment. If all went well, this day he would see something he had imagined and studied for years, but had never seen for himself—active volcanoes on the seafloor.

It still astonished him that they could be found at all at the bottom of the cold ocean, pumping out hot lava from deep inside the earth. He understood very well that they were there; he worked with the small group of scientists who had discovered and mapped these volcanoes off the northern California coast. But that he might see them, see this display of the earth's primal, hidden forces first-hand, made him feel a kind of awe. And made him, he admitted to himself, just a bit nervous.

He was forty-two years old and had been an ocean scientist for twenty years, and this would be his first dive in a submersible. That in itself was not so surprising. Most ocean scientists never get in one at all. To obtain the information they want they may not need to.

Today a researcher can find out a great deal about the ocean by lowering a variety of electronic instruments over the side of a ship at the surface. Sometimes marine geologists, the specialists in the sea-floor, don't even have to go to sea. Satellites can give them certain kinds of images of the ocean floor that there's no better way to get.

For some scientists, though, the sophisticated electronic instruments were fine as far as they went, but they didn't go far enough. Yes, certainly, you could admire remote-controlled drones for their precision, their capabilities, the data they brought back. But the Voyage of the Instruments, these scientists felt, shouldn't be all there was.

No machine, no matter how sophisticated, could replace a human observer, they argued. No machine could make sense of a place as a human could, as something more than data, as something whole unto itself. And only a trained observer could begin to decipher the importance of a place in the larger, infinitely more complex whole of this grand exception in our universe, the mysterious, dynamic, ocean-bathed, living earth. Humans needed to go to the bottom of the sea.

That was the argument. It had its points, and Steve Hammond believed it. He had taken the instruments, the best there were, and coaxed every last bit of information out of them until they let him visualize landforms in the sea that had never actually been seen. But now, with his maps and a submersible, it was possible to go to this eternally dark world of the seafloor and see it for himself. Shed some light on it, he told himself. He wanted to. Today, though, might not be the day.

Sure, he liked diving, of a sort. He enjoyed scuba diving in coral reefs, poking around with the colorful tropical fish. He even liked the idea of adventure just fine. It was the reality of squeezing into an oversized metal can and dropping out of sight that made his head hurt.

To begin with, there had been the whole business of going to the bathroom.

He had thought it was totally crazy. Apparently you were expected not to relieve yourself during the dive.

Here you were in the middle of the Pacific Ocean, going off on this potentially dangerous mission. First you stayed down inside the sub for twelve hours. *Twelve* hours. Then you were to come up, calmly walk across the deck, chat with the crew . . . and then, only then, go to the head. That's what Hammond thought; and he had to wonder.

He had read about the astronauts on Skylab, how they had managed their bodily necessities while floating upside down, under zero gravity. He hoped the *Alvin* crew cabin had some kind of arrangement; it wouldn't need to be anything nearly as exotic.

He was probably just being anxious, he told himself; there was no doubt a simple solution. But just in case, he had developed a plan to try to keep his needs limited. He had spent a good part of the day before, July 9, 1984, helping to fix the ship's position some 120 miles off Crescent City, California. But he had also taken himself to the head more often than he actually needed to. You couldn't be overprepared.

Then last night, at the predive briefing, Hammond found out how the submersible actually worked. Diving was going to be quite an experience, he concluded. This was a sub with a style of its own.

For something that was going to carry humans around in its belly, the *Alvin* didn't look especially biological. Twenty-five feet long and weighing eighteen tons, the body looked like a swollen bathtub with a World War II submarine conning tower perched on the front end. The conning tower, or "sail," as it was oddly called, was just a narrow entryway down into the pressurized sphere, where the crew were carried.

When Hammond had lowered his five feet seven inches into the unlighted sphere for the briefing, he found Ralph Hollis, the pilot, sitting with his back to the instrument panel, clipboard on lap. He had met Hollis briefly before on the *Atlantis*, and he had taken him to be a shy, reserved, unprepossessing technician. Nice enough, but sort of gray. Here, Hollis looked different. Sitting cross-legged, a corona of tiny colored lights surrounding him, Hollis looked like some casual Buddha of technology.

Hammond, feeling like a novice, took a seat on the cushioned deck facing the other man, only a couple of feet away. Everything, he noticed, was only a couple of feet away. A big man would scarcely have been able to lie down in the crew cabin. And standing up was easy only in the center of the sphere, under the hatch.

Hammond shifted on the cushioned deck, trying to get comfortable in the new dimensions.

"Just one thing I want to know, Ralph," he said, posing his question. "Do you go to the bathroom in this tub, or do you hold it?"

Hollis allowed himself a small smile.

"Number two," he said, "you'll probably want to hold." His voice was deadpan.

"For number one"—he reached onto one of the back equipment shelves—"we use these."

"Human Element Range Extenders we call them—HERE," he said. Hollis handed him a quart plastic bottle with a funnel top that twisted open and closed. Hammond laughed. The voyage could go on.

Hollis had gone on to talk about what he called the "safety features" of the *Alvin*, which he livened up with anecdotes about the sub's history.

The sub had not had a fatal accident in its twenty years of operation. That was good. It had been in some pretty iffy positions, though, Hollis said. Once it had slipped off *Lulu*, its mother ship, and sunk 5,000 feet. The two scientists and pilot on board got *one* chance to get out when it rolled in the waves. They did. The *Alvin* wasn't recovered until a year later.

And there was the sub's very first mission, in 1966. The sub had attempted to find an H-bomb a B-52 had dropped into the Mediterranean by accident. The bomb hadn't exploded, and the Navy had to get it back. After weeks of searching, the *Alvin* found the bomb and attempted to hoist it, but the twenty-megaton-yield deadweight turned ornery and slipped free of the hoist cable. Everyone in the sub and up on the surface held his breath. But the bomb just rolled down deeper into the sea. The crew got it back, "eventually," Hollis said.

The *Alvin*'s "primary life-support system" was the crew cabin, maintained at a constant one atmosphere pressure, the pressure of sea level. The sphere was two to four inches of titanium alloy, lighter and stronger than steel and welded in precise hemispheres. The Navy, which owned the sub, had tested it out. The tests, conducted at the Navy's submarine lab in Annapolis, satisfied their engineers that the titanium belly wouldn't implode at 4,000 meters—wouldn't buckle and collapse and turn the crew into sardines in a crumpled can, sealed at a pressure 400 times normal. The Navy rated the *Alvin* for operating at depths of up to 4,000 meters—13,000 feet—making it the deepest-diving submersible used for research in the United States. In 1984 it was twenty years old.

Hammond's dive that morning would take him to at least 3,500 meters, assuming the depths he had helped calculate were correct. Three thousand five hundred meters was just over two miles. As he toyed with his breakfast eggs, not really eating them, Hammond thought about the Styrofoam mannequin head that some joker had put on the outside of the sub during a dive on another research cruise. It had become the size of one of those shrunken heads from some cannibal ritual.

Abruptly, Alex Malahoff stuck his head inside the door of the galley. Malahoff was chief scientist on the research cruise and Hammond's companion on the dive this morning. That is, *would* be, Malahoff's face said, if Steve got moving.

He paused. "See you there, Steve," he said.

Hammond put down his coffee mug and went out to the men's room.

Out on the deck the submersible's technicians were making final preparations for the dive. All of his personal belongings had been given to Hollis the night before, so Hammond ambled empty-handed across the deck into the *Alvin*'s hangar. Giving all your gear to the pilot was part of procedure; the pilot approved everything that went on board.

Who knows, Hammond mused, maybe Hollis had nixed the *Chariots of Fire* cassette. Maybe he would think the title was too sensational, that it would make a bad omen. As he walked over the catwalk to the conning tower, he heard a thud underneath him. The technicians were placing 900 pounds of steel weights onto the sides of the *Alvin* to make the sub sink, like a stone.

Hammond paused, halfway to the sail.

A laugh rose from the opposite side of the sub. A couple of the crew, wearing goofy T-shirts and manic grins, had just unstuck their noses from the outside of Alex Malahoff's port window. From the looks on their faces, Malahoff inside had done something goofy in reply.

Suddenly Hammond just wanted to stay out there, under the sun, watching the water shine.

Lake Quivera. He thought about driving out to Quivera, outside of Kansas City, with his rented scuba gear. In his father's Ford pickup, 1958. He had waded right in the very first time, gone straight down to the bottom.

Coming out, he saw the high school girls in their swimsuits on the beach watching him. The sun was shining hot. His black wet suit glistened.

Now with his feet on the ladder inside the sail, he took a last slow look around. Out beyond the stern, a light wind was rippling the Pacific into foam. With a shrug of his shoulders, Hammond stepped down into the sphere.

Inside, Hollis was finishing the checkout. "Glad you could make it," he said, over his shoulder. Hammond went to his bench, found his gym bag with his gear. Extra socks, sweater, gloves, sandwiches, milk. Everything was there. He looked a second time, absentmindedly.

Anyone, he told himself, would probably think twice about diving in a tiny submarine two miles down to the bottom of the ocean. Perhaps into a volcano, no less. He had the impulse to laugh, but it sounded wild now, wrong.

You climb into a small capsule and drop out of sight, to a place where nobody could come get you. . . .

The shaft of sunlight coming down the sail abruptly snapped off. A technician had lowered the hatch cover. Hammond suddenly found it hard to breathe.

No sounds came from outside, which seemed to have vanished. The inside of the sub began wheezing softly.

"Air scrubbers," said Malahoff, looking at Hammond. Hammond was looking at the faces now pressed up against his own window. He smiled, absently.

The wheeze . . . it was only the sound of the carbon dioxide scrubber. For an instant, Hammond remembered diving, chasing the lemon fish deep into a coral reef. The sudden cold of the depth, the sound of the blood in his ears, the hiss of the scuba tank.

"Well, we're set." It was Hollis.

"You all set, Steve?"

For a long moment Hammond said nothing.

"You know, I'm not sure."

The sphere was small, so small it was hard to disentangle your thoughts from the others sitting in there, breathing in there with you.

"Why don't we just sit then, for a moment," said Hollis.

Hammond sat, feeling a little foolish, inept. This wasn't science—something you could sit down with coolly and work out.

His mind stuck on the three days. *If they got stuck on the bottom, the* Alvin *carried enough air for three days. And in the end, if they couldn't get free any other way, they could separate the pressure sphere from the rest of the sub and it would rise to the surface. Quickly. An uncontrolled ascent.*

A glorified body bag.

"You don't have to go today. We'll be diving again tomorrow and you can try it then, Steve."

Hammond looked at Malahoff.

It was as if he had never seen the man before. The hazy light coming in through the plastic port made a silhouette of his face, sculpting it oddly. A mask.

"What do you think, Steve?"

Hammond saw his hands on the bottom of the lake that first time, grabbing a handful of mud. Then, everything in slow motion, he saw his feet tuck under, then push off straight up toward the light, breaking the surface with his fist over his head. . . .

He looked around, straight at Hollis.

"Let's go," he said.

Hollis spoke on the intercom to the winch operator on deck, and with a lurch of metal the *Alvin* was hoisted off into the air, then lowered, and quickly released into the water.

Most people never get far enough under water to notice the change, but sunlight fades rather quickly as you descend into the ocean. Under the clearest conditions in the open ocean, it's gone completely at about 400 feet. Steve Hammond watched the light fade and the bubbles rise past his window. Watching, he became quiet.

The green gauze of plankton near the ocean surface had abruptly given way to a sparse fabric of fish, dimly shuttling away from the sub on their unknown courses.

When he could no longer see out, Hammond busied himself

checking the gear he would use to record his observations on the bottom. He loaded a roll of high-speed color film into his camera. He had twenty rolls with him, but he didn't know how many he would shoot. The videocamera mounted forward on the hull would give the scientists continuous coverage of the dive, but it wouldn't give total coverage. Hammond didn't want to be in the position of seeing unbelievable things and, upon returning to the surface, being unable to show others what he had seen. An explorer travels with the world looking over his shoulder.

Of course, the visibility would have to be good enough on the bottom for any of the photography to work. The bottom of the ocean is pitch-black—and who knew what else it would be like in the Escanaba Trough, the section of the Gorda Ridge to which they were going.

The maps they had made from the surface showed a deep floor at the bottom of a valley, with sheer cliffs looming above. The sub might kick up clouds of sediment that had been deposited in this valley as they went through it. They might find themselves among plumes of black smoke, rising out of volcanic chimneys in the valley floor. The *Alvin*'s strobe lights would put out enough illumination to at least momentarily penetrate most conditions of blackness, Hammond knew. With that he would have to be content.

He turned to things he could do something about. He cleaned the Nikon's lenses and loaded and advanced the film, checking that it wouldn't rip in the sprockets. He put on a heavy wool sweater. As the *Alvin* sank beyond the reach of the sun, it had gotten cooler inside the sub. The only heat was from the electronic instrument panels and the bodies of the crew.

Hammond had just picked up his tape recorder, looking for something to do with it, when Hollis let out a little cry of amusement.

"Get ready for some entertainment," he said. "I'm going to slow our descent a bit. Just flash the strobe out your port, Steve, will you?"

Hammond pressed the trigger switch, then whistled softly in surprise. Outside the port the light revealed something he would never have imagined. Hanging in the perpetual night of the ocean were tiny orbs of light.

He whistled again under his breath. "It's *amazing*," he said.

Squinting through the glass, Hammond could make out brighter and fainter points, which were arrayed, as if by magic, into unexpected patterns.

"Do you see the ones that are arranged in a kind of wheel, with spokes?"

Hollis turned and nodded.

"Some of them, they look oddly like constellations," Malahoff said. Out their windows the three looked again. The *Alvin* had passed into a zone of luminescent sea creatures. Some were zooplankton, colonies of tiny animals. Others were small fish. All of them pulsed to the sudden flash of light.

"God, I wonder what they think is going on," said Hammond. Hollis laughed.

With a grunt, Hammond flashed the strobe again, making it brilliantly light and then abruptly dark outside the window. The tiny lights outside glowed in response.

It was like falling through space. It was like a separate universe out there.

Hammond smiled, and flashed the strobe again.

The sub sank steadily now, and Hollis began to monitor their distance off the floor continuously. The approach to the bottom was always critical and hazardous, he knew. They had lowered a transponder, a signal beacon, to the floor the day before, and when Hollis sent down an electronic pulse on the right frequency, the transponder recognized the signal and responded. The delay between the transmission and response told Hollis how far off the bottom they were.

Still, the technique was not foolproof. Hollis knew you could be coming down at 100 feet per minute and the altimeter would be telling you that the bottom was still 600 feet away, but the electronics would have failed to notice a cliff that was coming rapidly up to meet you. You had to be ready for anything.

Hollis was. He was the quintessential pilot; he thrived on performance but made no effort to show it.

He had been in electronics in the Air Force for twenty years, but quit in 1971, and leaped into civilian life by managing a McDonald's hamburger franchise on Cape Cod. He quit that when the Woods Hole Oceanographic Institution, nearby on the Cape, needed an electronic technician for the *Alvin*. Hollis had quickly advanced to being a pilot. Now he was the sub's chief pilot, with more than 300 dives to his credit. It was obvious why he was the chief pilot; it only took seeing him working one of the sub's mechanical arms.

Toggle switches inside the sub moved the arms, which were mounted to the bow. The switches were spread out around either side of the pilot's window, but there would be Hollis, face pressed against the window, rapidly turning the switches on and off without looking at them, without fumbling in the least. He looked like some virtuoso organist deftly traversing the keyboard, putting the mechanical arm just where he wanted it.

Now Hollis sat looking intently at the instrument panel, and at a depth of 9,700 feet, about fifty feet above the floor, he stopped the descent by releasing half the ballast steel. A thud from outside told Malahoff and Hammond that the weights had been dropped, and they moved closer to their observation windows, awaiting the moment when the ship would stabilize at neutral buoyancy and Hollis would turn on the lights.

At 10:30 A.M., July 10, 1984, 120 miles west of Crescent City and nearly two miles under the surface of the Pacific, Ralph Hollis turned the *Alvin*'s floodlight on a place no human being had ever seen.

When the television crews turned their floodlights on at the back of the conference room, Alex Malahoff, who had just arrived at the podium at the front, squinted. He dropped his eyes from surveying the full room of reporters to glance at his typewritten notes.

He looked up. "Ladies and gentlemen," he began, "this is the culmination of many, many years of effort: to finally go down on the Gorda and Juan de Fuca ridges with a manned submersible."

The scientist looked out over the crowd of reporters. It was a quiet, confident look. More than thirty reporters, representing the mainstream media—the *Los Angeles Times*, *The New York Times*, Cable News Network—sat expectantly. They were almost all of them far from their newsrooms, and far also, this Saturday morning, from their homes and bedrooms. They had come all the way out to a remote spot on the Pacific coast, to the Marine Science Center of Oregon State University, in hopes of getting an unusual story. But the scientist understood that reporters want something else, too— the feeling that they are not just observers, but in some measure a part of significant events.

He confided in them.

"The ultimate goal in our research is to get the human eye onto the ocean floor," he continued. "Because, although we use sophisticated instrumentation, it is ultimately the human eye and the brain behind it that interprets the phenomena on the ocean floor."

He paused. A New Zealander, he spoke with a slight accent that called attention to his voice. But there was something more to it, something in the way he spoke. It seemed a scientist's habitual manner, straight-ahead, accustomed to stating facts; yet there was an undercurrent, a hint, of the histrionic. Out in the audience were Malahoff's colleagues in the National Oceanic and Atmospheric Administration. Several were wearing little grins of expectation. They had seen Malahoff perform before.

Malahoff continued, setting the stage. He explained that the Gorda and Juan de Fuca ridges were the local continuation of a chain of volcanic mountains on the seafloor that snaked around the globe. The outline of the chain on the earth was like "the strings on a baseball," he said.

The very first exploration of these underwater mountains had begun in the mid-1970s. Several expeditions to submerged mountains in the Atlantic and Pacific oceans had occurred since then. From 1980 the scientists in his team had worked preparing for the dives onto the North Pacific ridges, from which they had just returned. First they had gone to sea to get depth soundings of the ridges. Then, back at their computers, they had turned those depth soundings into maps.

Malahoff turned to a large easel at the side of the podium, where the maps were pinned up. This was the first time they were being shown in public. In shades of red, green, and blue, they looked at a distance like striped flags as much as maps: flags to new territories. Malahoff used a pointer to tick off the spots on the map; all eyes in the room followed its movement. Starting in the south on the Gorda Ridge and working up north through the Juan de Fuca, he recounted the dives in the *Alvin*.

The dives on the Gorda had provided many interesting rock and water samples, he said, but had not yielded what the researchers had hoped to find. They had not seen evidence of volcanic vents on the seafloor.

But then, two researchers—Malahoff himself and Hammond—had dived on a site on the Juan de Fuca, off the Oregon coast, opposite the Columbia River.

"One could just drive out two hundred and fifty miles, if you had a submarine, drop down and see for yourself," Malahoff said, teasing. A few reporters laughed, nervously. The scientist smiled.

"Well," he said, "we found there this rather remarkable scene, if you can imagine it. On the ocean floor, which is normally very cold, you have hot springs—hydrothermal vents.

"They are like oases, and inside these oases you find the most unusual sort of animal communities. We found, for example, five-foot-long worms, hydrothermal worms."

He paused. The room was very quiet. "It is quite extraordinary how you find them," he continued. "They stand in great masses, tall, undulating in the water. They sort of look as though they are part of a field of wheat."

No smile from Malahoff, no underlining of the improbable, bizarre aspects of the scene he was describing. These are facts, please. Poker-facing it.

"When you go past the worms, you come into a hot vent area. This looks like a geyser valley . . . like Yellowstone underwater. But instead of geysers spouting you have chimneys with black smoke coming out of them. The chimneys rise up to heights of forty-five feet and are twisted, grotesquely."

Malahoff pressed on, describing the next dive site, speaking more rapidly. The fluids coming out of the smoking chimneys, he was saying, were at a temperature of about 600 degrees Fahrenheit. "So when you go down into these worm fields, you have to approach very cautiously, because the submarine has a plastic window on the bottom of its hull. You don't want to land on a smoker, and thereby wipe yourself out.

"The visibility is very poor here . . . but what you see is eerily beautiful. The visibility is poor because you have large flocks of bacteria—bacterial clumps the size of snowflakes—floating around."

Abruptly, a small clatter in the room: someone had dropped a pen or pencil. No one turned, no one gave the slightest reaction.

"Underneath this snowstorm of bacteria you see jellylike, translucent, whitish mats on the ocean floor. These are also bacteria."

The reporters could almost be heard struggling mentally to assimilate what they were hearing, to put this information into some familiar context. *Snowing bacteria swirling above a field of worms crowded around* underwater *hot springs carpeted by more bacteria.*

Malahoff wasn't stopping. "All in all," he was saying, "the life per cubic foot exceeds anything we know of on the surface of the earth." Eyes blinked, almost audibly. "The life density here was just"—he chose his word—"incredible."

He paused then. He wasn't quite done.

"Now in this bag," he said, raising a small plastic bag from the shelf of the podium into view, "I have some specimens."

Immediately, a press photographer who had been standing at the side of the room moved in toward Malahoff, the motor drive on his camera whirring, a second camera around his neck thumping his chest as he walked. At the same time, the reporters in the front row leaned forward to get a better look. People in the back moved forward. Malahoff took clams from the hot spring out of the plastic bag. He took off his glasses. A broad smile transformed his scientist's mask.

When, in 1493, Columbus returned to Spain from his first voyage, he brought with him Indians; and the Spaniards lined the streets to look at these new sorts of beings, naked, red-skinned. Columbus always brought the Indians with him when he visited royalty. They were the token of discoveries that could only, as yet, be talked about. But to king and commoner alike they were signs of something more; they were real, tangible presences to unfetter one's sense of limits.

The reaction of the reporters to the odd little clams was as Malahoff had hoped, because he shared the feeling himself.

This is what anyone wanted from exploration: new worlds to wonder about.

CHAPTER TWO

FEATS OF SCIENTIFIC IMAGINATION

I was one of the reporters at that press conference in 1984. I responded to what I heard and saw in a way that hadn't happened to me for a long time about something in science. What I heard brought back the feelings I had had as a fifth-grader when my class filed down to the elementary school auditorium and we sat with all the other kids in front of the big television sets listening to Walter Cronkite. Then a man with a crackling voice began counting down "Ten—nine—eight—" and his voice went up, and so did the rocket with Alan Shepard inside it, that day in 1961.

I had felt something new then. I didn't have a word for it, but it had to do with a new sense of what people will do, of what things they are capable of doing because they want to know.

These scientists going to the bottom of the sea struck me the same way in 1984, and I was interested in them and also in what curious things they were finding and how they were going about it. I didn't know much about this undersea exploration at the time, but

I knew enough to recognize that activities like those that Alex Malahoff described must be supported by a substantial background of experience and knowledge.

I was curious. I decided to try to find out how ocean scientists came to be exploring deep-sea hot springs off the Pacific Northwest coast of the United States.

Going to the bottom of the sea in a tiny submarine may sound like the stuff of a Jules Verne armchair fantasy, but, it became clear, it is a complex business under any circumstances. The sea is notoriously indifferent to human aspirations. The people who struggle to understand it confront all the difficulties of working in a slippery, treacherous, infinitely changeable world—in short, an alien world.

Locating a small opening in the ocean floor two miles beneath the ocean's surface and diving directly there in a submarine are feats enough. It is something else again to know what to do once there— what questions to ask, what tools to use to answer them.

Scientists could not be doing any of this today if it had not been for a series of major scientific discoveries that came earlier, during the last seventy years. These discoveries are now often described as fomenting a "revolution" in the understanding of the earth, an understanding which constitutes one of the major developments in twentieth-century science. While this is almost surely so, the label "revolution" has a way of mystifying the process. Scientific discovery, like other sorts of investigation, really involves the opposite— the patient exposure of mysteries. In fact, in many ways the discovery of the seafloor vents is like a detective story.

In this story, a miscellaneous group of investigators, in different countries, working on separate mysteries, spent these last seven decades solving parts of what has turned out to be the same riddle. The riddle is big, it should be added right away, and has been around a very long time. It is: How is the earth put together?

The question is probably interesting enough that the search for a solution would be intriguing even if the detectives were bumblers, which they clearly weren't. However, one of the qualities that give this tale the modern stamp is that these investigators—a meteorologist, several odd oceanographers, an assortment of specialists in the magnetic behavior of rocks—were by no means always aware they were working on the same puzzle. And, as an added challenge, our detectives were all, in a sense, blind. They could not physically see the ultimate subject of their inquiry, the seafloor.

Still, they possessed the indispensable two qualities that made them, as investigators, as insightful as Sherlock Holmes. They had resourcefulness and imagination. Face to face with a good big puzzle, they knew it and had the wit to try to make sense of it.

Their resourcefulness showed itself in the tools and techniques they assembled to help them see. Their imaginations helped them to go beyond the mystique of the data, to see through what others only observed. As it happened, what one of them discovered and then surmised, another would use to fire his own imagination. This combustion would sometimes take years, even decades to occur. But from it the mystery was finally illuminated.

The discovery of vents themselves—small, remote features in the seafloor—came, of necessity, very late in this story. Before this could happen, some understanding of the context of the vents—the crust of the earth and the floor of the sea itself—had to be built up.

The first protagonist and the first witness in this twentieth-century detective story are a curious duo: a German scientist with some time on his hands, and a 270-million-year-old reptile waiting to be understood.

In 1915, Alfred Wegener, recently a lieutenant in the German army, was convalescing from a wound that had removed him from combat in World War I. A bullet had become lodged in his neck. A meteorologist by training, he was taking the opportunity of bedrest to think about a topic he had considered before.

Lying in bed he reflected, as he wrote later, on the "congruence of coastlines on either side of the Atlantic." Wegener was certainly not the first person to have noticed this curious congruence between the west coast of Africa and the east coast of South America. For as long as good maps of the world have existed, since early in the seventeenth century, the match-up between the bulge of Brazil and the dent of southwestern Africa must have struck a number of observers.

Antonio Snider-Pellegrini, an Italian-American essayist, published a book in 1858 that, almost in spite of itself, went further. *The Creation and Its Mysteries Unveiled* was partly earth science derived from Scripture, and given over to such pursuits as explaining Noah's Flood. But Snider-Pellegrini also produced a pair of global maps which showed how all the continents had at one time fit together and had later come apart. These paired maps achieved a life of their own, and were reproduced in other, popular scientific texts which served to keep this idea of continents coupled and uncoupled in circulation. Prominent in Snider-Pellegrini's global perspective was the match-up of South America and Africa.

So it was not unusual to conjecture that the continents might have been joined. The question, in scientific terms, was how. As perhaps many before had also done, Wegener admitted that at first he "did not pay any attention" to what he had noticed. Then in 1911, Wegener "came quite accidentally," he wrote, "upon paleontological evidence for a former land bridge between Brazil and Africa." How interesting it is that lying in bed with a foreign object lodged in his body, Wegener suddenly began to wonder about the meaning of fossils imbedded forever in rocks.

In particular, he was impressed by the fossil remains of a toothpick-toothed reptile that lived in the Paleozoic era, 270 million years ago. Fossils of the diminutive dinosaur, which was known as the mesosaur, had been found only in Brazil and South Africa.

Wegener knew that the standard explanation for this coincidence was that there once had been a very long and very wide land bridge joining the two continents. He, however, was unconvinced. Land bridges are not a totally bankrupt concept, it should be said. American schoolchildren are not being sold some romantic tale when they are taught that the ancestors of the American Indians came across a land bridge from what is today Soviet Siberia. But the idea of an extensive land bridge between Brazil and Africa, Wegener had the good sense to argue, was not a very sharp one.

Its proponents said the bridge was no longer visible at all because it had sunk out of sight beneath the seafloor. Not possible, Wegener replied. Terrestrial crust, out of which the land bridge would be made, is lighter than ocean crust; it rests on top of it. Therefore it can't have sunk beneath it. In any case, if the supposed intercontinental bridge or bridges had been able to sink, "the water displacement would be so enormous," he wrote in *The Origin of Continents and Oceans*, "that the level of the world's oceans would rise above that of the whole continental area of the Earth and all would be flooded, today's continents and the bridges alike."

Having thus dispatched the arguments for a land bridge, Wegener turned around and argued—perversely, it would seem—that the two continents had indeed been joined by land. They had been, in fact, the same land, Wegener said, and then they had come apart.

For part of his evidence, Wegener trotted out the mesosaur. Fossils of the 270-million-year-old creature were found only in Brazil and Africa because "Brazil" and "Africa" had come apart, about 125 million years ago. They became part of two continents, and they drifted, slowly separating the mesosaur population.

Wegener cited other lines of evidence besides fossil remains, marshaling insights from several different scientific disciplines. As *The Origin of Continents and Oceans* went through four editions between 1915 and 1929, Wegener added to his argument and rebutted criticisms from other scientists. The basic insight, however, remained arrestingly simple. The surface of the earth is in motion. The continents of today drifted apart from one original supercontinent, which Wegener called Pangaea.

The theory, it is not inappropriate to say, had an earth-shaking effect on the geological profession.

The novelty of the concept alone would probably have been enough to gain a certain amount of puzzlement and resistance from other scientists. But what happened was more extreme. Continental drift became viewed as heresy.

True, critics of the theory did find a central flaw in it. To the question of how the huge continental slabs manage to drift, Wegener claimed essentially that they plowed through the seabed. In the 1920s, influential scientists were arguing convincingly that this mechanism was not possible.

What is curious, however, is how antagonistic and wholesale the dismissal of the idea of continental drift became. After about 1930 it became a professional liability for a geologist in the United States, for example, to espouse, or in some cases even to betray too close a familiarity with, the theory of continental drift.

Why was the reaction so strong?

This rejection has been, for some, the skeleton in the closet of modern geology, for if Wegener's theory had been accepted earlier, some argue, the understanding of the earth might have progressed more rapidly, with untold advantages to science and human affairs.

The rejection is hard to explain simply and by a single cause. Instead, two explanations together seem to make most sense. One, the "objective" explanation, is that Wegener left his major insight vulnerable to rejection by making crucial errors in specific claims, like the "plowing continents" argument. This line of criticism is advanced persuasively by H. W. Menard, an eminent marine geologist whose career spanned from the 1950s to the 1980s.

Wegener, Menard observes, "could have emphasized the simple beauty and integrating power of the continental drift theory without insisting that it offered the *only* explanation for any *particular* observation. It did not, and the experts quickly proved it."

But one senses even with Menard, who always strives to be judicious, that the objective argument really covers a deeper, subjective, complaint. Elaborating his argument, Menard adds that Wegener "could have focused on gaining acceptance of the basic theory, instead of casually tossing off the explanation of every great puzzle that was vexing geologists."

Wegener, it seems, did not follow an accepted code of professional conduct.

The roots of this impertinence can be seen in a letter he wrote to a friend in 1911. This is a significant year, because it is the same year Wegener learned about the fossil data but before he wrote his book. And already he is wondering out loud, "If we now find many surprising simplifications and can begin at last to make real sense of an entire mass of geological data, why should we delay in throwing the old concept overboard? Is this revolutionary?"

Indeed. Wegener apparently didn't see that "throwing the old concept overboard" might not sit well with the geologists, climatologists, paleontologists, and other professionals who were challenged, even threatened, by his work. While he plowed ahead, they dug in their heels.

Their resistance, one can speculate, may have been as strong as it was because it came from someplace even deeper than professional training and expectations. The idea that *terra firma* might just not be so firm after all seems deeply troubling to a certain sort of mind, and, conversely, attractive to another sort.

This phenomenon of different mind-sets, apparently recognized among geologists themselves, was the subject of public speeches by a Swiss geologist, Emile Argand, in the 1920s. Speaking in support of Wegener at the International Geological Congress in Brussels in 1922, for instance, Argand observed that two opposing camps struggle for supremacy in describing the physical world. They are the "fixists," who believe in fixed continents, and the "mobilists," who believe the continents have moved across the earth's surface.

Argand's insight was that scientific beliefs are not held in a vacuum, but instead are formed in the crucible of experience and shaped by imagination. The temperaments of some scientists favor fixity, it would seem; the temperaments of others are open to motion.

Why was Wegener rejected, then? Was it the "objective" limits of his own work or the "subjective" limits of those challenged by him? There were probably elements of both.

In the 1920s, in any case, the opposition of the fixists and mobilists would have to remain unresolved, the question of if and how the continents move remain a conundrum. It would take better investigative tools to decide the argument. Over the next two decades those tools would begin to be assembled.

In 1943, out in the middle of the Pacific Ocean, U.S. Navy Commander Harry Hess put down his earphones. He had been listening to echo signals coming back from the seafloor, and he was momentarily confused. It was that hour before sunrise when the Pacific becomes still, and tired from being up so late, Hess wondered if the echo he was receiving from an object not far below his transport ship could be an enemy submarine with its engines off.

More likely, he thought, it was another of those oddly located undersea mountains. Hess wondered which it was, and for a moment in the cool night air, the potential threat of the one balanced with the curiosity of the other. He lit a cigarette. He was discovering some very interesting things about the floor of the sea.

Fortunately for Hess, and ultimately for science, that evening's discovery concerned the seafloor, not an enemy submarine.

Although it occupies more than two-thirds of the surface of the earth, the floor of the sea has mostly been a vast unknown until this century. Up until the 1940s the seafloor was still under the shadow of the British *Challenger* expedition of 1872–76.

As the most comprehensive and most influential oceanographic expedition taken up to that time, the voyage of *Challenger* covered nearly 70,000 nautical miles of the globe. The voyagers returned with the impression, based on depth soundings taken every 100 miles, that the deep sea was a tranquil environment, mainly flat and covered with mud. In short, it was not the sort of place likely to attract a great deal more curiosity. Seventy years after *Challenger* one of the most widely read oceanography texts still said, "From the oceanographic point of view the chief interest in the topography of the sea floor is that it forms the lower and lateral boundaries of water."

But in the 1940s all that was about to change. Again, as with Alfred Wegener, it was a world war that provided the occasion for the advance of science.

World War II, waged by the United States over most of the world's oceans, placed a new premium on accurate, detailed information about the ocean environment, and the few U.S. oceanographic institutions then in operation found themselves suddenly overwhelmed by an unaccustomed bounty of government contracts. One important field of research was the use of sound underwater. The need for surface ships to be able to locate and track enemy submarines provided an incentive for significant improvements in the techniques of echolocation, or sonar, as it was now called. One of those who aided the military with one hand and science with the other was Harry Hess.

On the day after Pearl Harbor, Hess left his job in the Geology Department at Princeton University and reported for active duty in the Navy. His first responsibility was organizing detection of German subs in the North Atlantic. Hess showed his ability to think around the conventional edges of a problem in the system he developed. The system involved calculating such factors as the U-boats' fuel capacity, speed, and ocean currents, but the ingredient that Hess recognized would drive the German operations was a certain military passion. "U-boat captains were constrained by German ideology to maximize all efficiencies," he observed.

During this stint Hess also showed how absorbed he could become in a problem. Long hours were common, and one apocryphal story has it that once, after working all night, at 4:00 A.M. on his second night someone approached his desk. Hess didn't look up but said only, "Can't you see I'm busy? Go away."

"Pardon me, young man," came the reply. "I know you're busy, but could you just tell me where my flagship is?"

Presumably the man Hess had ordered away was the admiral.

When he successfully finished his submarine detection office work, he was assigned to command the *Cape Johnson*, an attack transport, a position in which he made time to pursue his research interests. He obtained the most powerful model of echo sounder available, and he ran it almost constantly during his Pacific missions. So intent was Hess on obtaining data that crew members had occasion to doubt that the routes that he took between points were the most direct.

In his soundings, Hess discovered and mapped about 100 flat-topped submarine mountains. This was to be perhaps the key event in shaping his thinking about geology. After the war, back at Princeton, Hess theorized how these mountains originated as pointed-top volcanoes. This drew him into considerations of the life cycle of underwater mountains, which continued to be his focus throughout the 1950s. His major insight and his major contribution to unraveling the mystery of the earth's structure occurred in 1960 as a result again of echo soundings. These echo soundings, though, were of a nature unimagined at the end of the war.

Following the war, Columbia University became the home base for a vigorous marine geology research program, headed by a Texan, former oil prospector Maurice Ewing. Ewing kept the research ships of Columbia's Lamont Geological Observatory at sea throughout the year, collecting all sorts of oceanographic data, including numerous depth soundings taken across the Atlantic Ocean. In 1952 the Lamont researchers began the task of assembling a map derived from these soundings. What they saw startled them.

Out in the middle of the Atlantic, rising above a broad flat plain to either side, was a mountain range whose peaks jutted up 10,000 feet from the Atlantic floor. Not only was this midocean ridge high, it was long; it ran nearly the full length of the ocean from north of Greenland to south of Africa. Some 9,000 miles long, the ridge stretched farther than the Rocky Mountains and the Andes combined. But the feature most unexpected of all was the presence of a deep valley in the ridge's center, forming a rift between the ridge's two flanks.

The rift valley descended an average of 6,000 feet from the ridge crest, and ranged in width from eight to thirty miles. This meant that at its deepest and widest, the Mid-Atlantic Ridge could hold the Grand Canyon inside it. The Grand Canyon of the Colorado River is 4,000 feet deep and not more than eighteen miles wide.

A map of the North Atlantic showing such features was published by Lamont researchers Ewing, Bruce Heezen, and Marie Tharp in 1959. Since the Navy had slapped a security classification on all deep-ocean soundings done by U.S. researchers in 1952, the map was executed as an illustration, not as a relief map with measured depths. As it happened, the power of the image was probably even greater because of this. In the map the earth was shown naked, with the ocean drained. The landforms under the sea achieved a prominence they had never had before.

In these last years of the 1950s, echo soundings in the other oceans produced similar profiles of the seafloor throughout the world, and from them, an extraordinary pattern emerged. The soundings showed that the midocean ridge was one of the planet's three dominant physical features, along with the continents and the oceans themselves. It was 33,000 miles in length, long enough to circle the equator one and a half times. Overall, its heights were impressive too. Many peaks rose 10,000, 12,000, or 15,000 feet.

The midocean ridge system was not only a major but a fundamental discovery about the earth. The discovery was more than astonishing. It was a provocation to geologists and geophysicists.

What did it mean? What was the ridge system doing there? Three lines of evidence about the ridges themselves were being accumulated during the 1950s, but as yet they remained unincorporated into any larger explanation of the structure and function of the ridge system.

Studies of rocks collected at the ridges and on the neighboring seafloor indicated that the rocks became older as the distance from the ridge crest increased. Meanwhile, measurements of heat flow showed a similar pattern—the central ridge valley was significantly hotter than outlying areas. And earthquake studies revealed two prominent zones of earthquakes: one was right along the ridges, the other was at sites often hundreds of miles across the ocean floor from them, which were identified as oceanic trenches. Age differentials, heat differentials, motion differentials across the ocean floor: Could they be related in some way? It was about time for a mobilist to give a motive force to these phantoms of motion.

Through this dizzying period of revelations in the 1950s, Harry Hess had kept abreast of the mountain of data about the seafloor that was piling up. In 1960 he invited Bruce Heezen, of Lamont and the North Atlantic maps, to lecture at Princeton. Heezen spoke about his theory that the earth was "coming apart at the seams." He argued that at the midocean ridges, volcanic rock—magma—welled up from below the crust.

Here was the hint of a mechanism that could explain the mid-ocean ridges, Hess believed. Drawing together all that he knew about the formation and structure of the earth and of the seafloor, he offered a new synthesis. Where Wegener had called his *The Origin of Continents and Oceans*, Hess would go beyond Wegener. He titled his essay "The History of Ocean Basins."

Hess first wrote the article in 1960 and privately circulated it; it was finally published in 1962.

He began the essay diffidently. "The birth of the oceans is a matter of conjecture, the subsequent history is obscure, and the present structure is just beginning to be understood," he wrote. Given this state of incomplete knowledge, the most that can be expected from a scientist is plausibility, a kind of exercise of the imagination grounded in fact. Or as he put it, "an essay in geopoetry." He proceeded by setting out the assumptions underlying his conceptual framework.

After the earth condensed into a solid planet, the decay of radioactive particles began to generate heat in its interior. (That the natural radioactivity of the earth's rocks produces heat was discovered in 1904, following on research by Pierre Curie.) As the heat increased, elemental iron began to melt and fall toward the center of the earth, forming a molten core which further heated the earth. As the non-iron rock continued heating, it became less dense and began slowly rising through the earth. Eventually it reached the surface of the planet and formed a single continental landmass. There was then a crust, a core, and a zone of ferment in between, the mantle.

Hess saw that as radioactive decay continued to the present giving off heat, heated rocks would continue to move upward through the mantle. Approaching the crust the heated rocks would lose energy, cool, and descend again into the mantle. This is a clear example of convection, in which heated material rises and cold material sinks. If a continuous heat source is present, the cooled, sinking material is reheated, establishing a convection "loop" or current. Water being heated in a pot provides a commonplace example of a convection loop. To Harry Hess, the movement of heat in the mantle provided another example.

The development of this idea of a convection loop in the mantle was Hess's breakthrough. Other scientists had discussed the possibilities of mantle convection, but Hess envisioned it entire, as the prime mover of his imagined world. From it, everything else flowed.

Once the earth's core and crust formed, mantle convection subdivided into several loops that flowed out from the core along different radii, like petals on a daisy. These powerful currents of rock broke up the original continent. Where these convection currents of hot rocks broke into the crust, they formed the midocean ridges. And at these ridges, the ocean floor itself is continuously created when magma emerges from the mantle and cools.

As the convection loops flow in their circles, they act like conveyor belts, moving the ocean floor slowly away from its origin at the ridge to either side. The ascent of the loop injects magma to create the ocean floor. The floor is pushed away as new magma rises behind it. Ultimately it is destroyed as the loop descends into the mantle at seafloor trenches. The process is continuous but slow, Hess theorized; the rocks in the loop move about a centimeter per year, roughly a half inch.

This continuous mechanism of the conveyor belt suggested explanations for much of the puzzling seafloor data of the 1950s. The moving conveyor belt could account for the collision of rocks implied by the earthquake maps. It could account for the increasing age of seafloor rocks out from the ridge. And a moving seafloor could explain why heat-probe measurements showed the seafloor becoming cooler out from the ridge. By also introducing a means by which the seafloor could be destroyed, the conveyor belt could account for observations that seafloor rocks are relatively young—none older than about 200 million years—and that sediments, which need time to accumulate, are relatively sparse on the seafloor.

More important still, with his argument for mantle convection, Hess resolved the main complaint against Wegener. "The continents do not plow through oceanic crust impelled by unknown forces," Hess was able to assert. "Rather they ride passively on mantle material as it comes to the surface at the crest of the ridge and then moves laterally away from it."

At the end of the essay Hess put together his vision of the earth. The prose offered no fanfare, only nineteen assertions, rendered tersely. The next-to-last read: "The ocean basins are impermanent features, and the continents are permanent although they may be torn apart or welded together and their margins deformed. . . ."

Hess had placed the two main observed features of the earth, the oceans and the continents, into subordination to the motions of his third invisible feature, the moving seafloor.

With similar understatement Hess concluded, "The Earth is a dynamic body, with its surface constantly changing."

While it was compelling, perhaps even disquieting as a vision, Hess's theory lacked direct proof. How could one observe the seafloor spreading away from the ridges when the rate that Hess proposed—one centimeter per year—was so slow? No one at the time expected that that amount of movement would actually be observable directly. The proof would have to come indirectly.

In the summer of 1961, two recently hired geologists with the U.S. Geological Survey were up in California's Sierra Nevada mountains collecting samples for their work. Allan Cox and Richard Doell were developing a new approach to another geologic mystery. They were trying to understand a curious aspect of the magnetic behavior of rocks.

It had been known since 1906 that rocks on land could be magnetized in either a north or south direction, but for a long time the phenomenon was unexplained. Gradually, as the evidence grew that rocks from different locations and from different geological strata could show such positive or negative polarity of the magnetic field, it became natural to ask if there was some pattern to these apparent "reversals" of the field.

Cox and Doell framed the question of pattern in terms of time. The discovery of magnetized rocks in different strata suggested that the rocks were formed at different times. Dating by fossil evidence—the standard means that had assisted Alfred Wegener—had indeed been done in a limited way, but the dates obtainable for the age of rocks by correlation with nearby fossils wasn't very precise. The two geologists believed that an accurate time scale of the reversals of the magnetic field would require a more precise technique. Cox and Doell were aware of such a technique, but as researchers relatively new to the Survey, they had two problems. They weren't able to get people who worked with the new technique to assist them, and furthermore, they needed to collect samples in order to have data to work with.

So, up in the Sierras in the summer of 1961, the two men collected basaltic rocks. Basalt is lava that has emerged from the earth and in cooling has become magnetized in one direction or another. It has also hardened, so to get their samples, Cox and Doell needed to drill into solid rock. In those days the drill system they carried with them was a cumbersome affair that linked a four-horsepower Briggs & Stratton engine to a diamond drill bit on a flexible shaft. This rig was heavy and awkward to pack, but it worked.

After a summer day in the mountains drilling like this, geologists have been known to enjoy a chance to relax and drink a beer or two. Berkeley faculty and students had a base camp for their geology studies in the Sierras, and Cox and Doell, Berkeley graduates of a few years before, were visitors there.

One evening sitting around the campfire drinking beer, Cox began telling one of the grad students, Brent Dalrymple, about the work that he and Doell were doing. Cox's beers with Dalrymple were about to put all of earth science into a ferment, for Dalrymple was becoming proficient in the technique that the two Survey researchers believed would give them their time scale of magnetic reversals. Dalrymple knew about radioisotopic dating, and he agreed to help.

This meeting was one of several that was to occur in the next couple of years among scientists of the younger generation, those then in their twenties and thirties. They would crack the problem that Hess, the summarizer of the previous generation, had presented to them; and they would go further.

Any discussion of radioisotopic dating exposes one to the odd world of geologists' time. It is like a dream world of immense crowded vistas in which objects are so far away that they should have long before blurred and vanished, but instead they stand out uncannily, distinctly. A geologist today routinely confronts the notion that a particular rock is, say, three million two hundred thousand years old. Three million years becomes a real age; the rock is hard in the hand.

It must do something to one's imagination to be exposed to remote time like this. With some people, it even seems to be the compelling reason for working as geologists, to acquire this perspective on time that is so different from personal experience. "The world as seen on our time scale is like a single frame in a movie that has played for over 4,000 million years," a marine geologist wrote in 1977. The statement seems characteristic.

Whatever the motive, the ability to have this kind of knowledge of deep time did put the geologists who were capable of "dating" rocks into a frenzy of productivity when the necessary tool was brought to bear on the problem. The period began in 1962; the tool was the mass spectrometer, and Berkeley was the training ground for many of the geochronologists. Ever since the involvement of Berkeley scientists nearly a generation before in the Manhattan Project, the university had continued to pioneer in research activities relating to nuclear physics. Research with the mass spectrometer advanced there during the 1950s.

The principle behind the operation of the spectrometer in radioisotopic dating is simple enough.

Isotopes are minor variations on the theme of atomic parts. An atom has a central nucleus, made up of protons and neutrons; electrons whirl about the nucleus. Isotopes of an element have the same atomic number—the same number of protons and electrons—but a different atomic weight, representing a different number of neutrons. There are three isotopes of potassium, for instance, with atomic weights of 39, 40, and 41.

Some isotopes are unstable; that is, they are radioactive. Over time they break down into more stable elements, and this decay occurs at a constant rate peculiar to the particular radioactive element. For example, potassium 40 is the radioactive isotope of potassium; it decays to argon 40 in such a way that one-half of the original quantity of potassium 40 has become argon 40 in 1.25 billion years. This is known as the half-life of potassium 40.

As it happens, potassium is a common component of rocks, so to determine the date of a rock one basically needs to know the amount of potassium 40 in it and the amount of radiogenic argon 40—derived from decay of potassium 40. This gives the total potassium 40 that was in the rock originally, and since the potassium 40 that remains and the rate of decay of the isotope are known, the age of the rock can be calculated.

The laboratory procedures are, of course, not so simple as this makes it sound. At the start of the 1960s, much of the hardware for the spectrometer was not available ready-made. Brent Dalrymple's apprenticeship with the instrument involved learning how to blow glass into complex shapes. Working with the rock samples themselves also took some technique. Plain and dumb as it might appear, a rock possesses tricks that can make a mass spectrometrist squirm.

Dalrymple had to learn the techniques to get the argon gas sample out of the solid rock and measure it accurately. To free the argon from the rock, the rock was melted in an extraction device, but the melting released other gases along with the argon. Since the mass of the rock was measured in grams and the mass of argon 40 in billionths of a gram, a scientist first had to separate the argon from the unwanted gases.

The other problem with the extraction system was contamination of the sample by argon from the atmosphere, but by the time Dalrymple was learning his craft, procedures were in use to overcome this problem.

The operation of the mass spectrometer itself was straightforward. The mass spectrometer that Dalrymple learned to use at Berkeley was basically a specialized glass tube. Through valves at one end, a gas sample was introduced to the device; a collector at the opposite end allowed components of the sample to be measured. In between, the gas was subjected first to an electron beam, which put an electrical charge onto the gas, then to various voltages to accelerate and focus the ions, and finally to a magnetic field, which deflected the ions into separate paths depending on their mass. By applying the right amount of electrical charge and magnetic field, ions of argon of any particular mass could be made to strike the collector and produce a tiny electrical signal.

Dalrymple could compute the abundance of the three isotopes of argon from their electric signals, and could then determine the geologic age of the sample by adding the argon 40 amount to the potassium 40 amount and calculating.

In June 1963, Dalrymple, Cox, and Doell published the results of their first analysis of rocks. The rocks, magnetized in opposite directions, were shown by potassium-argon dating to have been created at different times. The earth's magnetic field, the three researchers found, had in fact reversed itself at least nine times in the last 3.5 million years.

The announcement of the time scale was not exactly greeted by trumpets of welcome and cheers of approbation from the geological community. The results were admittedly preliminary, inasmuch as the data didn't permit the three to say definitely whether duration of their magnetic periods was a million years or only half a million. But more important, most geologists were still not convinced of the reality of a reversing magnetic field.

For a short time, this geologic time scale based on magnetic reversals went unnoticed by most scientists. It did not go completely unnoticed, however.

In early 1963 a graduate student in marine geophysics at Cambridge University was starting work on a research project which had been assigned to him by his supervisory professor. This is a standard event in the career of a budding researcher, but twenty-three-year-old Fred Vine's efforts drew the kind of response that would have made most graduate students pause. When Vine showed the first results to the head of the marine geophysics group, the older scientist offered little encouragement.

"I think he thought it was rubbish," Vine, now a professor himself, recollects.

What Fred Vine had done was to give a novel interpretation to some data that his supervisor, Drummond Matthews, had collected on a research cruise in the Indian Ocean. The data were a detailed magnetic survey over a seafloor ridge.

The technology of magnetic surveying was not new. Like echo sounding, it had been developed during World War II as an outgrowth of the effort to improve detection of submarines, which it did. Detecting the faint magnetic signals of rocks, however, took even more subtle equipment, which was first available in the 1950s. Vine was the intellectual beneficiary of this earlier technical achievement.

The first magnetometers used in marine science were hand-built by researchers at the Scripps Institution of Oceanography in California. It was a pioneering engineering effort, almost quaint. To try to escape the effects of magnetic objects while calibrating and testing the new equipment, the magnetometers' designers worked inside plywood geodesic domes in which the fittings were brass and all the paint was aluminum. The remarkable thing, however, was not that the magnetometers worked well, but that there was a phenomenon that caused them to work at all.

Why the earth has a magnetic field was pretty much an unresolved question in the 1950s, and for that matter, still is today. The traditional explanation, however, has been that the core of the earth is the source of the magnetic field. The core is thought to be divided into a solid inner section, most likely of iron and nickel, and a liquid outer section of the same elements. It is the liquid outer core that is important to magnetism. Since the liquid is metallic, it conducts electricity. Theory has it that an electric current is induced in the outer core by a weak and stray magnetic field, and this flow of electricity generates a strong magnetic field.

In turn, rocks become magnetized when they melt and then recool; this notion was suggested three centuries ago by British chemist Robert Boyle. Like any other rocks, those melted through volcanic processes and placed on the seafloor would be magnetized. Such rocks produce detectable signals that enhance or detract from the earth's background magnetic field strength.

Such variations from the magnetic norm were first documented off the west coast of North America by the Scripps researchers in the mid-1950s. In charting their survey, Ronald Mason and Arthur Raff assigned shadings of black or white to the stronger and weaker signals, and then examined the results. The results virtually leaped off the page.

The chart showed a giant black-and-white-striped pattern running from Canada to Mexico, along primarily a north-south axis. "A single glance was enough to show that we had something quite new in geophysics," Raff observed. The question was what.

The magnetic survey had been done in conjunction with a mapping survey for the Navy, which was gathering information to protect its submarines as they navigated the West Coast. Mason and Raff didn't have access to the classified mapping, so they didn't know the shape of the seafloor in the area of their "zebra stripes." If they had had the map they might have been able to make some additional interpretation, or see some relationship, but they didn't. And they didn't know what to make of such a zebra-stripe pattern.

In 1963, Fred Vine believed he knew. The Mid-Atlantic Ridge also showed this curious pattern of stronger and weaker magnetic signals in parallel on either side of the ridge crest. So did Drummond Matthews's survey of the Carlsberg Ridge. The stronger and weaker signals were not the results of some difference in original magnetic force, Vine believed. This quantity should be relatively constant over time. The difference must be due to some other factor.

It's perhaps easiest to understand what Vine realized with a straightforward case, the Mid-Atlantic Ridge, a ridge running north-south in a northern latitude. The weaker signals there would be indications of rocks that were magnetized in a direction *opposite* to the current magnetic field. The opposition effectively would cancel out some of the signal strength. Conversely, stronger signals would indicate rocks magnetized in line with the contemporary field.

Starting with this conceptual framework, Vine proceeded to elaborate a new theory. "The theory," he wrote in a September 1963 article, "is consistent with, in fact virtually a corollary of, current ideas" in two areas.

One of the ideas was "ocean floor spreading." Vine was referring, of course, to Hess, whom he had heard lecture when he was an undergraduate at Cambridge, and whose writings he had studied. The other current idea was that of "periodic reversals in the Earth's magnetic field." Vine had read the journal article by Cox, Doell, and Dalrymple published three months before.

Vine's breakthrough was to put the insights on seafloor spreading and reversals of the magnetic field together. Ocean crust is formed from rocks emerging under the seafloor, he wrote. When the rocks emerge they are magnetized in the direction of the earth's field at that time. It followed that over time, "if spreading of the ocean floor occurs, blocks of alternately normal and reversely magnetized material would drift away from the centre of the ridge and parallel to the crest of it."

Vine had conceived a physical model which could be used to test Hess's geopoetry. If magnetic bands were discovered running parallel to the ridge, it would suggest that the seafloor was spreading, as Hess had theorized.

It might be thought that Vine's proposal would have been taken up quickly by other researchers and put to the test. But the concept drew little attention, and primarily criticism at that.

Typical of the initial scientific reaction was Matthews's own. He appeared on the paper as coauthor, largely because the data were his, but Vine recalled later that he said little about the idea until a year or so afterward, when he was working up his own separate paper on magnetics over seafloor ridges.

"One day," Vine remembered, "he came in and said, 'You know, that was a damn good idea you had just over a year ago.' I really felt that he hadn't believed it until then."

The problem was the evidence, Vine realized quite clearly. Originally he had wanted to focus the paper on the idea itself, which he felt was strong and provocative. But the head of the marine geophysics group had urged him to focus the paper on Matthews's data, which Vine thought was unconvincing. What was needed was two additional findings.

One could make an argument for seafloor spreading from the Carlsberg Ridge data, but it did not show pronounced symmetry. A symmetrical pattern would suggest spreading to both sides of the ridge at a constant rate, as Hess had proposed. Then, once such symmetrical bands of magnetic signals were found, there needed to be a way to show that the bands moving outward from a ridge actually emerged during different geologic time periods. Symmetry and a clock were needed.

But the challenge was not taken up by the scientific community, and the idea languished. Sometimes Vine himself lost hope of proving the idea, or what seemed worse—to an eager researcher in his mid-twenties—he thought he would spend the rest of his life trying to prove it. But ultimately he had faith in the idea, in what physicists like to call its elegance. Physicists, in particular, are quite convinced that Nature is very simple, he would say, and when you have a simple model, an elegant model, it has to be right. The data just needed improving.

In 1965, an extraordinary couple of meetings proved Vine right. In January of that year, Harry Hess arrived at Cambridge on sabbatical leave from Princeton. J. Tuzo Wilson, a geophysicist from the University of Toronto, had also come to continue some research on midocean ridges. Virtually all the other Cambridge marine geophysicists were at sea that January, except for Fred Vine, who had stayed behind to finish his Ph.D. thesis. Hess and Wilson, senior scientists in their fifties, and Vine, the precocious student, soon found common ground.

At that time Wilson was developing an explanation for a curious phenomenon revealed by the seafloor maps of the 1950s and early 1960s. The great 33,000-mile midocean ridge was not in a straight line. Rather it was offset into sections broken up by cracks running perpendicular to it. Wilson proposed that such cracks, which he called transform faults, were in fact caused by the segmenting of the ridge.

Between the two segments the spreading seafloor would be moving in opposite directions, which would increase earthquake activity. Such activity and other structural clues might indicate the presence of the ridge segments.

At Cambridge in the spring of 1965, Wilson was examining some maps of the seafloor area off the coast of Vancouver Island south through California, and he theorized that the maps showed transform faults and a ridge.

He was explaining his interpretation to Hess and Vine at Madingley Rise, the geophysics building, when Hess spoke up.

"Well," he said, "if you're going to put a ridge there, it's one of the few places where we have a decent magnetic map. Fred's magnetic anomalies should show up, if there's a ridge."

Vine rushed upstairs two flights to the departmental library and pulled the journal with Mason and Raff's magnetic maps off the shelf. He brought it downstairs, and he and Hess and Wilson stared at what was now obvious as a symmetrical zebra-stripe pattern in the area southwest of Vancouver Island. Now they knew what to make of the Scripps maps. In an essay published in October 1965, Vine and Wilson laid out an improved theory of seafloor spreading. Before launching into the data, however, the two diplomatically struck a conciliatory note.

"At the time it was put forward, the Vine and Matthews hypothesis was particularly speculative," they wrote.

But now they had the Pacific coast seafloor maps and the magnetic surveys to work with. And they also had the improved magnetic-reversal time scales produced by the trio of researchers at the Geological Survey and others. "Clearly," they wrote, "we now have information with which to reexamine the original suggestion of Vine and Matthews."

They identified a ridge off Vancouver Island, naming it the Juan de Fuca Ridge, after the nearby strait of that name; then they produced two charts. Placing the ridge crest at the center of the first chart, they plotted the pattern of the anomalies, the stronger and weaker magnetic signals observed by the Scripps researchers.

The magnitude of the signal was marked on the vertical axis of the graph; the distance out from the ridge crest was shown along the horizontal axis. This first chart showed a roughly symmetrical wave pattern obtained from the magnetic data.

Lined up underneath the first chart, the second one also had a vertical axis showing magnetic values. In this chart, however, elapsed time was marked along the horizontal axis. Here Vine and Wilson displayed the wave pattern of the magnetic-field reversals identified by Cox, Doell, and Dalrymple.

Examined in this way, it was clear that the waveforms in the two charts were very similar. The magnetic signals associated with the *positions* of rocks on the seafloor and the magnetic reversals associated with the *ages* of rocks on land indeed appeared to be closely related. Taken together, the charts suggested strongly that the seafloor was spreading out over time.

And yet, while similar, the charts were not perfectly congruent, and so not beyond skepticism.

In November 1965, Vine and Wilson presented papers at a meeting in Kansas City of the Geological Society of America. Brent Dalrymple was also there. Meeting him for the first time, Vine learned that the Survey researchers had defined a new polarity-reversal event and named it Jaramillo, for the location in New Mexico where the rocks had been recovered. The reversal was the youngest yet; it had occurred 900,000 years ago. The Survey researchers had not yet published this new finding.

This new reversal was a revelation to Vine, for he realized that the record as written by the spreading was clearer than he had seen so far. His and Wilson's magnetic-reversal chart had been based on the Survey's earlier time scale—which had not included the Jaramillo reversal. Its absence caused the reversal chart to differ from the Juan de Fuca Ridge magnetic-signal pattern. Now the reversal chart could be corrected. Vine was convinced that he could do it.

He was turning this effort over in his mind two months later when in February 1966 he went to visit a friend, a researcher working at Lamont. Vine found Neil Opdyke all caught up in his work, enthusiastic about the data he had obtained from analyzing sediment samples. The samples were from long vertical cores, sixteen to forty feet in length, that were obtained from the ocean floor in the South Pacific.

Whereas Vine had theorized that the passage of geologic time could be shown in a horizontal dimension by a magnetometer towed over the ocean floor, Opdyke's core samples of the floor actually *showed* the same passage of time vertically, in the rocks and sediments that had piled up over time and had been magnetized in the direction of their particular period. The time period of a section of core was determined by comparing fossils in the section with known fossils that had previously been dated by other means.

Opdyke's first notable result was that the vertical core sections showed all the same reversals as the last published time scale of the

Survey researchers. But, beyond this, he told Vine that he had discovered a new magnetic reversal. It occurred, he said, about 900,000 years ago.

Vine was stunned.

"Neil," he said, "I hate to tell you this, but the Menlo Park group have already discovered it."

Opdyke's jaw dropped.

"They've named it the Jaramillo event."

"You're joking," Opdyke said. He had not been to the Kansas City meeting.

Opdyke might have been disappointed, but he would not be displeased. The fact that the depths of ocean floor revealed the same time scale as did the mountain cores on land was powerful, independent confirmation of the validity of the time scale. For Vine, meanwhile, the visit to Neil Opdyke's office that day was doubly momentous. For there, pinned to the office wall, were profiles of magnetic anomalies obtained in a just-completed research cruise to the East Pacific Rise, a ridge system west of South America.

Some graduate students who had gone primarily to collect information about seafloor structure had also kept the magnetometer running during their cruise. What Vine saw in their profiles was the last piece of the puzzle falling into place.

Line for line, the magnetic signals obtained on board the research vessel *Eltanin* matched the magnetic time scale of the Geological Survey researchers. Even more important, Vine saw, the pattern of magnetic stripes taken over the East Pacific Rise was perfectly symmetrical. He realized at once that this new, symmetrical pattern over a seafloor ridge—a pattern which exactly matched the time scale obtained on land—meant he had his proof. Symmetry and the clock had come together. The seafloor spreads out from the ridge over time. Vine was ecstatic.

Before long, other scientists would show how the continents, embedded in the seafloor, are moved by Vine's spreading seafloor. They indeed drift, just as Wegener had theorized. Only now the mechanism was known.

With the theory of seafloor spreading confirmed, scientists, it would appear, held the key to a whole new way of understanding the earth. But this is talk from the vantage of hindsight. For those working in the earth sciences in the mid-1960s, the situation was far less resolved. A handful of their peers—Hess, Cox, Vine, Wilson—

had just had some very exciting insights. But accepting these insights for what they were, assimilating them, and putting them to use were separate matters. In the study of the earth the mid-1960s was to be an exciting time, a revolutionary time. It determined everything that has come since.

CHAPTER THREE

MAKING
THE REVOLUTION
IN EARTH SCIENCES

At the same time that Harry Hess was publishing his radical theory of seafloor spreading and Cox, Doell, and Dalrymple were about to unveil their first geomagnetic time scale, another work was being published that would put their efforts into a new perspective. It was *The Structure of Scientific Revolutions*, by philosopher of science Thomas Kuhn. First published in 1962 and instantly provocative, Kuhn's book can serve as a guide to the revolution in earth sciences that was about to occur.

In the book, Kuhn introduced the idea that a revolution involves a "paradigm shift." The practice of a particular science, he wrote, is organized around a paradigm, the bundle of accepted theories, methods, shared interpretations, and values that scientists in a particular field use to direct their research. Under "normal" circumstances, when a particular paradigm is widely accepted, research goes forward quite comfortably. Researchers appear to know which questions are the important ones and how to go about answering them. "One of the reasons why normal science seems to progress so rapidly," Kuhn observed drily, "is that its practitioners concentrate on problems that only their own lack of ingenuity should keep them from solving."

Eventually, however, observations arise that the prevailing paradigm can't explain. The observers question its authority, and as more instances arise, a state of crisis begins. Kuhn likened the situation to the start of political revolutions, when existing institutions no longer seem able to resolve pressing contradictions in the society.

Out of the scientific crisis, a new paradigm is proposed. It arrives offering two main attractions. Primarily, say its proponents, it can solve the problems that have led the old paradigm to a crisis. But more than that, the new paradigm often has an "aesthetic" appeal. "The new theory," Kuhn observed, "is said to be 'neater,' 'more suitable,' or 'simpler' than the old."

At its headiest, this aesthetic pleasure can crystallize into a new way of perception. It is like seeing the pattern in the familiar psychology experiment as not just a wine goblet but also as two faces in silhouette. The understanding expands. New totalities are perceived. There is something akin to a religious experience of enlightenment. Often something else typical of a religious awakening occurs—there may be a rapid conversion of former unbelievers. A sober scientific community will sometimes be embarrassed by the spectacle.

By February 1966, when Fred Vine visited Neil Opdyke, such a revolution was coming to a head in earth sciences. The prevailing worldview was that the surface of the earth was static in a certain way—prevented from horizontal structural movements. But this "fixist" paradigm could not explain such observations as the odd pattern of seafloor magnetic signals. They could be understood adequately, for the first time, only within the newly emerging paradigm. In it the horizontal motion of seafloor spreading was a key force in sculpting the planet's surface.

Fundamental conceptual differences divided the two paradigms. But scientific revolutions, Kuhn was at some pains to point out, are not merely affairs of the abstract intellect, merely disinterested weighings of "facts" taking place in a social vacuum. Instead, as the controversy over Wegener's theory of continental drift showed, they are also affairs of intellectual disposition, power, and persuasion. They involve the struggles of flesh-and-blood people.

"Like the choice between competing political institutions," Kuhn observed, "that between competing paradigms proves to be a choice between incompatible modes of community life." A revolution involves a "change of worldview," and the choice between worldviews cannot be resolved under the old worldview. It is as if one expected England's King George III to be the arbitrator of Thomas Jefferson's convictions.

In a scientific revolution, as in a political one, the crisis finally comes to dominate the life of the community until it is resolved. The stages of the crisis are predictable. At first, the scientific revolutionists struggle to publish and proclaim the outlaw truth, while those who have an investment in the old way of seeing and doing things resist the new worldview and its advocates. The pressure builds. If the revolutionists are to be successful they will persuade some others. Eventually, armed with more new data and new interpretations, the revolutionists will make more and more converts until what political scientists are pleased to call "revolutionary fever" will grip the community, and the new paradigm will be swept into power.

In the aftermath, the community will often enter a period of fruitfulness, marked by rapid new discoveries. Unexpectedly great advances will be made beyond what might have been anticipated under the old regime just a short time before. Meanwhile, for their part, the lingering adherents of the old paradigm may well be forgotten and discredited, and the old worldview itself consigned to the dustbin of history. As Mao Zedong would say, "a revolution is not a tea party."

From the early 1960s to the late 1970s, earth science went through all these phases, each of them dominated by strong individuals who seized the particular moment of the revolution that they found themselves in. First came the revolutionary vanguard, proclaiming a new order. Next came the early converts, substantiating the vision with their work. Then came the explorers, assimilating the new worldview and forging ahead, making discoveries that were the first fruits of the new regime.

Science is a collective enterprise; one of its beauties is its sprawling, collaborative, gregarious nature, colleague talking to colleague beyond the limits of place and time. And yet, while acknowledging that every new advance in knowledge won by any individual scientist depends on knowledge gained by colleagues, science, as any other field, has its trailblazers. These leaders of science make creative use of their tradition; better, they create with their tradition.

Those who thrived during the "revolution in earth sciences" shared certain qualities, though in different proportions. The qualities were boldness, insight, tolerance for ambiguity, and a certain sense of timing.

From the 1920s through the 1950s, most scientists were skeptical, if not hostile, to ideas associated with continental drift. S. Warren Carey, an Australian drift sympathizer, reminisced in 1976 about the tone of those years and the difficulty of getting a hearing for the idea of drift.

"Any loose statement denigrating or mocking continental dispersion got easy passage and approval for publication," he wrote. "Any who was unwise enough to argue for displacement of continents was cold-shouldered by referees and editors [of professional journals] and became the butt for snide comments."

Such dismissive attitudes ultimately failed to subdue the right sort of independent, self-possessed type. J. Tuzo Wilson was such a man. Fifty-four years old in 1962, at the peak of his career, Wilson was a man ready for large challenges. A geophysicist rather than a tradition-bound geologist, and a Canadian, rather than a perhaps more cautious American scientist, Wilson became the champion of "the revolution in the earth sciences." In fact, he was the one who coined the phrase.

Wilson had read Kuhn's *Scientific Revolutions* and agreed with much of it, taking its insights to heart, confirming his own instincts. Wilson wound up playing the roles of this revolution's Patrick Henry *and* Thomas Jefferson. Both as proponent and as theoretician, he had a knack of getting his ideas into circulation, which is exactly what a revolution needs from its vanguard leaders.

Wilson is remembered by those who worked with him as always the center of ferment. A revealing example of his engaging the opposition dates from 1972, when he was invited to give a guest lecture at a small college in northwestern Ontario. He told his inviter, a former student, that he didn't just want to give the lecture; he said he must come up early to talk with the earth science faculty.

On the morning before the lecture he met with the department members and told them that he suspected they were having a tough time with the "so-called pure scientists, the physicists and chemists."

"They are trying to tell you what to do," Wilson said. He asked his colleagues to identify their antagonists at the college. They did so, willingly.

Then at a cocktail party after his talk, Wilson went head to head with each of these physicists and chemists, pointing out how their scientific disciplines were, as he put it, really just adjuncts to earth science.

The effect was galvanic, as James Franklin recalled.

"I remember it well, because when he left the university to catch a plane home, we were all up in the president's office—we had broken into his wine supply, and were having a tremendous time which went on for hours after Wilson left—and were saying things like 'We really should hire a geophysicist rather than another particle physicist.' "

In the late 1980s, when Wilson was approaching eighty years old, an age when all but a few have lost their creative fire, he was continuing to write scientific papers. Perhaps at least some of his energy came from a fundamental outlook. "I have always thought a change in ideas is healthy," he wrote in 1987. "Most people don't like it."

A key factor that prepared him for his role in the 1960s revolution, Wilson said, was his training in more than one academic discipline. He started in physics and later took up the study of geology, with the result that he "always viewed geological ideas skeptically." Although continental drift was considered suspect when he began his studies in the 1920s, his later work at Toronto, Cambridge, and Princeton, where he worked with Harry Hess, brought him into contact with scientists who would be influential as questions touching on drift were periodically reexamined.

For a long time he was unconvinced about drift. An essay he wrote in 1960, for example, finds Wilson preoccupied with the idea that the earth may have expanded during its history. He appears quite sympathetic to this idea, but rather less sympathetic to drift. By 1963, however, his own research and that of Hess, notably, had changed his mind.

In April that year he used the forum of an article in *Scientific*

American to set out his complaints against the prevailing theory. The article was titled baldly—provocatively, given prevailing opinion—"Continental Drift."

"The traditional rigid-earth theory," Wilson began, "holds that the earth, once hot, is now cooling, that it became rigid at an early date, and that the contraction attendant on the cooling process creates compressive forces." These forces "squeeze up mountains," but the rigid-earth theory otherwise holds that the continents themselves were "frozen in place."

"On the other hand," Wilson advanced, "a number of formidable objections have been raised by those who have studied radioactivity, ancient climates, terrestrial magnetism and, most recently, submarine geology."

The burden of their objections was that the continents may move laterally.

Wilson proceeded to spell out the argument for drift on the merits of the existing, admittedly incomplete, research.

Having pulled off the minor coup of getting a discussion on drift into the most widely read general science journal published in the United States, Wilson then sought out opportunities to promote the idea to his colleagues directly. He used the occasion later in 1963 of the annual meeting of the International Union of Geodesy and Geophysics to address a large number of them.

At the meeting, Wilson could hardly be considered the wild-eyed outsider; he had been the professional society's president from 1957 to 1960. In a major speech, he discussed the current opportunity by comparing it to previous revolutions in planetary science.

"I believe that earth science is ripe for such a revolution," he exhorted his colleagues. "In a lesser way its present situation is like that of astronomers before the ideas of Copernicus and Galileo were accepted."

This was a bold stroke on Wilson's part. Even though rigid-earth theory may have looked a bit stodgy in 1963, its explanations somewhat threadbare, the crucial scientific studies of Vine, Cox, Doell and Dalrymple, and Wilson himself had not yet been put together. Wilson's sense of "ripeness," however, was acute. Three years later, because of his own efforts and those of Vine and the others, the revolution that Wilson had called for was at hand.

For many scientists, the moment of conversion to seafloor spreading occurred in April 1966 at a meeting of the American Geophysical Union. First Neil Opdyke presented his research on core samples, confirming the magnetic-reversal time scale. Then James Heirtzler of Columbia showed the magnetic profile obtained over the East Pacific Rise aboard *Eltanin*. The symmetrical plot of leg 19 of the cruise was what the scientific community had been needing— but not expecting—to see.

The shock of recognition followed directly.

Richard Doell of the Geological Survey looked at the magnetic profile from the *Eltanin* and exclaimed, "It's so good, it can't possibly be true. But it is."

Allan Cox later recalled his reaction. "I hadn't really believed in seafloor spreading up until then because the magnetic data hadn't been very symmetrical. But suddenly there was the incredible symmetry of the *Eltanin* 19. I remember my reaction, 'Good grief! Vine is right after all.' "

With the core group of geochronologists and marine geophysicists convinced, from that moment the revolution proceeded swiftly, with little overt resistance. Testimony to just how fast the conversion occurred is that by January 1967 nearly seventy proposals for presentations on seafloor spreading had been submitted to the American Geophysical Union for the professional society's next meeting. Four whole sessions in the four-day conference focused on aspects of the dynamic seafloor. So great was the enthusiasm for the topic that when Harry Hess gave a speech entitled "History of Seafloor Spreading," not even the largest auditorium could hold the crowd.

Wilson was triumphant. "It seems that we know what is going on in the earth," he crowed in a speech later that year. He offered another historic parallel. Seafloor spreading, he said, "could be as important to geology as Harvey's discovery of the circulation of the blood was to physiology or evolution to biology.

"This is the most exciting event in geology for a century and every effort in research should be bent toward it."

Just the same, in the mid-1960s those who were beginning to think of themselves as earth scientists still had some rather basic questions to answer. A skeptic might well have asked, Just what is it exactly that spreads over the surface of the globe? Do segments of the mountain ridges move, relative to other segments? Or do the mountains stay put and the flanks of seafloor adjacent to them move?

And seriously, the skeptic might have continued, it's fine to simplify the discussion by talking as if the spreading happens on a flat surface; but really, if you say we have spreading on the sphere of the earth, would you explain how it works?

Again, Tuzo Wilson, this time as theoretician, was the major influence in answering these questions. In 1965 he had been the first to propose the key idea of crustal plates. This idea resulted from his attempt to explain seafloor fault lines.

The seafloor faults that concerned Wilson are cracks observed perpendicular to spreading ridges around the globe. They break the ridges up into apparent segments. When Wilson took up the question, the favored interpretation was that the faults were evidence of the tearing of the ocean crust as the ridge segments moved independently left or right with respect to each other. Wilson, however, didn't see it that way.

The ridges themselves were stationary, he argued. It was the new ocean crust, formed at them, that was moving, albeit slowly. The perpendicular cracks—transform faults—were caused by this movement. Wilson gave the name "plate" to these large masses of moving rock. He further proposed that the surface of the earth was divided into several large plates.

This notion that the surface of the earth was made up of rigid plates implied that these plates were of a certain depth and moved as a unit. The reality of this concept came under scrutiny by researchers at the Lamont Geological Observatory. Under Maurice Ewing's direction, Lamont had always been in the forefront of a certain kind of oceanographic research that could determine whether such large "plates" did, in fact, exist. This was seismic research, the study of earth structure through sound waves.

Maurice Ewing himself had pioneered the use of explosives to understand the structure of the ocean floor. A stint in the late 1920s as a petroleum prospector in the swamps and lakes of the Louisiana coast taught Ewing how to prepare homemade bombs, detonate them in the mud, and record their return signals on a seismometer. The explosives would send out powerful sound waves which would penetrate the ocean floor and be deflected in certain characteristic ways depending on the nature and depth of the rock structure. As with echo sounding, the plot of the returning sound waves made a picture of this invisible structure.

Getting this sort of information became a main mission of Lamont during Ewing's tenure from 1949 to 1972. A photograph of the 1950s shows Ewing on board a research ship looking like a man possessed, lacing up a canvas rucksack full of dynamite. The rucksack would be dropped overboard and detonated; up would come the signals; advanced would be Ewing's never-ending quest for data. "We're paying for this ship twenty-four hours a day," Ewing would say on a cruise, "so damn it, we're going to *work* twenty-four hours a day." Explosives would be detonated through the night, if that was what Ewing's schedule required.

Seismic work at Lamont had produced important insights over the years, notably the first documentation of the existence of the global midocean ridge. But as the revelations of the 1960s unfolded, Ewing remained cool to the growing arguments in favor of seafloor spreading, and for a time he appeared to take the role of counter-revolutionist. It could have been expected that Wilson's idea of plates would fall under the scrutiny of Lamont researchers and be tested by their main tool, the seismometer.

As had been the case with the development of the echo sounder, the magnetometer, and the mass spectrometer, it was the needs of the military for more sophisticated detection instruments that brought about the development of more refined seismometers. These instruments were conventionally used for earthquake identification and geological prospecting, but in the late 1950s the U.S. government had deployed a global system of seismometers to monitor nuclear weapons explosions.

This monitoring system of 125 stations could reveal the direction of motion associated with earthquakes. With data from this network at his disposal, Lynn Sykes of Lamont was able to determine that movements of the ocean floor under natural conditions were just as Wilson predicted. The seafloor was moving away from the ridges; the ridges themselves were staying put.

From other earthquake studies, Sykes contributed another piece to the emerging picture of the plates. Since the 1930s it had been known that deep earthquakes were concentrated in areas around the edges of oceans close to volcanoes on land. Studies in the 1950s showed that those ocean areas were the location of deep trenches.

But this puzzled seismologists. Trenches descended into the mantle, where the combination of high heat and high pressure should have melted anything solid and ruled out the possibility of earthquakes.

Beginning in 1964, Sykes and two Lamont colleagues, Bryan Isacks and Jack Oliver, had examined the earthquake activity near the South Pacific island of Tonga. There they measured the earthquake zone and found it much narrower than they had supposed—only twelve miles wide. Furthermore, the vibrations of the earthquake traveled along a plane tilting down from the ocean floor on about a 45-degree angle. This suggested something unexpected—that there was some hard, cold, planar substance in the trench.

Suddenly Sykes and his colleagues realized that the seafloor itself was being bent, and pushed or pulled—they didn't know which—down into the trench, creating the earthquake zone. Just as Harry Hess had predicted, the seafloor was descending into the giant "jaw-crusher" of the ocean trench.

The Tonga Trench research added another major piece of information that cleared up some of the unanswered questions about the seafloor. The descending slab of seafloor had thickness—sixty miles. What was spreading was not just the surface of the floor, the crust alone, but a thicker block. It seemed fair to call the object that spread what Wilson had, a plate.

So, there were moving plates. But what were their shapes, where were the outlines of these blocks of the earth, and what determined their movement and location on the globe?

The seafloor relief maps of the early 1960s, drawn on Mercator projections (like conventional maps in an atlas), offered some hints. The seafloor ridges were identified, and the ridges would clearly be considered one boundary of adjoining plates. But where were the other boundaries? At first it seemed impossible to say. And without determining the outline of the plates it would be impossible to describe where they moved.

The maps did seem to be giving another clue, however. Fault lines ran perpendicular from the midocean ridge system toward continental landmasses. There appeared to be some connection between the length of the fault lines and the distance from the ridge to the continents. Northern Africa and northern South America, for example, were closer together than the southern parts of those continents, and the fault lines coming off the Mid-Atlantic Ridge were shorter in the north, longer in the south. What did the pattern mean?

The answers were found in 1967 by young geophysicists who visualized seafloor spreading as it actually occurs, over the surface of a sphere.

Dan McKenzie and Jason Morgan were young researchers in 1967; McKenzie, at Scripps, was only twenty-five, Morgan, at Princeton, was thirty-two. First McKenzie, then Morgan published articles explaining how the spreading seafloor conforms to classical laws of motion on a sphere.

Though Morgan's article was second by a few months, it was more detailed. His presentation, like McKenzie's, rested on the laws of motion outlined by an eighteenth-century mathematician, Leonhard Euler.

Euler explained that on a sphere any two blocks of material in motion could be thought of as rotating around some point. This point, the pole of rotation, could be extended by drawing an imaginary line from it through the center of the sphere, forming an axis of rotation. Around this axis the blocks would move on the sphere at a speed proportionate to their distance from the pole of rotation. Their relative motion, and therefore their displacement from each other, would be greatest at the position farthest from the pole, the "equator" of this sphere of rotation. The displacement would vanish to zero at the pole itself.

Morgan took Euler's theorem and applied it to the blocks of the earth, which he defined according to the latest insights, those coming from Wilson and Sykes and Vine. While the old worldview divided the surface of the globe into continents and ocean basins, Morgan divided the planet's surface into contiguous blocks. Between blocks were three dividing lines: ridges, where the blocks are created; trenches, where they are consumed; and certain "great faults," where they slip past each other. He examined the fault lines shared by adjoining plate blocks.

From Euler's theorem, Morgan predicted that these fault lines would lie on "circles of latitude" about some pole of rotation. When he used the terms "latitude," "poles," and "equator," Morgan was not referring to the familiar north and south poles and the tropical equator, but instead to hypothetical positions that may be easiest to think of as superimposed on the familiar sphere of the earth.

So Morgan examined the positions of the faults in the African and South American plates that intersect the Mid-Atlantic Ridge. If these faults really outlined blocks that behaved according to Euler's geometrical law, they would lie along circles of latitude on an imagined sphere or rotation. That imaginary sphere would have a pole around which the blocks would move.

Morgan found that the faults did overlie "circles of latitude" that corresponded to a pole of motion. The pole of this South Atlantic sphere was a spot off the southeast coast of Greenland. From Euler's theorem, locations in the two blocks that were closer to the pole should be closer together than locations that were farther from the pole, and indeed northern Brazil and Guinea in Africa were closer together than were Cape Horn and the Cape of Good Hope. Brazil and Guinea were nearer the pole of rotation. The southern continental capes were nearer the equator of this sphere of rotation. The significance of all this: a fundamental principle of geometry confirmed that the earth was divided into moving blocks.

Morgan went on to show the poles of rotation for other blocks (or plates) of the earth. In the process he demonstrated that something humankind takes to be both fixed and mysterious—the positions of the continents—could be predicted by elementary geometry.

The young scientist's spin around the globe with Leonhard Euler pushed the revolution in earth science to a climax and ushered in a new regime. "Plate tectonics" was the name given to the new paradigm, and if it sounded technical and academic at first, it also had oddly familiar echoes.

"Tectonic": the word imitated in its rhythm and sound something of its meaning—the rise of construction, the slap together of objects. "Plate tectonics": the study of how the earth's geological features are constructed by the action of the plates.

In an introduction to a collection of essays about plate tectonics, Tuzo Wilson memorably described the new worldview.

"Formerly, most scientists thought of the earth as a rigid body with fixed continents and permanent ocean basins," Wilson wrote. "But now most of them consider the brittle surface of the earth to be broken into six large plates and several smaller ones, which very slowly move and jostle one another like blocks of ice on a river that is breaking up in the spring thaw.

"They believe that the thin plates of this surface layer are 'floating' on a deeper layer that is slowly deformable. Each continent does not constitute one plate, but rather each is incorporated with surrounding ocean floor into a plate that is larger than the continent, just as a raft of logs may be frozen into a sheet of ice.

"These plates have repeatedly collided and joined, broken apart, and rejoined in different patterns. As they have done so ocean floors have been reabsorbed, but the continents have been modified and remain."

Thomas Kuhn might well have complimented this new vision of the earth for its simplicity and comprehensiveness, its "elegance." The earth's surface was seen to be the result of the movements of just a few main structural elements, the plates. Their motions, moreover, were limited in kind. Plates are created at seafloor spreading zones, where material for them emerges from the innards of the earth. They are destroyed—their material descends back into the earth—at seafloor trenches and at the margins of continents. And this crustal material may rise again, for once under the continents the descended material melts, and may reemerge later in volcanoes, creating a new crust for the earth. Eventually this continental crust, too, will erode and return to the sea and perhaps ultimately to the hot mantle beneath the seafloor, where it will be melted and return again, in a grand continuing cycle.

In the tens of millions of years between creation and destruction, the moving, spreading plates slip slowly past or collide with each other, like late-night dancers in a crowded ballroom. These are events of more than middling significance. The sliding moves continents around, and the collisions wreak earthquakes and force up mountains.

Plate tectonics theory was quickly accepted by the scientific community for at least a couple of reasons. The straightforward, objective reason was that the theory was supported by data, of which there was a significant amount by 1968. But the subjective reasons were surely also strong. One influence was "revolutionary fever."

While scientists may not like in retrospect to think of themselves as being swayed by something other than data, evidence of at least one academic study points to a kind of state of contagion in the community.

This study of 300 geologists found that at the time of their conversion to plate tectonics there was a "relative lack of familiarity with the relevant literature" among them as a group. The sociologists who analyzed the responses theorized that a "chain reaction" occurred within the profession as a whole, and the conversion of the profession was not "the result of individual judgments of the evidence."

One could quibble with this study and still admit to the influence of subjective factors. The new worldview was simply very compelling. It presented a unified picture of the planet. It accounted for geological phenomena from the great, like the drifting of continents, to the comparatively small, like the genesis of earthquakes. It was, in a word, suggestive. It inspired the imagination.

As Wilson wrote in 1972, the new worldview could be expected to open lines of inquiry unimagined before. "Just as the aftermaths of earlier scientific revolutions have proved to be exciting times in the history of science, so the immediate future promises to be a period of excitement and discovery in the earth sciences."

One of the foundries of the new regime was the Scripps Institution of Oceanography, in La Jolla, California. In the middle years of the 1960s, La Jolla, in the backyard of San Diego, still had the character of a small seacoast community. The explosive growth that was soon to deposit high-rise apartments on the beachfront had not yet begun. Instead, graduate students still could afford to live on the beach, some of them in quaint old cottages that were rumored to have once been retreats of Hollywood stars.

Living near the beach was very much the thing at Scripps in those days. You could spend all month in La Jolla without ever going into San Diego, up over the winding mountain road that led back to town. What would be the point of leaving? This was southern California in its heyday. The Beach Boys were crooning the siren song of fun in the sun to all of America, and they were doing it right from here.

The southern California style seemed, at first glance, to be at odds with academic seriousness. For male graduate students coming to Scripps from some conservative university back East it was a bit of a surprise to find professors wearing shorts and Hawaiian shirts to class. The women students wore halter tops and suntans, and as the early 1960s became the later 1960s bikinis became the fashion. The popular walkway outside the lunchroom became known as Bikini Plaza.

At Scripps the course of study had a certain informality as well. With professors off at sea on research cruises on an unpredictable basis, there was no such thing as a set program of courses in a particular discipline. Students were pretty much on their own to obtain a program that suited them. Scripps accepted only about the top 10 percent of applicants, and the general idea seemed to be that if you were good enough to get in, you were expected to be smart enough to take care of yourself and do well, regardless.

Under the surface informality, though, was a place conscious of itself and of its mission. Under the leadership of Roger Revelle, its director of the time, Scripps in the late 1950s became the nucleus of a new university, the University of California at San Diego. By the early 1960s, the oceanography institute campus was expanding dramatically, and with physical expansion came new aspirations.

During any year from the late fifties through the sixties, about 10 of the Scripps faculty could be expected to be members of the prestigious National Academy of Sciences, and several scientists who contributed to the development of seafloor spreading and plate tectonics ideas did their research there.

Scripps, however, had not been in the vanguard of the earth sciences revolution. It was not Princeton, Cambridge, or Columbia's Lamont. But people there were able to see the implications of the work of Wilson and Vine, and when the time came, they were eager to move Scripps into position for new opportunities. Faculty member H. W. Menard commented in 1966, "Marine geology and geology as a whole are at a turning point. It will be a very exciting time for participants but a sad time for onlookers."

The year after that observation, Dan McKenzie and Robert Parker developed their essay about motions of plates on a sphere. They were working in a Scripps office overlooking the Pacific, virtually astride an ancient seafloor spreading zone.

It was—just about any of them would have acknowledged— stimulating to be a graduate student there. For those with motivation there were real opportunities. Most grad students worked as research assistants, and though the $270 monthly pay wasn't exactly the big time, budgets for equipment and research projects were generous. The largesse of the moment was partly spurred on by a sense of a new manifest destiny for the United States towards the sea and its riches.

In the mid-1960s, American scientists and politicians became fond of jawboning about the exploration of the "inner space" of the ocean in the same way that President Kennedy had earlier ballyhooed the exploration of outer space. The oceans, furthermore, had a down-to-earth appeal that fit into the social conscience of the time. In 1966, for example, when Vice President Hubert Humphrey came to campus, he spoke as if oceanography might be enlisted in creating the Great Society.

"We're on the threshold of a new age of exploration," Humphrey was moved to say. "Our dreams for the oceans are not those of the poets and the prophets. They are practical dreams. . . . We intend to develop the bountiful resources of the sea to serve man's needs."

For someone starting out in a career in oceanography, the time and the place couldn't have seemed better, if you knew how to play the time and the place. To succeed in an environment like this it helped to be informal—*cool*—in a southern California style, and yet single-mindedly creative when it counted. John B. Corliss was that kind of person.

Unlike many other married students, who lived in the married student housing on campus, Jack Corliss and his wife lived in a big old house in town, formerly owned by the Scripps family, the local business magnates. The Corlisses, who arrived in town in 1963, shared the house with other Scripps grad students, and it became the scene of many parties and discussions that went on late into the night. Jack was always willing to talk, and would talk well on many topics, not just science, with a kind of delighted, inquisitive manner. He relished exploring the connections between seemingly disparate things. Corliss was a man indulgent with possibilities, but with his science he also had the ability to become deeply absorbed.

He was one of the bright lights in the orbit around Tjeerd van Andel, a marine geologist born and trained in Holland. Jerry, as he was known, had had a good deal of experience in both industry and academia, and he was making a name for himself with his studies of the Mid-Atlantic Ridge. It so happened that on a research cruise to the Atlantic with van Andel, Corliss was diverted onto a course of study that would ultimately point him in a new direction. That direction would ultimately have its influences on marine science.

The cruise was dedicated in part to Corliss's thesis project, and one morning he and van Andel were up on the bridge of the *Thomas Washington* discussing Corliss's plans, which were to do some geologic mapping of the ridge. Suddenly from down below in the ship came a boom.

The ship continued to move ahead on its course, so the two kept talking, realizing that if there was a serious problem they would only be in the way of the crew who had to deal with it. But after a few minutes they decided to go below to find out what had happened. On the floor of the kitchen, they discovered the aftermath of an accident. There was the cook, lying on his back, his leg being put into a splint.

During the night before, the cook had placed a large can of sweet potatoes, sealed, in the oven, and on this morning, preparing to bake bread, he had turned on the oven without taking the can out. When the can got hot enough it exploded, blowing the door off the oven and apparently breaking the cook's leg in the process.

The cook was in pain, and the doctor on board couldn't tell exactly if and where the leg was broken. So a decision was made to bring the cook to land to have his leg X-rayed and try to find a new cook. It was five days of precious research time later before the *Thomas Washington* was back on site.

And then a new mishap occurred.

Jack Corliss smiled whimsically as he talked about those events more than twenty years later. Corliss is a big man, with a generous girth, a large face, and a swarm of white beard. But it is the eyes—bright, even merry—that one notices. They seem to be looking over events, looking at them easily, quizzically, as if for a pattern.

"It was then that the *Washington*'s engineers noticed an apparent malfunction in the thruster motor on the bow of the ship," Corliss told me. "And just at the same time"—his smile broadened—"an urgent message came from the sister ship of ours, the *Thomas Thompson*. They had been heading into a storm off the Oregon coast when *their* bow thruster had completely dropped out of its housing and disappeared." The bow thruster helps a ship in critical maneuvers.

The crew of the *Washington* became seized with anxiety, and cables were rigged around the hull to hold the ship's bow thruster in. The cables, however, vibrated against the hull and banged horrendously, which would have ruined any echo soundings of the seabed and Corliss's efforts to make a map.

The result of the mishaps—the exploding can and the banging cables—was that Corliss had to make last-minute changes in plans for his thesis. He dredged some rocks from the seafloor; back in the lab he would analyze them.

The rocks, it turned out, were the result of a sort of bang themselves.

When Corliss did this dredging, in December 1965, no one had ever observed underwater hot springs. In a general way, though, one could infer from Harry Hess's theory of seafloor spreading that they would exist. The argument would go something like this. If the seafloor was being spread apart by the action of hot rock underneath it, there were probably also cracks in the seafloor accompanying this spreading, and cold seawater would no doubt slip down into those cracks. Once under the surface, the cold water would be heated by the rock, and then if there were openings back up to the surface, the heated water might be expelled, creating hot springs.

Key parts of this model had been recognized during the nineteenth century. The existence of submarine volcanism, of the circulation of seawater through the seafloor, and of mineral deposits on the seafloor was known. Still, no one until the advent of seafloor spreading had put those three elements together with hot springs.

In the year of Corliss's cruise, 1965, J. W. Elder of the University of Manchester published the first article linking thermal springs and midocean spreading centers. A few other scientists soon followed, speculating about the cause from its apparent effects. At Scripps, for instance, Kurt Boström and Melvin Peterson made the connection between unusually high concentrations of certain chemical elements in seafloor sediments and hydrothermal activity and volcanism. However, they didn't offer an explicit model of how the pieces fit together. This Jack Corliss did from the rocks he had dredged.

Examining them, he saw that they were all basalts, rocks of volcanic origin. From that it was clear that they came from eruption systems, from caldrons of magma under the seafloor. That was the first clue. The second clue was their appearance. Some were glassy, while others were crystalline. The third clue was the kicker: the chemical composition of the two kinds of rock was slightly different. The crystalline ones were depleted in some substances that were present in the glassy ones.

As he worked on the rocks, the three clues came together. The crystalline basalts were depleted in some chemicals, Corliss reasoned, because they had formed at depth. There seawater, seeping downward through the seafloor, had slowly penetrated into the hot rock and leached chemicals out of it. Crystals formed as the rocks slowly cooled. Conversely, the glassy basalts were not depleted because they had been formed when molten magma came quickly into contact with cold seawater above the seafloor.

Two important inferences could be drawn from his analysis, Corliss saw. First, the cracking of the hot rock beneath the floor would create heated-water solutions—"hydrothermal" solutions. These fluids would carry the chemicals leached out of the rock. Second, the temperature difference between the cold surface of the seafloor and the heated interior of the sub-seafloor would establish small convection loops between the seafloor and subfloor. These loops would carry the hydrothermal solutions from beneath the seafloor out through cracks in the floor. The result? There must be seafloor hot springs.

In 1970, the year he completed his doctoral thesis on the basalts and the hot springs, Jack Corliss believed that the springs were important primarily because they could help explain this mineral composition of the ocean floor and of seawater itself. Since sea life as a whole was presumably adapted to the specific chemical composition of the sea, if the hot springs played a role in this composition that would certainly make them important. And minerals had been collected by Boström, Peterson, and others; such minerals might have commercial value.

Such considerations warranted direct inspection of seafloor hot springs. But that involved mounting an expedition in search of phenomena that had not been seen before and that, moreover, might be unusually hard to find. The scientific community was not quite ready for this. It would be another six years before Corliss got his chance.

Instead, the attention of seafloor researchers—the geologists, geochemists, and geophysicists who converged on the new scientific territory—was still on the grosser physical manifestations of seafloor spreading. The major research program of the late sixties, which began in 1968 and was ongoing in 1970, was the Deep Sea Drilling Project. This was a global study initially designed to put the theory of seafloor spreading to a conclusive test. Cores were taken of the seafloor at intervals out from ridges and then dated to see if the seafloor's age was indeed related to its distance from the ridge, as the theory predicted.

By the time it was completed in 1983 this era of the Deep Sea Drilling Project would be referred to as the "most successful experiment ever done." Six hundred and twenty-five holes taken during ninety-six cruises would abundantly confirm the theory. Already in 1970, though, the confirmation was clear, and some scientists were setting their sights on the next challenge.

It was becoming time to go beyond piecemeal surveying and sampling of ridges, they felt, time to mount a comprehensive expedition to a seafloor rift zone to examine this critically important region in detail.

A group of scientists from U.S. academic institutions and government agencies, in collaboration with French colleagues, began organizing such an expedition to the Mid-Atlantic Ridge in 1971. The Americans foresaw that the dives would draw both a great deal of attention from the public and scrutiny from funding agencies. They were determined it would be a success, but there was sharp disagreement about what tools would be best to study the ridge.

Among the planners of the expedition were Xavier Le Pichon and Charles Drake of Lamont. Drake, who had used manned submersibles, wanted to use them for the Mid-Atlantic expedition, but there wasn't much initial support for them.

One reason was practical: Mounting an expedition with submersibles is costly. The operation of the submersible during a dive is a considerable expense in itself, but the sub also has to be maintained by a technical crew; and both they and the research scientists usually need to be housed on another ship during the course of the expedition. Operating costs of $10,000 to $25,000 per day were commonplace. The problem was that scientific administrators had begun to feel that in too many research projects, submersibles weren't being put to best use.

A small research submarine is an ideal tool for going to a particular, preselected location and giving scientists an opportunity to observe and sample it firsthand. But it is not an efficient tool for reconnaissance work, for attempting to scout and survey a quantity of unexplored terrain. For an individual dive, a submersible such as the *Alvin* is limited to working an area of a few square miles, both by mechanical limitations, such as its relatively slow cruising speed, and by the endurance of the divers. Reconnaissance was not the *Alvin*'s forte. But all too often since it had been put in operation in 1964, the sub had dived in locations where thorough reconnaissance work had not been done, because the right tools were not available.

The other objection to subs was more philosophical. Geophysicists had a good deal of influence in earth sciences in the United States at the time. Many of the insights into plate tectonics had come from the broad-scale perspective common to geophysical studies, including seismology and geomagnetism, and there was a certain professional skepticism about the narrower approaches favored by geologists. A submersible was viewed as an awfully expensive jeep just to go to a location where some geologist would use, essentially, a rock hammer on the end of a robot arm.

The debate over the use of submersibles came to a climax at a planning meeting for the expedition at Princeton University. The year was 1972. One of those asked to speak about the uses of submersibles was a thirty-year-old graduate student in marine geology, Robert Ballard.

Ballard was a student of K. O. Emery, a geologist at Woods Hole. Before the Princeton meeting, Le Pichon of Lamont had written Emery a letter asking about the appropriateness of using *Alvin* for a deep expedition, and Emery had asked Ballard to respond. Despite his youth, Ballard had a good deal of experience with submersibles, much more than many senior researchers.

He had begun designing submersibles when he was still a high school student. As a college student he had bid, unsuccessfully, on the design of the *Alvin*. As a grad student at the University of Southern California, he worked at North American Aviation on submarines for Mobil Oil. In 1967, after duty in Vietnam, he was assigned to Woods Hole as a naval officer, as liaison to the *Alvin* program. And he resumed his graduate studies under Emery by doing research in the Gulf of Maine.

Ballard wrote to Le Pichon enthusiastically about *Alvin*. The sub was reliable, he said, with navigation, sampling, and data-logging skills.

At the Princeton meeting, Ballard was asked to make the case for *Alvin*. He spoke from a lectern at the bottom of a steeply rising amphitheater. When he looked up, a host of scientific luminaries was looking down on him, and he was scared to death. But in a straight, matter-of-fact way, the youthful-looking grad student went about explaining to his audience how he had been using the submersible to do his mapping work. The presentation was all straightforward, or so it seemed to him.

Ballard finished speaking, and Frank Press, a leading geophysicist from MIT and a Lamont graduate (and later president of the National Academy of Sciences), rose up like a Roman senator. "Please name for me," said Press, "one significant thing a manned submersible has done."

Press made a brief, dramatic pause, said, "I rest my case," and sat down.

Ballard was mortified. An uneasy silence filled the amphitheater.

Then Bruce Luyendyk, a young geophysicist, rose to his feet, picking up the gauntlet tossed down by Press. "It's not the fault of the technology," he addressed the crowd. "The scientific community has not tried to use the sub as a significant tool. I rest *my* case."

And he sat down.

The debate spilled over into dinner that night, where Ballard felt worked over by the "heavyweights," the institute and program directors. And he said, "Look, I'm not advocating a submersible in every garage; I'm advocating *one*."

Finally, a consensus emerged, articulated by the flinty, powerful Maurice Ewing, the Lamont director. "We'll let this happen," Ewing told Ballard, "but if you fail, we'll melt *Alvin* down into titanium paper clips."

In this context of a life-or-death test for manned submersibles, the organizers put their best foot forward, dubbed the expedition with an auspicious name, Project FAMOUS—for French-American Mid-Ocean Undersea Study—and proceeded to get the critical reconnaissance work done with the appropriate tools for the job. They spent two years, from 1972 to 1974, surveying part of the ridge, and ended up producing a photographic map of the seafloor off the Azores Islands, west of Portugal, where the dives were planned. Those who were to be involved in the dives spent hours in a Navy gymnasium in Washington, D.C., walking around on the photographic map shot by underwater cameras, studying the terrain.

Thanks to such detailed preparation, the FAMOUS dives in the summer of 1974 lived up to the expedition's name. The researchers dove right onto a seafloor spreading zone, a region several miles across. There they gained some direct insights into spreading and the geologic processes associated with it. Even before the scientific research papers were published, however, the expedition was judged a success, not only by scientific administrators but by the public. Submersibles had shown their value in exploring the sea-floor. And they captured the imagination.

National Geographic magazine heralded FAMOUS with a thirty-page feature story. "For the first time in history," the magazine extolled, "men have gone down in the sea to prowl and study firsthand the largest mountain range on this planet—a system greater than the Rockies, the Andes, and the Himalayas combined."

Bob Ballard had the key role of teaching the other scientists how to use the *Alvin*, which was no simple matter. The success of Ballard's efforts can be measured by their effects on one of the five American scientists who had the chance to dive in the sub.

Jerry van Andel was involved with the expedition because of his expertise on the ridge, but his earlier studies had all been done from shipboard; he had never been diving in a submersible before this expedition. Still, van Andel's expertise led to his being named chief scientist of the American diving team, and FAMOUS put him two miles down seven times over. He came away impressed by the quality of scientific observation that was possible in a sub compared to what could be obtained from shipboard and instrument studies.

Something else happened to him. He was enchanted by diving.

In his journal he wrote, "The seafloor is so beautiful, so out-of-this-world beautiful. The misty, grandiose, mysterious landscape of craggy black and snowy, pillowy white set in the foreground with brilliantly lit small, sharp and perfect vignettes of rock, coral, and sponge is unforgettable."

He could not do the vision justice, he wrote. He wished he could draw it. Back on land he told a reporter that diving on the ridge "was like walking across the top of New York City skyscrapers. . . . the cliffs were straight up and down—some 50 to 200 feet high or more."

The experience was a tonic for both his intellect and his soul. When van Andel returned to his university he was determined to extend this experience, to make something more of seafloor exploration.

The institution that Professor van Andel returned to was Oregon State University; he had been there since 1968. One of those he shared his enthusiasm with was Assistant Professor Jack Corliss. Corliss had followed his major professor there from Scripps.

In some ways, Oregon State would have seemed an unlikely choice for ocean scientists with ambition. The university, located in

Corvallis, a modest little town in the heart of farming country, was known for its agriculture and forestry research. But until 1959 there had been no oceanography program there at all. The fact that the Pacific Ocean off Oregon, sixty miles away, was scientifically a virtual unknown, however, had ultimately piqued the interest of the federal and state governments, and they began funding marine research. In less than a decade, the operating budget for the school of oceanography, which was $34,000 in 1959, had jumped to over $2 million.

During the same period, the academic staff had grown comparably. The open territory and the growing program drew certain types, both younger researchers, like Corliss, who saw a chance to make their mark, and mid-career people, like van Andel, who saw new options and higher academic rank. From Scripps alone came not only those two, but by 1970 a half-dozen others.

Van Andel realized that FAMOUS had raised many new questions for research. But he was concerned that answers would be slow in coming, since there was no funding to use the *Alvin* in a major research expedition after 1974. Van Andel and Richard Von Herzen, of Woods Hole, who had been with van Andel during FAMOUS, came up with the idea to propose a next step in seafloor submersible research. It must be one, they knew, that was so interesting it couldn't be denied. They felt they had both such an idea and a place to work on it.

In 1972, before FAMOUS, Von Herzen had been the leader of a shipboard research expedition to a spreading ridge near the Galapagos Islands. There he and his colleagues had lowered a heat probe into sediments of the ridge and spotted a warmer-than-normal area. To confirm their probe measurements they suspended a chain of ultrasensitive thermistors above the ocean bottom in the same location. The temperature recorded closest to the bottom was warmer than the one above it, which was warmer than the blip recorded above it, which suggested that there was a little rising plume of heated water. Von Herzen believed that this was evidence of a hot spring. To the National Science Foundation he and van Andel proposed studies of the Galapagos Rift to find out. With the *Alvin* they would explore part of the rift.

CHAPTER FOUR

THE PATH OF DISCOVERY

Van Andel and Von Herzen's proposal to explore the Galapagos Rift was bold. Hot springs had not been found during the FAMOUS expedition. Yet the two men believed that hot springs were likely to be found on midocean ridges. When they were at Scripps, they were familiar with the geochemical studies of their colleagues Boström and Peterson, and with Corliss's work, of course, but they were also persuaded by the geophysical studies of Clive Lister, of the University of Washington.

Lister was a specialist in heat flow at the ridges, which he had begun studying as a graduate student at Cambridge University in 1959. Working on the Mid-Atlantic Ridge, Lister first encountered a very puzzling phenomenon. The heat flows he and others measured at the ridge crest didn't match the theoretical values that had been calculated. Although sometimes high in comparison to the flanks of the ridge, they weren't nearly as high as would be expected in the vicinity of molten rock, which had raised the crest. What caused the temperature shortfall?

Heat can be dissipated from the earth's interior in three ways: conduction through the earth; convection, by way of a fluid; and radiation. Lister gave his attention to conduction, which appeared to be the most likely mechanism, and when the shortfall appeared, he systematically began examining several possible explanations for it.

He considered ways in which errors could have been introduced by the way the sampling was done. Von Herzen had suggested that measurements might be depressed because they were always taken in ridge valleys. Measurements were taken in valleys because the probe could go into sediment there; a heat probe wouldn't penetrate the hard rock of a ridge crest. But Von Herzen's concern was that sediments might be cooled if they had mixed with water. One way that could have occurred was if they had been deposited as a result of slumping from off an elevation. This would place a cool layer on the top.

To test this hypothesis, Lister began by attempting to measure the depth of sediments. At Washington he spent some time designing a suitable instrument, a high-resolution seismic profiler, and by the late 1960s he had found that, contrary to some expectations, sediments on the Juan de Fuca Ridge were thin. They were also old enough, on the order of thousands of years, that even if they had slumped and cooled at one point, they would likely have become warmed again from below.

From these pieces of evidence, Lister saw that some characteristic of the sediments didn't seem to be disturbing conduction and causing the ridge measurements to be cooler than theory indicated. He was beginning to believe that conduction wasn't the only cooling mechanism operating at the ridge. He became convinced of it when he managed to get heat-flow probes into recently formed seafloor on the Explorer Ridge, north of the Juan de Fuca Ridge, and discovered that this very youngest seafloor was still not as hot as theory required.

The solution to the puzzle of the missing heat, he felt, was that water was flowing through the rocks of the seafloor and taking the heat out of them, by convection. That rocks are permeable seems hard to believe, but Lister showed in detailed theoretical calculations how water could penetrate into hot rock. The cold seawater would cause a thermal stress in the hot rock, just as a very hot glass will crack if put into a pail of ice water. In the sub-seafloor, the rocks would fracture along a "cracking front," where temperatures were thought to be about 500 degrees Celsius, or more than 900 degrees Fahrenheit. A typical crack is a millimeter wide, and with only one crack every meter, Lister calculated, the permeability of rock is equal to that of coarse sand. With more frequent cracks the permeability of rock exceeds that of sand.

Lister argued that hot springs would arise in a permeable ridge crest environment because of the difference in density between the water heated to more than 350 degrees C. in the subfloor and that of ordinary cold seawater at the seafloor surface. The hotter water is about half as dense as cold water, so it rises, and the cold, denser water descends. Lister showed theoretically that the heat taken out of the seafloor by convection would approximately equal the missing heat not accounted for by conduction.

By a separate route, Lister, the geophysicist, had arrived at the same conclusion as Corliss and the other geochemists: There must be hot springs.

With the potential for hot springs buttressed by such arguments, the National Science Foundation provided the first stage of funding for Von Herzen and van Andel's Galapagos Rift expedition in October 1975. The challenge of the first stage of the project was to pinpoint the actual dive sites.

During this part of the planning, Jack Corliss became increasingly involved. Oregon State and Woods Hole were identified as the main participants in the project, and when van Andel took a new job at Stanford University, Corliss, though he had only junior faculty status, took his place as chief scientist and expedition leader from Oregon.

Work began over the proposed area, 500 miles west of Ecuador, during the summer of 1976. Researchers from Woods Hole and Scripps joined thirteen researchers from Oregon State to search a section of the rift zone. They used a variety of instruments to zero in on the most likely spot. They used sonar, thermistors, water chemistry samplers, sediment traps, and earthquake-detecting seismometers placed on the bottom.

When they were done, Corliss, as chief scientist on the cruise, fixed the location by navigating a marker buoy into place and anchoring it. The buoy was suspended above the bottom in such a way that it could be found by a submarine. The date was the Fourth of July, 1976, and the mood on board the research ship was running high. One of the technicians filled some weather balloons with acetylene and oxygen and set them adrift with a fuse. As the sun sank in the Pacific, the research party celebrated their success with a bang.

During the next eight months, the scientists who would be involved in the expedition busied themselves in final preparations. The main thing they were about to do—attempt to observe and understand the activity of a seafloor hot spring—no one had exactly done before, and Corliss set himself the task of designing the device that would give them the information they wanted once they actually found a hot spring.

The device that evolved was a computerized flow-through water sampler, designed to be placed directly into a hot spring by the claw hand of the *Alvin*'s mechanical arm. Eight nine-liter bottles were arranged in a rectangular frame and fixed with independently operable, remote-controlled valves. Once the sampler was in position at a hot spring, any number of the bottles could be filled; inside the *Alvin* a researcher would be able to simultaneously monitor the characteristics of the hot spring's water.

One sensor on the sampler could measure water temperature to thousandths-of-a-degree accuracy. Others measured minutely the oxygen content, water acidity or alkalinity, and conductivity, which is an indicator of the concentration of metals in the water. At the same time, other sensors would also give precise information about the seafloor depth, the altitude of the spring above the bottom, and the time. All this was recorded in computer memory, ten times per second.

The dives were scheduled for February and March 1977. On February 15, the *Knorr*, the scientific support ship, carrying most of the expedition's twenty-five scientists and twenty-six technicians, arrived on site over the Galapagos Rift. The crew got right to work placing transponders on the seafloor, for navigation.

Under the direction of Bob Ballard, the youthful veteran of submersibles, the navigation group made echo soundings of the bottom in the vicinity of the transponder left the previous summer. They compared the depth measurements obtained from these soundings with a detailed map the U.S. Navy had produced. When the depths began to match they knew roughly what the floor under them looked like. They dropped three more transponders onto the bottom.

The movements of all the vessels and of the camera sled, ANGUS (Acoustically Navigated Geological Undersea Surveyor), were to be guided by these beacons. Ballard dubbed the three tiny sources of seafloor intelligence Dopey, Sleepy, and Bashful.

On February 17, the *Alvin* arrived, carried in its mother ship, *Lulu*, a makeshift 100-foot catamaran that was made of two Navy surplus pontoons. Right away, Corliss and van Andel took the first dive in the *Alvin*, found the marker buoy left the previous summer, and then headed out exploring along the bottom. The *Alvin* had its water sampling hose at the ready, and in one place Corliss, watching the digital display, saw the temperature jump several thousandths of a degree. It wasn't much, but he and van Andel were sure that they had found a hot spring, and they attempted to get a water sample. The sampler, however, balked. The scientists continued to cruise about on the floor for a while, observing crabs, clams, and mussels, and surmising that the animals were associated with heated water, since most of the ocean floor is cold and supports little life. Finally they decided to return to the surface to adjust the water sampler.

Meanwhile, on February 15, the *Knorr* had towed the ANGUS above the bottom, taking photographs by strobe light every ten seconds and recording the temperature in that location. Up at the surface, Ballard and his group kept a vigil, monitoring any temperature changes, alert for a sudden spike. They drank Coke and mugs of coffee, ate bowls of popcorn, cracked nervous jokes, and watched the monitor.

Six hours into this routine a temperature blip suddenly appeared. They marked the location with coordinates on the Navy map—and returned, hopeful, to the vigil. Six hours later, no second temperature spike had occurred. The camera, though, had run out of its 3,000 frames of film. The ANGUS was hauled up and the film was processed.

Scientists gathered around to check the pictures. Fifteen hundred color photographs in a row looked down on a slate-blue seafloor covered with lava flows and volcanic rocks. This was worthwhile information, but not what they wanted. There was no sign of hot springs.

But then, above the familiar slate-blue background, one frame showed a suspended cloud of misty blue water. In the next frames, shapes different from rocks emerged through the mist. There were clams, dozens of them, and dozens of mussels. The time imprinted in the bottom of the picture was the same time the navigation group had noticed the temperature anomaly.

This confirmed the impression Corliss and van Andel had gained from their dive that animals and hot springs were related. On February 19, Corliss climbed back into the *Alvin*, hopeful that when he reached the bottom he would find that reality confirmed his prediction about hot springs.

On board the sub that morning was MIT geochemist John Edmond, an old friend of Corliss's from Scripps days, and pilot Jack Donnelly. An hour and a half below the surface, at 9,200 feet, the *Alvin* reached bottom. Donnelly turned on the searchlights and set the sub to find the coordinates that had marked the temperature blip.

They were cruising slowly, just above the seafloor, when abruptly, up ahead, they spotted several clusters of clams, and some other animals that looked like they might be worms, though they were standing upright in the water. The scene was strange. Donnelly set the sub down near some animals.

Corliss leaned forward to get a better view. Out the port, he saw a silkiness, a kind of silvery sheen in the water, and he stared.

Donnelly, peering out his window also, turned some controls and extended *Alvin*'s mechanical arm toward the shimmering water. In the grip of the claw was a sensitive thermometer.

Edmond called out, "It's seven point five degrees, seven point five six, seven point six." Corliss looked up at the computer readout in the sphere. It showed 7.6 degrees Celsius, about 43 degrees Fahrenheit. He sang it out.

It was not exactly hot water by the normal standards of sea-level earth. But at the bottom of the ocean, where water lies near freezing, where everything tends to inanimateness, these few degrees clearly represented a significant difference. Besides, as Corliss and Edmond stared transfixed at the shimmering water, it was streaming. Up.

They had found hot springs where the seafloor spread apart. Inside the tiny sub the three of them were shouting and cheering together.

*   *   *

When Jack Corliss and John Edmond surfaced in the *Alvin* that February evening there was no fanfare. There were no television crews recording the success as there would have been for a space shot or, say, an ascent of Mount Everest. But the scientists of the Galapagos Hydrothermal Expedition realized immediately the importance of what had happened. They had discovered a new ecosystem on earth. The hot springs were a new world of life that had not been known before. This was in itself a rare event; the discovery alone contributed to knowledge.

But these scientists had come to the Galapagos prepared for discovery. For the next four weeks, they crowded eighteen-hour work days with the exploration of this newfound world. They studied in detail a ten-square-mile section of the rift zone, which lay between the Galapagos Islands and the coast of Ecuador. To reconnoiter, they took 70,000 color photographs with the ANGUS camera sled; they made twenty-four dives in *Alvin*; and on each dive they took measurements and brought back samples. They worked intensely. It was clear as soon as Corliss and Edmond had completed their discovery dive that the cruise represented an extraordinary opportunity for research.

They accomplished an enormous amount. In the course of the cruise they examined five hot springs areas, along the actual line of ridge spreading, the axis. The environment of the seafloor hot springs quickly showed itself to be more than just new. It was odd. And dynamic.

Use of the water-sampling gear which Corliss had adapted revealed that the springs were the site of a two-way flux of chemically enriched fluids, not just a one-way flow. Up through the springs came chemicals from inside the earth; down through these vent areas went other chemicals from the land and the sea. Starting during the cruise the geochemists—John Edmond, particularly— saw that the springs were a major source of some elements, like manganese and lithium, and a sink for others, like magnesium. It seemed clear that the springs played a significant role in the chemical composition of the ocean, and by extension, of the whole planet.

The small, previously unknown springs also appeared to have a major effect on another critical element of the planet, its heat. Using a coring device which provided them with temperature measurements, the scientists estimated that heat flowed out of the Galapagos Rift at about 110 calories per second for each centimeter along the ridge's spreading axis.

Extrapolating this local heat flow to the total global seafloor ridge system over a year's time resulted in a huge number: 1.5×10^{19} calories per year. This quantity of heat is equivalent to about 1.3 million megawatts, about three times the power usage of the entire United States at peak periods during the summer. The seafloor ridge system, it appeared, provided an important avenue of escape for the heat that builds up inside the earth. About 20 percent of global heat was estimated to escape through the seafloor ridges, an escape which contributed to the overall temperature-regulation scheme of the planet in a way not thoroughly appreciated before.

These findings about chemical and heat fluxes were clearly important news. But in the course of the cruise they began to be overshadowed by discoveries of another sort. These concerned the animals.

The *Alvin* that carried Corliss, Edmond, and Donnelly back to the surface after their dive also carried some unusually large clams and some long wormlike creatures. However, that night the animals didn't get much attention. None of the main scientists on the expedition was a trained biologist, so the excitement was over the geological discoveries.

But by the next day, questions had begun to dawn on this preoccupied group of geologists, geochemists, and geophysicists. What were these animals? Where had they come from? How were they managing to survive in the dark bottom of the sea, far from the light of the sun?

The closer they looked, the more astonishing the animals seemed. There's a revealing photograph of Corliss holding a clam in front of his chest. His head is slightly tilted and his expression says he's just been shaking it in disbelief. The clam is easily four or five times the size one expects to see, perhaps a foot in length. The shell's surface is white, smooth but slightly textured, almost as if it were a wrap or blanket for what is inside.

In the photograph, Corliss holds the clam gingerly under its back. For all the world, he looks like a proud, somewhat incredulous father holding his firstborn.

Perhaps, though, he was holding it gingerly for another reason. The clam stank. It smelled like rotten eggs.

So did the strange tube worms, the red-tipped, white-bodied, three-to-five-foot-long animals that were found abundantly around the vents, their tubes anchored to the seafloor. They too had the odor of rotten eggs, hydrogen sulfide.

The gas, the geochemists realized, had been formed when sulfate in seawater became exposed to the heat of the subfloor. Transformed by the heat and modified by the contact with rock, the sulfur emerged from the hot spring as hydrogen sulfide, part of the hydrothermal fluid. But why the animals smelled so strongly of the gas was at first unclear. Hydrogen sulfide is toxic to most organisms, and by any normal expectations, animals would have been scarce around the hot springs, if present at all.

But there they were. Not only were the giant clams and worms abundant, but different sites appeared to have their own distinct communities. The scientists named the sites accordingly, with a touch of irreverence: "Clambake," "Clambake II," "Oyster Bed," "Garden of Eden," and "Dandelions." The last one was named after some strange, unknown organisms that looked like the flower.

Each new encounter with the life of the springs brought new surprises, some of them bizarre. When they opened the clams to examine their flesh, they found red blood in their vessels. When they looked closely at the worms, they noticed that these animals had no apparent mouth. When they examined rocks by some of the springs, they found thick strands of microorganisms woven into their cracks. They also collected and cultured bacteria that came jetting out with the warm water.

With each new day they became more convinced they had come upon something very important. When David Perlman, the science editor for the *San Francisco Chronicle*, joined the expedition during its second half, he immediately got caught up in the excitement, filing six lengthy news stories in eighteen days. One of them quoted Corliss saying, "I think that what we are finding here will prove to be the greatest discovery in the history of benthic biology since the discovery that life was even possible in the deep sea."

A measure of how remarkable—or improbable—the findings appeared even to scientists who weren't there was the response that Perlman's stories received initially at Woods Hole. The reporter had made arrangements to send his stories via radio from the *Knorr* to Woods Hole, which would transmit them to the *Chronicle*. But when his stories about the animals reached the director of Woods Hole, Paul Fye, he "flipped his lid, as far as I can understand,"

Perlman remembered. Fye thought Perlman must be exaggerating.

The director radioed to Bob Ballard. As Perlman recalled the event, the director said, " 'Can't you stop that guy from writing those articles?' And Ballard came to me at last and said, 'Look what's happening. You're causing consternation.' "

Although those on the cruise were fascinated and surprised, they weren't totally unprepared for the animals. In 1976 Corliss had been contacted by John Isaacs, a teacher at Scripps with wide-ranging interests, one of which was thermophilic bacteria. Isaacs had suggested that Corliss arrange for some equipment to preserve samples in case they found such heat-loving microorganisms on the Galapagos. For the cruise, Corliss asked an Oregon State colleague, geochemist Jack Dymond, to take charge of collecting and preserving some samples, and Dymond did so.

Given how abundant and widespread the bacteria seemed to be, it began to appear that they must somehow be involved in the food web of the higher animals, perhaps as the basic food supply. Although it was not their field of expertise, several of the cruise party—Corliss, van Andel, and Dymond among them—recognized that the hot springs communities were probably not getting their nourishment in the usual way, since sunlight didn't reach down to the deep sea. Photosynthesis of food was very unlikely to be a factor. The animals were more likely tapping into the chemicals coming out of the vents for their nourishment. This process, known as chemosynthesis, was not unknown in nature, but it wasn't known to operate in anything like the scale that might be involved at the hot springs. It was clearly going to be another major field for examination, and it was apparent to Perlman on the cruise "that deep-sea marine biologists will be competing wildly for the privilege of examining the samples."

All told, the voyage was rewarding beyond expectation. Perlman's account of a dive by Corliss and Ballard conveyed the astonishment and the adventure. The scientists dove to a mountain they had named—with their usual whimsy—Mount Shazaam. "Shazaam," Perlman reminded his readers, was "the magic exclamation that Captain Marvel uses in the comic book to mobilize his unearthly powers."

Alvin flew six feet above the top of Mt. Shazaam, and suddenly its altimeter went wild. From a reading of six feet, the red digital numbers raced to 90, then went blank. *Alvin* was hovering on the edge of the mountaintop, and below was an unmeasurable void.

So Donnelly flew the submarine down, and down some more, for hundreds of feet, cautiously feeling his way. . . .

For 1000 feet Donnelly took *Alvin* down, until the submarine hovered above fresh pahoehoe lava again. The side-viewing sonar sent out its pinging acoustic signals, and the scientists read the echoes.

They were on the floor of a lava lake barely 100 yards across, with towering cliffs on either side. The lake stretched ahead to invisibility. Its floor was flat pahoehoe, and at its edges pillows of basalt licked the cliffs like rounded waves frozen in their instant of motion.

Perlman's six stories attracted a good deal of attention to the cruise, and when the researchers returned to land and to their university campuses other publications picked up the story. The crescendo of media attention reached its climax in October that year with the publication of a feature story in *National Geographic* magazine. The magazine showcased the dives with color photographs of the kind the magazine specializes in—photographs of rarely seen, in this case *never*-before-seen, locations. Corliss and Ballard, who coauthored the article, and the other scientists became demi-celebrities in their college towns.

Partly the attention was for the feat itself, the daring, the apparent teamwork, and the precision involved in setting a submarine down on a tiny crack in the ocean floor, down a mile and a half in the pitch dark. It could be imagined as rather like being in a helicopter at night, without lights, and dropping from 8,000 feet right onto a geyser in mountainous Yellowstone Park. The difference is that the Galapagos Rift would have been harder because the terrain was completely unfamiliar.

But if the expedition had just been a feat of courage—like a solo flight across the ocean, or the first ascent of a mountain peak—the discovery of the hot springs might well have been ignored by the world of science. Instead, the scientific community picked up on the discovery right away. That this was a once-in-a-lifetime opportunity to be in on the ground floor of a new field of research wasn't lost on other investigators. Requests from scientists for biological samples, as Perlman had noted, were quick in coming, and a struggle over the allocation of them ensued.

Corliss felt some obligation to Scripps for having provided the sampling equipment that obtained the bacteria. When the cruise was over, however, some Woods Hole scientists took the position that since the *Alvin* is operated by Woods Hole, and since no biologist was on the cruise, the samples should go to them. However, there had been a meeting on the *Knorr* at the end of the first leg of the expedition, attended by the scientific party, at which it was agreed that the samples should not be obligated to Woods Hole. The opportunity ought to be spread around, was the opinion.

When Corliss returned to Oregon State after the cruise, he was approached by a microbiologist who made a convincing case that he should be given some of the bacterial samples. John Baross, who specialized in bacteria that live under extreme conditions, was subsequently given them; and while the Scripps researchers said that was okay with them, some at Woods Hole were, predictably, not pleased. To forestall further disagreements and to get the needed work of taxonomic description accomplished by neutral, competent parties, Corliss asked curators at the National Museum of Natural History, the Smithsonian Institution, to help.

Academic scientists weren't the only ones who saw the opportunity in the aftermath of the Galapagos expedition. Up to this point in the study of the seafloor, most of the research and been done piecemeal by university scientists with a particular, specialized interest. On occasion these interests were collected into an expedition like FAMOUS, or the Galapagos, but these were the exceptions. Generally the science was conducted by individuals, acting separately on projects of their own initiative.

If the research done by the U.S. Navy is put to the side—and academic scientists had little opportunity to do otherwise, since most of it was classified—then this grant-writing entrepreneurial mode was the main way ocean science was organized in the United States in the 1960s and 1970s. This was different from the system in most other countries, whose governments usually attempted to focus the available money on coordinated group efforts, often overseen by some agency of the government.

But two new developments began in the wake of the Galapagos expedition. Expeditions to seafloor ridges began to be mounted with greater frequency, bringing together scientists from different disciplines and different institutions. Much of this funding came through major federal agencies, the National Science Foundation, NOAA, and the Navy's Office of Naval Research.

The federal government became active in a second way. The agencies that had an interest in the consequences of these seafloor processes became involved in the research. In time, this involvement would change the conduct of seafloor research dramatically, as programs would be established within the agencies and would develop from year to year. At the beginning, in 1976, though, the programmatic involvement of the first agency, the U.S. Geological Survey, came casually. It was really almost an accident.

William Normark was a marine geologist with the Survey in 1976. Like Corliss, Dymond, and Edmond, his path to the hot springs began at Scripps in the mid-1960s.

As a new graduate student in 1965, Normark attached himself to Professor Fred Spiess, who was working on an engineering problem that fascinated Normark. Two years earlier, the nuclear submarine *Thresher* had been lost with its crew of 127. The sub had gone down in over 8,000 feet of water, and as the world waited anxiously, the U.S. Navy found it lacked equipment to locate the sub. In the aftermath, the Navy's top brass were intent that such a loss would not happen again, and they provided funding to Spiess to continue developing a transportable reconnaissance system that could be used for seafloor missions.

Spiess and some engineers at Scripps set about adding new instruments to this Deep Tow system, which they had begun developing in 1961. Deep Tow was the first generation of remotely operated mapping and observation vehicles that could be towed near the bottom by a surface ship, and its great usefulness was that it could provide a good deal of information over an area relatively quickly. A continuous set of depth measurements, a rough idea of seafloor topography and magnetic characteristics, and a color photographic survey of the bottom could all be obtained with one tow.

Deep Tow's straightforward design placed the instruments onto a metal bed which was towed through the water on a cable. The Scripps oceanographers called the package a "fish."

Over time, succeeding generations of these underwater instrument packages would be placed in tubular steel housings, or "gorilla cages," as they are unceremoniously called. Costly trial and error over the years taught scientists to make these things as tough as gorilla cages to withstand being towed behind a ship and inadvertently bounced off underwater promontories.

One of these learning experiences involved Normark. In 1967, with Normark along on the cruise, Deep Tow was lost in over 9,000 feet of water when the tow cable broke. This was not the sort of performance the Navy had had in mind for the unit. Spiess and the Deep Tow group, however, were determined not to be sunk by the mishap, and they set out to build another Deep Tow.

Oceanographers like Spiess and Normark are the sort to take adversity as a challenge. Once, on another project, Normark was trying to complete a study of the distribution of particles in the bottom water of Lake Superior. He had been unable to get a transmissometer, the sophisticated device with which such measurements are normally done. But not to be undone, Normark drove down to the local variety store and bought himself a dozen magnets. Back at the lake, he weighed them carefully, tied them along a string so they would be suspended in the water at different depths, then dropped this homemade sampling gear overboard.

When he pulled the magnets up after an hour, he weighed them again and got his results: a measure of the magnetic-particle abundance at the different depths.

The Deep Tow group showed the same kind of pluck, returning six months later with their new Deep Tow system to the spot where the first camera sled had been lost. They made physical maps of the seafloor, in which contours represented elevation changes; and they made magnetic maps, in which contours represented the magnetic values of the floor. Using the two data sets and comparing them to the data gathered by the first Deep Tow just before it stopped sending signals, Normark picked a location where he felt the Deep Tow was likely to be sitting.

Meanwhile the Scripps engineers had been making plans to retrieve the lost "fish." They had quizzed telephone company engineers about how they retrieved submarine cables when they broke, and they modified the design particulars to fit the broken cable of the Deep Tow. Working from a research ship at the surface over the location that Normark had identified, they lowered their special cable catcher to the seafloor. The operation went slowly, but they managed to snag the cable of the lost Deep Tow and pull the instrument sled to the surface.

Examining the unit back on deck, the Deep Tow group found that most of the recovered gear was still operable and was not too much the worse for wear after six months underwater. They were elated. The recovery operation had taken less than one day. Noti-

fied about the success, Navy officials were also impressed; the Deep
Tow system had proved its usefulness. The good reputation of the
Scripps team and their gear was more than restored.

During that same cruise, the team used the new Deep Tow to
map a section of the East Pacific Rise off Mexico. In this map were
the traces of Normark's future.

After Normark finished his doctorate and moved on from
Scripps, he continued to stay in close touch with his mentor, Spiess.
Several years later, in 1974, the younger scientist had just gotten a
job with the Geological Survey when his former professor gave him
a call. He had a special request, he said. The chief scientist for a
research cruise to Mexico was suddenly unable to make it. Could
Normark jump in and take over?

Normark got permission to go, as the cruise presented an interesting challenge. The Deep Tow would be used to select a place on
a ridge from which the spreading of the seafloor could be measured
directly. To measure the spreading, the plan was to place transponders on the seafloor. The width of the zone of spreading was crucial, because the wider it was, the harder it would be for the acoustic
beacons to measure movement precisely. The section of the East
Pacific Rise off Mexico that Normark had earlier helped to map was
selected. It was at 21 degrees north latitude.

Normark's main job was to use the Deep Tow to produce a good
relief map of the seafloor rift zone; from such a map the important
geologic features could then be interpreted. When the cruise was
over, Normark took the sonar data, which had been collected in
digital code on the research ship's computer, and turned it into a
map to guide further exploration. This was 1974. In 1976, Normark returned to the site in his role as a USGS researcher, to collect
some rock samples. The next year Spiess resumed the experiment
on the ridge crest at 21 degrees north, bringing his mapmaker,
Normark, along with him.

That was 1977. The results of the Galapagos expedition were
galvanizing Normark and the rest of the oceanographic community.

Because Normark had made the best available map of the proposed diving area in the ridge crest, he was invited by the team of
French, American, and Mexican scientists to take part in the first
set of dives onto 21 degrees north in 1978. Those dives recovered
some interesting geological samples, including a mineral deposit
containing copper and zinc, and though the full significance of the

deposit was not at first appreciated, many of the scientists were eager to return to the area in 1979. By agreement among the research party, all those involved in those first dives would be welcome on a second set the following year. So, on April 21, 1979, as circumstances would have it, Bill Normark was preparing to get on board the *Alvin* for a dive. From the start it was unusual.

What had happened was that the National Science Foundation had funded twenty dives out of about forty that had been proposed by the scientists, and all the dives the NSF funded were focused on geophysical questions. But by the completion of the first group of dives a good deal of geophysical information had already been obtained, and a number of scientists on the cruise were interested in other features of the ridge crest. The sites where hot springs might be found were known.

In a brief segment of the cruise preceding the diving with *Alvin*, Bob Ballard and his Woods Hole colleagues had used the ANGUS camera sled to photograph the bottom, and they identified some twenty-five hot springs sites. With the geophysical work going well, the chief scientists felt that someone could take a look at some of these sites, but it would be impolitic to send down scientists who were on the cruise with funds from the National Science Foundation. Someone from "outside" was needed. A French scientist, Tierre Juteau, and Bill Normark were chosen. Neither of them was getting funding from NSF. The way they figured it, the science agency might try to slap their hands for taking an unplanned dive, but there wasn't really much the agency could do.

Having decided to be unconventional about the dive, Normark and Juteau were rewarded in kind. At the first site the *Alvin* brought them to, they encountered something that could have come straight out of Dante's *Inferno*.

Through a bleak, murky void, large rock spires suddenly loomed up. They were of macabre colors: red, yellow, orange, brown, and black. A superstitious person could have read something quite ominous in the scene, but Normark and Juteau forged ahead through the inky darkness of the bottom. Abruptly, up ahead in the *Alvin*'s lights emerged a sight that stunned them. Out of another of these twisted spires of rock billowed a thick column of black smoke.

Though the seawater above this chimney pressed down at nearly two tons per square inch, the smoke shot fiercely upward, showering yellow-, red-, and brown-tinged particles as it rose. No one had seen anything like this before in the ocean, and Normark and Juteau watched fascinated as the *Alvin* crossed and recrossed through the smoke, maneuvering for position over the chimney so that a temperature probe, gripped in the sub's claw, could be lowered into the smoking vent.

They watched in further astonishment as the temperature gauge inside the sub went off the scale. Quickly the two scientists took photographs, obtained some samples of the rock and of the black water, and got out of there.

On the way back to the surface they had time to think about what they had seen. This thick smoke was the earth disgorging itself of some of its mineral treasure. They had witnessed the initial stages of construction of those mineral spires they saw around them. The towers were formed, they realized, when minerals precipitated out of the hot springs' fluids as they mixed with cold seawater.

Back at the surface Normark and Juteau met more surprises. When they examined the temperature probe, they found that it had melted. The temperature of the black smoker was about 350 degrees Celsius, they calculated—some 660 degrees Fahrenheit. This was hot enough to melt lead, and they had flown the *Alvin* right through this smoke, exposing the Plexiglas windows to temperatures which could have melted them, too, if they had lingered perhaps only moments longer. Instead of triumphant scientists, they could have been merely dead ones.

Superheated water emerging into the near-freezing ocean depths: This rapidly became the stuff of newspaper headlines and invitations to guest speaking engagements. But, looking back on the event a decade afterward, Normark was unencumbered by a sense of his own importance in the discovery. "The only word for this kind of discovery," he said, "is 'serendipitous.' "

The expedition hadn't planned even to look at the vents, but once Normark had seen the minerals and the smoking chimney which deposited them, he was convinced that the seafloor hot springs were systems that the Geological Survey should find out more about. Returning from the expedition, he gave a seminar to colleagues in the Survey about the findings on the East Pacific Rise.

The seafloor research up to that point in the eastern Pacific had succeeded in raising many questions in geology, geophysics, biology, and mineralogy, he said. The importance of those questions was clear, and the time was ripe for the kind of investigation that would be possible under a concentrated program.

Normark was asked to propose such a program. He figured it could be designed in either of two basic ways. One way would focus on discovering additional hydrothermal vent areas and learning about the kinds of mineral deposits associated with them. The other way would concentrate on a particular vent site and probe such questions as how mineral deposits form, where the minerals come from, how they are precipitated. Normark proposed a five-year program that would meld the two approaches, beginning with the first and moving to the second. To start, the Survey would restrict itself to studying a relatively small area, and would proceed in phases. Mapping would be followed by sampling for the presence of mineral deposits. Later, the deposits would be drilled into to learn more about them.

The articulation of a research program that would extend over a number of years signaled a new phase for seafloor research. It was becoming institutionalized, and for a program to be endorsed by a government institution required that it advance that agency's mission. For the Geological Survey, the excitement over the possibilities of vent research had to do with what might be learned about one of the agency's main interests, the nature and genesis of mineral deposits.

In choosing a study area for his research program, Normark considered the Juan de Fuca Ridge and the Gorda Ridge, off the Pacific Northwest coast. The two shared one attraction. Despite the existence of spreading ridges all the way around the world's seafloor, not very much ridge area was close to the United States. These two, though, were relatively close, between about 100 and 350 miles offshore. Research could be done on them without inordinate expenditures of time and money just getting to the site. Normark, as the leader of the Survey's new Pacific Marine Geology program, ultimately chose to concentrate on the Juan de Fuca.

For him, scientific and practical considerations compelled the decision. Magnetic reversal data for the ridge, coupled with the radioisotopic time scale, showed that the rate of spreading on the Juan de Fuca was similar to that on the East Pacific Rise at 21 degrees north. Both were spreading apart at about two inches per year, which was considered medium rate. The Gorda was, on the average, spreading more slowly. Since, at the time, scientists believed that other interesting physical characteristics of the ridges were linked to a faster rate of spreading, the choice favored the Juan de Fuca.

The Juan de Fuca was also favored by practicality. The southernmost section of that ridge, which is opposite the central coast of Oregon, appeared—from the rough information that was then available—to be structurally rather uncomplicated, regular, and shallower than the Gorda, and so easier in which to work.

Normark's proposal to study the southern Juan de Fuca Ridge was well received by administrators within the Geological Survey, and they placed it in competition with the other principal candidate for major new project funding, a new volcano observatory. Then, in 1980, Mount St. Helens in Washington blew its top, and the volcano observatory was funded.

The Survey's Juan de Fuca research program also began in 1979, but without major funding, so Normark had to exercise his resourcefulness. To accomplish the baseline mapping and sampling work on the ridge, Normark had no separate budget to hire a ship, but he arranged to piggyback his work on a Survey ship as it passed over the ridge in returning from Alaska.

The month of this return was November 1980, and the weather at sea off the northwest coast was miserable. In fifteen days at sea, Normark and his colleagues completed only a portion of the mapping they had planned. But they got enough information to identify a ten-mile-long segment of the ridge crest about 240 miles west of Newport, Oregon. In the center of the ridge crest, which ran in a nearly straight north-south line, they mapped a valley about a half mile wide, with ridges that rose up 300 feet above the floor on either side. This information enabled Normark's group to return to the ridge more purposefully in the years following.

Meanwhile, during the same period, a complementary program for studying the Juan de Fuca and the Gorda was being developed by the other federal agency with an interest in the seafloor. Perhaps the National Oceanic and Atmospheric Administration would not have gotten involved when and how it did, however, if it had not been for someone who came from outside the agency and who saw an opportunity that others on the inside probably had not discerned yet. It helped that this scientist also had the ambition to get things moving.

Ambition was a constant with Alexander Malahoff, as his office of the mid-1980s revealed. By that time he had returned to academia from NOAA and had settled into a professorship at the University of Hawaii.

Large windows in two walls proffered sun-drenched views of the tropical vegetation outside. Beneath the windows, dozens of file boxes containing professional journals were neatly arranged on bookshelves. On one interior wall a bookcase held rows of books, arranged by subject and author; on the top shelf lay a special box cradling genuine Havana cigars. The other wall, behind the professor's desk, displayed plaques and mementos of his career. This much of the view might have given the impression one had entered the academic's Valhalla, a calm and well-ordered paradise beyond the political wars of Washington.

But at the entrance to the office the reality of the academic researcher's life à la Malahoff intruded. Four messages, marked "Pressing," were posted on the office door. On the doorjamb itself, another—"Urgent"—was stuck with tape. The time marked on it was several hours old.

The path between the door and the professor's desk chair was cobbled with piled-up journals and scholarly books, a series of land mines for an unwary walker. The desk, besieged by papers, rolled-up maps, and three-ring binders, left only a small unoccupied territory for new work. Though the bookcases of the perimeter might be secure, how was one to explain the battle zone of the office's interior?

A poster taped to the side of the filing cabinet appeared to offer a kind of explanation. "The Many Adventures of Winnie the Pooh," it once had read, and it showed the lovable, quixotic bear in full motion. A card had been placed over the name Winnie. "Alex" was the name on the card.

Malahoff had cultivated a taste for being caught up in the whirlwind years before. Raised in volcanic New Zealand and awarded a doctorate in volcanic Hawaii, Malahoff had in 1971 been led by his training in geology and geophysics to the U.S. Navy's Office of Naval Research, where he became director of a research division. His job was to forecast and propose solutions to problems relating to marine geology and geophysics that might have an effect on naval operations. The job exposed him to activities on the inside of the most advanced marine data-gathering operation in the world, activities which were only sketchily known outside the Navy, even to scientists working in the same fields.

A key experience for Malahoff was spending time on test cruises aboard the Navy's experimental nuclear-powered research submarine, known simply as NR-1. Malahoff became fascinated with submersibles during this time, and he worked closely with some key figures in marine geology. A colleague during one three-week cruise on the NR-1 was Bruce Heezen of Lamont, whose maps had done much to motivate Malahoff's generation of marine scientists.

Besides the experimental submersible, one other advanced piece of marine equipment that Malahoff became familiar with was a new kind of echo sounder. Unlike other existing sounders, which shot single beams of sound to the ocean floor, the Navy's new state-of-the art version shot ninety beams. The multibeam system was superior to anything else available. It could cover the ocean floor more rapidly and provide more detailed information than other systems.

Most people outside the Office of Naval Research knew little about SASS, the Sonar Array Survey System, since information about it was classified, This fact proved to be an advantage to Malahoff in his next job, as chief scientist of NOAA's National Ocean Survey, which he began in 1976.

Historically, the Ocean Survey's main job was nearshore, shallow-water mapping, but Malahoff was convinced that the new technology of the multibeam deep ocean mapping system would give the agency significant new opportunities. The challenge he faced as chief scientist was to persuade the administrators in NOAA. It was partly a conceptual task, Malahoff felt; the administrators were being asked to see things in a new way. But they were also being asked for $1 million, and they balked. An assistant administrator of the agency finally tried to discourage Malahoff, in a diplomatic way. Malahoff was told that if he could find $500,000 from other sources, the agency would come up with the rest.

That was the sort of wager that Malahoff liked. He enjoys recounting what happened.

"I took that as a challenge: hunted up the half million; forced them into it." Malahoff raises his eyebrows slowly.

The Sea Beam that NOAA bought from the General Instrument Corporation in 1979 was the first civilian multibeam system in the United States. To begin, Malahoff wanted NOAA to go beyond the Geological Survey's localized reconnaissance effort on the southern Juan de Fuca. He wanted to use Sea Beam to obtain a comprehensive map of the whole Gorda and Juan de Fuca ridges from Cape Mendocino to Vancouver Island. Once this ambitious task was completed, he would see that the maps were used to study the mechanisms involved at seafloor ridges.

He hired a research geophysicist whom he had known at the University of Hawaii, Steve Hammond, and he hired Bob Embley, an oceanographer who had received his doctorate at Lamont. Malahoff himself became particularly interested in studying the formation of mineral deposits.

This interest was whetted by his own voyage to the Galapagos. In 1979, after the first seafloor mineral deposits were discovered on the East Pacific Rise, new areas with deposits were also found on the Galapagos Rift. Malahoff was familiar with the multibeam surveys which the Navy had run there; these gave him a head start on understanding the geological structure of the area, which would be a big help in finding more mineral deposits. Malahoff saw the opportunity plainly.

"Having only a small research team, the only way I knew I could do my research and leave my mark on science," he said later, "was to jump onto the Galapagos." He bid for submersible time, got the *Alvin*, and in August 1981 commenced a series of dives. The results were another milestone in the exploration of the seafloor.

The NOAA team discovered the largest assemblage of polymetallic sulfides that had yet been discovered on the seafloor. Such deposits, among the most common type of mineral deposit on land, were what Normark and Juteau had encountered and sampled in 1979. These deposits get their name from being complex assemblages of minerals in which iron and sulfur are the main elements. Zinc and copper are other dominant metals.

The 1981 NOAA discovery consisted of more than twenty polymetallic sulfide chimneys located against a valley wall of the ridge crest. Malahoff described the ore body as 130 feet thick, about 650 feet wide, and 3,280 feet long; he estimated that it contained 25 million tons of sulfides. If it could be mined efficiently and then

successfully processed and marketed, Malahoff believed, it could
have considerable value. The quantity of copper contained in the
ore alone was worth $2 billion, he said.

The Galapagos discovery quickened Malahoff's interest in com-
pleting the mapping of the Gorda and the Juan de Fuca ridges,
which had begun in 1980. In the summers from 1980 to 1983,
NOAA expeditions generated enough mapping information to set
the stage for submersible dives in the following summers.

These maps were the key to further discoveries in the geology,
geophysics, biology, and chemistry of the ocean floor. In the 1980s,
the revolution in earth sciences would continue apace.

CHAPTER FIVE

IMAGES
OF A HIDDEN WORLD

The world that lies beneath the ocean waves has always been a subject of curiosity and speculation, even fantasy. The ancient Greeks had their Atlantis, the French novelist Jules Verne had his Captain Nemo, 20,000 leagues under the sea. In the earlier days of television the exploits of Jacques Cousteau aboard the *Calypso* and the *Diving Saucer* introduced millions of people to what really lies beneath the waves. More recently, in an era of instantaneous communications, scientist-explorer Bob Ballard has simultaneously shown viewers the floor of the Mediterranean via remote-controlled cameras and discussed it with them via satellite, all in "real time."

It is quite possible that the roots of our curiosity in the submerged world go deeper than our everyday selves, perhaps down to something truly primal. Perhaps, as some psychologists suggest, fascination with the underwater realms speaks to our origins in the wet and the dark. The water that nurtures the human fetus has the same salt composition as the sea. Something of the sea, it would seem, is deep in the blood.

Humans at the seashore, staring out to sea: It is easy to imagine the scene as a constant in human experience. A prehistoric human, dressed in animal skins, staring mute. A Homeric Greek watching rapt while the chariot of the sun falls below the rim of the wine-dark sea. A modern American family embarking on a cruise to watch whales, wondering about their mammal relatives and the different lives they lead.

What is it like out there under that changing surface: Is it menacing? Benign? What if you could see right down to the bottom?

Marine geologists like Steve Hammond have begun to find the answers.

By the last months of 1984, Hammond and his NOAA colleagues had finished moving from their offices outside of Washington, D.C., and into their new home at the Marine Science Center of Oregon State University. Located within sight of the Pacific Ocean, the laboratory, with its wood-shake roof and broad eaves, seemed to take its character from nature, the often wet and rainy nature of the Oregon coast. But the attitude inside the lab was something rather different, a spirit of overcoming nature's limits. In one of the offices Steve Hammond would sit at a computer console and with just the stroke of a few keys see, in effect, through the ocean.

Showing what he could do with the computer system one day in 1986, he called up on his computer screen an image of the seafloor, generated from data collected at sea. In an instant, in another room, a printer began drawing the map of the floor in a rainbow of colors. Although he did this sort of thing daily, it still appeared to delight him, and he talked about it readily.

"We've been making maps of part of the planet's surface that's never been seen before," Hammond said. "That's exciting. That's real discovery stuff. That"—he put on a gruff frontiersman voice—"is pioneer-type stuff." He laughed at his own swagger, and with it, too, happy as a child with a favorite toy.

From never having had a picture at all until a mere generation ago, scientists have progressed rapidly to having extremely detailed views. The gaining of this ability seems almost extravagant, something totally out of historical proportion, and Hammond has the sort of self-awareness that told him it was really an accident of circumstance, some kind of cosmic joke, that he should be the one sitting in this chair and able to see these hidden things.

The maps, as the offspring of computers from start to finish, may seem enchanted and effortless, like things of the imagination; like, for example, the map of Middle Earth in Tolkien's *Lord of the Rings*. Nevertheless, the making of undersea maps, as Hammond put it in his scientist's wry lingo, is "nontrivial." It is, in fact, the climax of a very long development of inventiveness. In marine geology, as in many sciences since the industrial revolution, technology has propelled discovery. Without the means to locate the vents, none of the scientific developments that have happened since would have happened at all.

To make seafloor maps, the mapmaker measures the depths of features below the sea surface, then connects places of equal depth into contours. This process sounds simple enough, and the resulting bathymetric map looks rather like a topographic relief map of land. But the making of a contour map on land is by comparison a fairly simple affair. Land mapmakers start with a good aerial view— a picture from an airplane, or, as has become commonplace, a satellite. For details and verification, they can go to the site, walk around it, and make measurements. It would be much easier if this approach could be taken for the contours below the waves.

The average depth of the ocean is about 12,000 feet; the greatest depth, at the Marianas Trench in the western Pacific, is about 36,000 feet. But by about 400 feet below the surface of even the clearest water, sunlight and visibility give out, and along with visibility goes any direct imaging of the shapes that fill the watery dark. Steve Hammond has an expression for the phenomenon. He calls it "hitting a wall."

Mariners have tried to punch a hole through that wall for centuries. In the 1520s the explorer Ferdinand Magellan tried to probe the ocean's depth by attaching a weight to a rope and throwing it overboard. When, midway through the Pacific, he hit a spot where he tied all his available ropes together and they ran out, Magellan declared he was over the deepest point in the ocean. He wasn't.

Later applications of the line-and-weight technique were stymied by two recurring problems. Either the weight was too light and wouldn't sink all the way, or it was too heavy and broke the line on retrieval. One solution, arrived at in the nineteenth century, was a spring-loaded cannonball. When the spring hit bottom, it opened a catch and the cannonball dropped off the line. The depth was measured from a mark on the line.

Variations on this technique plumbed a lot of ocean floor between 1850 and 1930. But in the vast, deep ocean, the technique was impractically slow and coverage impossibly spotty. Lines and weights were inadequate to give anything like a clear and complete picture. Further advances in deep-ocean mapping awaited a new technology.

As he did in other fields of inquiry, Leonardo da Vinci perceived the approach which later bore fruit. Working before the time of Magellan's circumnavigation of the globe, Leonardo observed that "if you cause your ship to stop and place the head of a long tube in the water and the other end to your ear, you will hear ships at a great distance from you." Leonardo recognized that distant objects in the water could be identified by sound, and also that sound traveled farther in water than in air.

To know the distance of some object underwater the speed of sound in water had to be known, and in the late eighteenth and early nineteenth centuries several gentleman scientists undertook to make the measurement. The first widely publicized measurement was made in 1826 on Lake Geneva. A Swiss physicist, Daniel Colladon, and a French mathematician, Charles Sturm, collaborated on the experiment, which involved striking a bell underwater at a known distance from an observer and recording the time it took the sound to reach him. A visual signal was given as the bell was struck, and after conducting some tests, Colladon and Sturm announced that the speed of sound in water of 8 degrees Celsius was 1,435 meters per second, or approaching a mile per second.

It took a disaster to move the study of sound in the sea from a scientific curiosity to practical application. The disaster was the wreck of the *Titanic* on an iceberg in 1912, which prompted Reginald Fessenden, a Canadian inventor, to develop an electronic device that could detect an underwater object by bouncing a sound wave off it.

In Fessenden's oscillator, a mineral crystal oscillated and sent out a high-pitched "ping" when an electric current ran through it. The principle of the oscillator's use in depth sounding was that the distance to an underwater object could be determined by measuring the time elapsed between when the sound wave was sent and when its echo was received. That two-way time in seconds, divided in half and then multiplied by the feet-per-second velocity of sound in water, would give the distance.

That was the principle, but in the view of Fessenden and the company he designed for, the Submarine Signal Company of Boston, a test on a real iceberg was required. So in the late winter of 1914, the inventor of the oscillator made a cruise off Nova Scotia in a ship hired for the occasion, which was about the size of a small schooner. The test brought Fessenden face to face with the hazards of work at sea, and the project might easily have been scuttled. Fessenden described the start of the journey in a letter to his wife.

> I was not sea sick but had an awful time the first night. The rolling was so bad that my mattress got thrown out of my berth four or five times with me on it. Then I got tired putting it back and left it on the floor and tried sleeping on the leather cushions under the mattress. But it got rolling worse till even these were thrown out several times. So I gave it up and tried the floor, but could not stick to the mattress even on the floor and in addition six or seven chairs, etc. took charge of the room, broke the ropes they were tied with, and started charging up and down the room. So then I tried sleeping on the bare planks of my berth, but soon the chairs started jumping up that and one of them gave me a bad crack on the ankle. . . . it was then 4 a.m. and dawn breaking I got up and dressed.

The test itself went fine, giving what was judged to be an accurate distance to a submerged iceberg. On the way back to Halifax, Fessenden experimented with bouncing the sound off the ocean bottom. This led directly to his development of a "fathometer" or echo sounder.

Fessenden's model and other echo sounders developed through the 1920s improved a great deal on the old technique of lines and weights. Depth measurements made with them were still, however, often approximations, for a number of reasons.

The common denominator of the problems, ironically, was seawater itself. Accurate depths required skill in listening for the echo and marking the time precisely. These tasks were challenges enough for the first operators of echo-sounding equipment. To make matters worse, the echo itself might be quite faint or be garbled among other sounds and hard to interpret. These were observational problems and were slowly overcome. But other problems, relating to the transmission of sound through ocean water, were more difficult.

Sound waves traveling through the ocean were found to go neither in a straight line nor at a constant speed. The sound waves bend, and their speed fluctuates in response to changes in the characteristics of the sea—its temperature, salinity, and pressure at different depths. These vary somewhat in each location. So the time that elapsed between signal and return, as users of the early echo sounders discovered, was affected by the particular makeup of the layers of water that lay above the features off which the sound reflected.

By the 1930s the British Admiralty provided a way out of this measurement quagmire. After collecting a good deal of data from various ocean locations, they developed tables of "average sounding velocity" for major parts of the ocean. Consistent and quite accurate soundings became possible.

In the next decade, World War II brought significant improvements to the use of sound underwater. The U.S. Navy's need to detect enemy submarines compelled refinements to techniques for measuring depth and distance. The war also introduced technical improvements like graphic recorders, which were image-making devices linked to the basic echo sounder. They provided much new information about the shape of the seafloor. Harry Hess on his transport ship out in the Pacific discovered flat-topped volcanic seamounts during his tour of duty using such a basic sounder.

Image production improved again after the war when the sounder was hooked up to a facsimile recorder, the same device used to transmit pictures over telephone lines. Good as it was, this mid-1950s system still had an inherent limitation, and if the technology of seafloor imaging had progressed no further than it, the exploration of seafloor hot springs would have been very much more difficult.

The limitation was in the coverage of the system. All the echo sounders in use through the 1950s employed only a single narrow beam of sound. That narrow beam could describe only a limited amount of seafloor at a time, and as a result, getting comprehensive coverage of an area was difficult.

If a researcher wanted to try to cover a broad area, he could run the survey ship in fewer, widely spaced sounding lines and then interpolate the features in between. Or alternatively, he could run a greater number of closely spaced soundings and have more confidence in the coverage. But this approach was time-consuming and costly. Detailed single-beam echo soundings were typically limited to very small areas.

By the early 1960s the U.S. Navy was deploying a dramatically more capable system, one which initiated a new generation of technology. This was the SASS system, which Alex Malahoff became familiar with during his stint with the Office of Naval Research. It provided both broad and detailed coverage.

NOAA's unclassified version of SASS, Sea Beam, mapped a good deal of seafloor in the early 1980s. All of the Juan de Fuca Ridge and all but a small portion of the Gorda Ridge were mapped by 1985, an area of some 10,000 square miles. The maps, moreover, were finely detailed.

At two miles, the typical depth of the ridge, their vertical resolution was about thirty feet, meaning that if two features adjacent to each other were different in height by more than thirty feet, they would be represented by different contour lines on the map. For shallower depths, of about one mile, even better resolution was possible, as good as five-foot contour lines.

The first step in making the maps is generating and collecting the data. To do this, electronic hardware is mounted on the hull of the surveying vessel. Clear fiberglass domes, about twenty feet long and three feet wide, enclose two sets of devices. Transducers, which send out high-pitched "pings" of sound toward the bottom, occupy one dome; hydrophones, underwater microphones which receive the echo, occupy the other.

The transducers of Sea Beam transmit the pings in twenty outgoing sound beams. Each beam is narrowly focused, but as a group they cut a fan shape below and to the sides of the ship. When the individual beams of sound hit the bottom in their particular path they are modified by the collision and return to the hydrophones in the hull.

This signal-and-return for the twenty beams happens very quickly. In deep water the pings are typically transmitted every five seconds and race through the water at 4,500 feet per second. So they are back at the ship in a matter of seconds. The result is that at the hydrophones, the sound beams are not distinct packages of information, but rather an abrupt cacophonous grab bag. To the uninitiated this could appear to be a serious problem.

Fortunately for oceanography, an eighteenth-century French mathematician, Jean Baptiste Fourier, developed a technique which identifies different phases of a wave of the same frequency. By using Fourier transform analysis, the Sea Beam system can pick out the sound wave representing the same bottom feature in different returning signals. It can also eliminate the redundant statements of other features and thereby isolate the dominant feature at each hydrophone. In this way the bottom at a particular angular position from the ship and a particular depth is knowable.

That is not the same thing as saying that the position on the globe of a particular feature is also known. To know that, some fixed reference point either on shore or on an orbiting satellite is needed.

When scientists only want to be able to go back to a seafloor feature that has been mapped before, crude position fixes are sufficient. In this case, when the return cruise comes to about the same position on the ocean where an earlier cruise has mapped the bottom, the scientists only need to turn on their depth sounders again, and when the new soundings match the previous map, they know that they have returned to the same place.

This technique has proved useful since the beginning of hot springs research. But more precise maps, accurately placed on the globe, were even more useful. The information they give about the arrangement of the seafloor can provide clues to the forces that form it. A fully developed Sea Beam map does this job well, but the complete production of one is not a trivial matter. For each ping, the Sea Beam system collects data not only for the position and depth of seafloor features, but also for numerous other variables, including the ship's compass heading, its pitch up or down, and its roll side to side, all of which affect the bottom reading. In all, fifty variables are tabulated per ping. Five seconds per ping means twelve pings and 600 pieces of information per minute, or 36,000 pieces of information per hour, and twenty-four times that amount in a round-the-clock day, which is how the system is run.

The goal of all this data, namely a precise location and description of the ocean floor, wouldn't be possible without a means to store, organize, and manipulate the numbers. To start this process, all of these 864,000 daily pieces of information are recorded and stored at sea on magnetic tape, 800 bytes per inch. A byte in this case is nine bits, or units, of data. A reel of tape contains 2,400 feet, or some 16 million nine-bit bytes, and at the end of a month-long surveying cruise, ten such tapes can be filled. By the beginning of 1988, the NOAA Vents Program had collected more than 100 of these tapes.

The job of making the most of this data came to Chris Fox when Steve Hammond became the program's leader. This hand-off of duties in 1985 was more than just a passing of the baton, however. As scientific research programs are wont to do, the Vents Program tried to progress by hiring people with the skills to refine the existing work and ratchet it up another notch. Chris Fox was chosen for exactly this quality. Fox had degrees in geology and climate history and a doctorate in geology and geophysics, but what made him particularly valuable was his specialty, which was as much of the late 1980s as personal computers and multibillion-dollar national debts. He was a numerical modeler.

Numerical modeling is a technique for making sense out of potential nonsense. In this case the nonsense is of a peculiarly contemporary kind—digital electronic data in such quantities that only very large computers avoid indigestion. Numerical modeling involves using a variety of statistical techniques to turn this data, produced by the Sea Beam as well as other systems, into visual products that scientists can use. Fox, a big man with an apparent gusto for organizing facts, seemed typecast for this role in the Vents Program.

In 1986 and 1987 he worked to clean up the Sea Beam data, to make it more useful for the group's scientific research. Everybody knew what he and the technicians working with him were doing, in a general sense, but improvements in the maps themselves would tell the story. There came an afternoon in 1988 when Fox was ready to show some new maps.

Fox was working in the main computer room, next door to his office. He often could be found there during the day, looking over the 100 magnetic tapes and the big machines with the air of a family man examining a well-stocked food freezer. Today he was going to serve up a new concoction.

The room was actually a bit like a walk-in freezer. Air conditioners kept the computers cool, setting up an obbligato of white noise above the constant thrum of the machines. Though the room had windows revealing the bush salal and wind-stunted shore pine of the Oregon coast, the scene outside seemed like part of another world. It might as well have been a mural. Inside the room, the machines dominated.

The problem that Fox and the technicians working with him had been grappling with concerned the precision of the maps. When the

Sea Beam data were collected at sea they were split into two branches, depth soundings and the ship's ocean positions. The branches were related to each other by the time of collection. Back in Newport the data on the original tapes were processed by computer routines and then transferred onto plastic-domed magnetic disks. The disks were about the size of medium pizzas, and each held the equivalent of about a month's worth of the seafloor data, some 200 million bytes of information. Nevertheless, the data on the disk were more accessible than they were on tapes.

This particular afternoon Fox loaded a disk of depth soundings and its corresponding navigation disk onto the drive shafts of the main computer. Then at a computer terminal he made a series of choices which defined the map. On the keyboard he indicated the latitude, the longitude, the scale of the map, and the interval between contour lines that he wanted to see. What he chose for scale and interval would determine how viewers' attention was focused.

He decided on a scale of 1:200,000, one inch on the map equal to 200,000 inches, or a bit more than three miles, on the seafloor. The interval between contours Fox set at 200 meters, or about 640 feet. A smaller contour interval would mean closer and harder-to-read lines on a map of this scale; a larger one would miss many local details. Choices like these become clearer with experience.

Then Fox had to choose the colors he would print the map in. He had at his disposal all the shades that a commercial color printing plant has, 512 of them, but so many shades are not necessarily an advantage. The gradations are too subtle; housepaint companies labor to distinguish tints, calling them "Golden Bisque," "Sun Shadow," "Pago Orange," and so on. Fox wouldn't let the Vents maps go blotto with too many colors; he restricted them to no more than forty. That was more than enough to create the illusion of different depths.

With commands to the computer and printer completed, Fox waited while the map was printed. It didn't take very long. The Vents Program has upgraded its computer systems regularly, and the computer it acquired in 1986 operated 50 percent faster than the one that was then two years old. The printer, technically known as a raster plotter, also had had a computer upgrade. A single map which took four hours to produce in 1984 took about eight minutes with the 1988 model.

The sophisticated plotter at work was dazzling to watch, but it was also uncanny, in a funny way. It brought to mind children in grade school coloring pictures with crayons. Like kids with crayons, the plotter lays its colors on one at a time. And like a child who doesn't yet know how to make a proper circle, a raster plotter doesn't understand curves. This would seem like a crucial limitation, since the seafloor contour information on the computer disk contains many curves. But the raster overcomes this apparent problem by laying its color on in a grid of extremely fine dots, forty thousand per inch.

The computer tells the printer precisely which spots on the three-foot-wide sheet are to receive each color. When they're all connected, the tiny dots make curves of colored contours.

The positioning of the dots is accomplished by a magnetic head, like a tape recorder's head, which puts electrical charges every two hundredths of an inch as the paper rolls over it. The charge attracts paint out of a narrow well that lies in the bed of the machine.

As the paper rolled over the bed, Fox watched it happily. He still got a kick out of seeing it operate. He shook his head. It was unbelievable how it worked.

After the black lines went on, printing the depths, the color washes of yellow, then dark blue, then purplish-red were added. Shapes slowly began to emerge, as from a huge Polaroid print. A deep purple belonged to the very deepest areas. Then blues, greens, oranges, and yellows ascended the color scale in lightness and warmth, indicating progressively shallower depths beneath the ocean surface. Bright yellows and reds were used for the highest areas. The perspective was immediately clear. The colors, from cool blue to excitable orange, seemed even psychologically appropriate. Fox rolled up the map and walked from the computer room to the charting room down the hall.

Inside, several maps were laid out on a big table that filled the room's center. Dozens of other maps, rolled up inside cardboard tubes or just cinched with rubber bands, sat on the floor or leaned against a wall. This was the organization's nerve center, the place where staffers often congregated, and most were in it when Fox entered. Steve Hammond came over as Fox unrolled his new map.

The major outlines of the setting were clear at a glance—the line of the ridge, the bulge of a seamount along it, the mountain's mainly conical shape. Hammond, who had studied versions of the map many times, saw a detail he liked.

"All *right!*" he said. "It looks good." He gave Fox an appreciative nod.

Fox unrolled an earlier map of the same region and began examining the two maps as others looked on. A newer staff member asked what was improved from the old version, and Fox pointed to a uniformly wiggly line on a contour in this map.

"See this feature?" he asked. He got a nod.

"Actually, it isn't there."

The wiggle on the old map was the result of electronic errors in the navigation signal as received by the mapping ship. Fox explained that a navigation system based on shore misread the ship's position. The system calculated, uncritically, that the ship was jumping 100 meters—300 feet—side to side, every *second*.

Fox smiled broadly.

"Now that *would* be interesting," he said.

The wiggle on the old map is an example of what happened when navigation fixes were inaccurate; some seafloor features got drawn that weren't actually there. This was a technical problem at least as old as the Renaissance; explorers then would succumb to it when, in their zeal for new territory, they elaborated the outline of a seacoast into the shape of a continent. It was easy to make an unusable map by extrapolating from limited information. Initially, the NOAA computer system didn't know that the navigation data was not reliable in certain places. But Fox had made it quite reliable by writing programs for the computer that reprocessed the data and interpolated more accurate positions.

For the future, Fox looked toward the day later in the 1990s when the Global Positioning System would be all in place. The GPS is a group, or as scientists like to say a constellation, of navigation satellites that will orbit the earth's poles. When this system is completed, with about twenty satellites, ships will be able to compute their distance relative to the satellites and thereby know their position in the ocean to within thirty feet.

Even without such future improvements, the appreciative voices in the Vents map room underscored the fact that the NOAA Sea Beam maps were highly useful scientific products.

The U.S. Navy itself appeared impressed. The Navy even gave the civilian maps a kind of compliment for their quality—backhanded though it was. In 1985, the Navy had some of the NOAA Sea Beam maps classified as national security risks.

*　　*　　*

The story behind the classification action has the makings of a mid-1980s potboiler military adventure novel. In fact, *The Hunt for Red October*, the best-selling military adventure novel written in 1984, described just the sort of scenario that made the Navy worry about the NOAA Sea Beam maps.

Early in Tom Clancy's novel of submarine hide-and-seek, the USS *Dallas* is being prepared for an assignment in the North Atlantic; it will patrol the deep sea near Iceland along the Mid-Atlantic Ridge. The Soviets, in this yarn of Cold War brinkmanship, predictably are up to no good. They have a new class of submarine that can elude the Americans. How do they do it? How can they maneuver through the dangerous peaks and valleys of the Reykjanes spreading ridge?

> Before the late sixties submarines could barely approach the peaks, much less probe their myriad valleys. Throughout the seventies Soviet naval survey vessels had been seen patrolling the ridge—in all seasons, in all weather, quartering and requartering the area in thousands of cruises. Then, fourteen months before the *Dallas'* present patrol, the USS *Los Angeles* had been tracking a Soviet *Victor II*-class attack submarine. The *Victor* had skirted the Icelandic coasts and gone deep as she approached the ridge. The *Los Angeles* had followed. The *Victor* proceeded at eight knots until she passed between the first pair of seamounts, informally known as Thor's Twins. All at once she went to full speed and moved southwest. The skipper of the *Los Angeles* made a determined effort to track the *Victor* and came away from it badly shaken. . . . The Russian submarine had simply not slowed down—for fifteen hours, it was later determined.

Part of the fictitious *Victor*'s elusiveness depended on its having access to high-resolution seafloor maps, charts produced by the "Soviet navy survey vessels." These would be Sea Beam–quality maps.

Although *Red October* was fiction, the U.S. Navy argued that the threat it portrayed was dangerously real. Soviet submarines in possession of detailed seafloor maps would be able to maneuver underwater near the U.S. coast without ever having to surface to check their bearings, they said. Nuclear missiles could be launched from precisely fixed positions. The Navy argued against inviting such dangers at all costs.

NOAA officials questioned whether the Soviets would need to

come as close to shore as was argued, within 200 miles, to launch their missiles. NOAA was also concerned about the constraint that classification would have on research and science.

The debate between the Navy and NOAA over classification went right up to a review before a panel of the prestigious National Academy of Sciences, who were convinced by the Navy's national security risk argument. The National Security Council took the initiative from there.

In early 1985, Ronald Reagan's National Security Adviser, Navy Vice Admiral John Poindexter, issued a letter to NOAA directing that NOAA multibeam seafloor maps were to be classified as "confidential." Although this rating is below other classified rankings of "secret" and "top secret," it had the effect of putting restrictions on civilian research, not only that of NOAA, but of academics who could benefit from the NOAA maps.

It was small consolation to the research scientists involved, but viewed from a historical perspective, NOAA's imbroglio with the Navy can be seen as just a recent skirmish in the ongoing battle between mapmakers and the authorities. Over the centuries some skirmishes have been worse.

When Galileo placed the sun, not the earth, in the center of his universe, the response of the authorities was clearly more severe. Since the placement of heavenly bodies was, in the Church's view, a matter of God's design and the Pope's decree, Galileo's indiscretion nearly cost him his life.

A case involving Sir Francis Drake was also more extreme. During Drake's epoch-making first voyage around the world, from 1577 to 1580, he kept an illustrated log. It no doubt showed information which would have been an advantage to England—and presumably a potential disadvantage if obtained by another country. Scholars suspect that the illustrated log was confiscated by Queen Elizabeth as a top-secret state document. "Suspected" is all historians can say. No record of its whereabouts exists. It may be an early example of one of those classified documents whose classification is itself classified.

For Steve Hammond and the Vents Program, the Navy action did not mean consignment to oblivion, a doom to working in the shadows. The Vents Program was not as directly affected as other programs within NOAA, since Poindexter's ruling only specifically affected the Sea Beam maps made after May 1984. Since most of the Vents data were collected before then, the main effect of the order was that staff and others using the data needed government security clearances, and the data needed to be stored under lock and key.

But there were contradictions and ironies in the constraints placed on the agency scientists. Their colleagues in academia were not restricted from producing Sea Beam maps of research areas. There was no difference in quality between their products, only a difference in quantity, the acreage covered.

The mapping arm of NOAA, the National Ocean Service, was embarked on systematic Sea Beam mapping of the entire U.S. offshore zone out to 200 miles, while academic Sea Beam mapping generally covered areas on the order of tens of miles or less. But researchers, whether academic or agency, in fact focused research on comparably small ocean areas, and the Navy treated them differently.

Meanwhile, another group of scientists was also producing sonar maps offshore without Navy classification. This group's activities were especially ironic, in light of the Navy's declared reason for keeping such seafloor information away from the Soviet Union. In 1986, Soviet scientists mounted an expedition to Axial Volcano and made their own sonar maps of it. Although the maps were not Sea Beam–quality, the Soviets were operating within the region the Navy was concerned about.

As high in quality and as valuable as the Sea Beam depth measurements can be, the NOAA researchers also employed other tools to hunt for the vents. Another important tool was, like Sea Beam, a sonar device. But SeaMARC used underwater sound in a different way.

Unlike Sea Beam, which is operated from the surface, SeaMARC is a torpedo-shaped "fish" which is towed a few hundred feet above the seafloor by a surface ship. The unit sends down sound beams toward the seafloor on an oblique angle. Rather than measuring the elapsed time of the returning signal, though, SeaMARC measures its strength.

A strong—energetic—return indicates a hard rocky bottom. A weak return indicates a softer, perhaps sedimented surface, or perhaps, given the angle of the incoming sound wave, one that is simply in the acoustic "shadow" of another feature. By assigning different colors to different signal strengths, a computer can make a virtual image of the seafloor from SeaMARC's digital information. Hence the instrument's acronym, which stands for Sea Mapping and Remote Characterization.

Mounted on the wall of the Vents computer room was an acoustic map produced from Sea Beam data and an acoustic image produced from SeaMARC, both of sections of Axial Volcano. The differences were striking. The Sea Beam map gave a representation of the contours of the seafloor, providing an overall sense of the shape of the land. The SeaMARC image for the same area gave a three-dimensional picture of the geologic features of the volcano, the eruptive cones, the sheer cliffs, the rubble-strewn slopes. By putting them together the researchers obtained a pretty good first impression of the volcano.

Sonar was not the only prospecting tool the NOAA researchers used to search for the vents. They also looked for indications in the ocean water surrounding the vents. They searched for hydrothermal plumes.

Plumes from the hot springs carry mineral particles and heat, which sensitive instruments can detect. The plumes also spread up into the ocean over a rather large area, an area that may extend from tens to thousands of square miles. For these reasons, finding plumes is considerably easier than finding springs themselves, whose scale is typically on the order of a few square feet.

The dispersal of a plume in the ocean, however, carries its own complications. The heat and particle traces of a hot spring will become vanishingly small as the plume mixes with seawater over space and time. As a result, this kind of prospecting involves looking for signals—differences in the characteristics of plume water from "normal" ocean water—that are very small. Typical temperature signals are on the order of hundredths of a degree centigrade; particle concentration signals are in the range of parts per billion.

The challenge to make this kind of prospecting successful is ultimately the job of ocean engineers. In fact, all oceanographic research involves the contributions of engineers at various stages. In this contribution, the 1980s were no different from the 1450s, when the first great oceanic expeditions of modern times were being organized by Prince Henry "the Navigator" of Portugal. Henry turned the port city of Sagres into the first research and development center, assembling there the finest ship designers and builders of the day. He had them build a new kind of vessel to fulfill his dreams of exploration.

The ship the prince wanted built was to be lighter and more maneuverable than the merchant ships that then plied the Mediterranean. The engineers and shipbuilders of Sagres responded with the caravelle, which became the preferred vessel of explorers for generations. The ships of Columbus's first voyage to the New World, the *Niña*, the *Pinta*, and the *Santa Maria*, were all caravelles.

For the scientist-discoverers associated with NOAA's Pacific Marine Environmental Laboratory, the equivalent of Sagres is Seattle, Washington. In Sand Point, not far from Puget Sound and the opening to the Pacific Ocean, the agency's engineers prepare gear for use in projects worldwide, including Vents.

For example, one project of the late 1980s was a network of climate-monitoring ocean buoys. The network girdled the equator and was known as ATLAS, for Automated Temperature Line Acquisition System. Another project, a warning system to protect people against the sudden onslaught of "tidal waves," was called THRUST—Tsunami Hazard Reduction Using System Technology. And while it might seem that the engineering division would exhaust its ingenuity in creating acronyms, at most times the engineers were working on perhaps half a dozen hardware projects, just about all of them identified with some snappy name.

At Sand Point, two large warehouses held goodly amounts of engineering supplies and equipment, much of it being refurbished for imminent use on some other project. Another building housed offices and testing labs. Inside of it was the electronic gear, the toolmaking machines, the computers for design work, and the handful of engineers who operated the stuff. Presiding over the operation was Hugh Milburn, leader of the engineering division.

Milburn began in ocean engineering in the late 1960s, when electronics played a smaller role in oceanographic equipment, and it helped if you were handy with your hands and wire and tape. The years of experience polished a temperament that was apparently well adjusted for engineering from the beginning.

In conversation, a question to Milburn was likely to be followed by a pause, during which he seemed to be contemplating the unique best solution.

"Well, you see," Milburn would explain to a first-time visitor, "we don't design instruments here as engineering experiments."

Not for these engineers the luxury of invention for the pure pleasure of it. Everything the NOAA engineers did, said Milburn, was "in response to the scientists' research needs."

The engineers used off-the-shelf equipment produced by others, recycled and retrofitted their own gear, or designed from scratch, depending on the needs of the particular project. When they took on the assignment of scouting out hydrothermal plumes, they put together what is known in the trade as an "instrument package." They did the job in close consultation with the scientists who intended to use the package. The design criteria were not "too demanding," Milburn said.

That would have been obvious only to an engineer.

For the instruments, the researchers needed ways to detect those temperature variations in hundredths of a degree and particle concentrations of parts per billion. Although these are indeed very small measures, such oceanographic instruments existed as off-the-shelf items in the 1980s. Measuring very small and very large quantities is the stuff of oceanographic research, and the continuing improvements in microelectronics since the 1970s made this sort of equipment available and affordable.

The Sand Point electronics workshop housed the two key plume sensors. It was a crowded room with ranks of workbenches topped with electrical components, testing instruments, wires and cords. Green and amber display screens of oscilloscopes and computers winked all around the room.

Thermistors lay in boxes on one shelf. They measured the tiny temperature changes as changes in electrical resistance. They cost three dollars.

Lying on another bench was a nephelometer, the instrument that would measure the change in particle concentrations. It worked by flashing a light through water. The reflectance of the light, captured on a photo multiplier tube, provided a measure of the particle content in the water. Although the nephelometer was expensive to buy, it was compact and it met all the design criteria.

With the thermistors and nephelometer in hand, the engineers were on the way to building the plume detector. Selecting the instruments was the easy part, however; the more demanding task was building a device to carry them.

Something that almost qualified already existed, known as a CTD. A CTD measures the three main characteristics of ocean water: conductivity (a measure of salinity), temperature, and depth. It is standard oceanographic gear, and the standard method for deploying it is what oceanographers call "punching holes in the ocean." That is, a CTD is customarily lowered vertically into the water from a ship.

However, punching holes in the ocean would not be very effective in finding plumes, which spread out laterally in the water column. So the Sand Point engineers decided that a new housing would be needed. It needed to be towable and move laterally.

Towable housings for oceanographic instruments were themselves not new when the engineers began their task in 1984. For a standard device like a "gorilla cage" camera sled, which is towed on a winch-operated cable, the setup was pretty well known. "It's like taking a dog for a walk," as Milburn liked to say. But the Vents scientists had called for a new approach for water-sampling gear. It needed to be something light, mobile, able to be yo-yoed up and down through the water. The prototype design looked like an exciting, even a dashing design solution.

Black, compact, four feet across, with downswept bat wings and upright tail, when seen out of the water it looked rather like a scale model for an experimental jet fighter, or perhaps a mutant manta ray. The streamlined winged design was supposed to fly through the water smoothly and with a minimum of drag. That was the idea, and in a flush of enthusiasm Ed Baker, the scientist who would use it, gave it one of those trademark acronyms, SLEUTH. It stood for System for Locating Eruptive Underwater Turbidity and Hydrography.

Hopes were high for it, but SLEUTH ran into trouble in the ocean. The bat wings tended to make it kite around in the water near the surface. It was also skittish near the bottom. The combination gave its operators conniptions. They were constantly running the risk of crashing it, and only frantic last-ditch hauls on the winch averted disaster more than once.

The bat got its chance in 1984, but afterward the engineers abandoned it. They replaced it with a design better known underwater, a torpedo.

There were two reasons for the choice. An elongated cylinder is stable in the water; and the researchers had also decided that they wanted to carry more instruments.

One of the pieces of gear added to SLEUTH 2 was a second

particle sensor, a transmissometer. Somewhat like the nephelometer, this device works by continuously shining a very-low-level light through the water. It detects particles by measuring a change in the transmission of light through a tube (rather than by its reflectance). The transmissometer is simpler in design and cheaper than the nephelometer, and it gave the researchers another way of detecting a plume.

SLEUTH 2 also incorporated gear for navigating, some acoustic transponders. When asked, Milburn would explain the need for them by highlighting the difficulty of seafloor research.

"Vents are very small features, and it's very hard to put an instrument down on a vent, even under the best circumstances," he would say, by way of introduction.

"Imagine standing on top of the Empire State Building and dangling a piece of string with a rubber ball on the end of it, and trying to stick it into a coffee cup on the sidewalk. That's the idea. It's difficult under any circumstances. It's impossible if you don't know where you are."

Once shipboard researchers figure out where they are on the globe by calculating their distance from known reference points on land or in space, they set up within the study area, on the ocean bottom, a net of other reference points. Transponders make up this reference net.

Usually three or more of them are placed on the bottom and tuned to different audio frequencies. A submerged vehicle within the net interrogates them in turn and fixes its position by measuring the time it takes for the sound to return from them.

Just as manned submersibles carry transponders to interrogate a bottom network, so did SLEUTH 2. As a result, shipboard operators could maneuver SLEUTH, but they did well not to have total confidence in transponders alone. For greater security, two last pieces of equipment were used.

To avoid crashing into the seafloor, the vertical distance from the seafloor is needed, and SLEUTH operators used an echo sounder to measure this height. At the same time an operator would check the depth of the SLEUTH by using the pressure sensor of the CTD instrument. The depth of the instrument combined with the height off the bottom equals the total depth, which could be checked against bathymetry to stay within a prudent range.

Sometimes, though, the echo sounder measured zero. "Then we

know we've crashed," Milburn explained. He laughed, but it didn't sound like getting this measurement was particularly funny.

All the pieces of transponder assemblies were housed in one of the Sand Point warehouses, a big, high-ceilinged shed large enough for a helicopter.

A transponder is moored to the ocean bottom on a line; it's the valuable piece on the line, the special charm on a sort of equipment charm bracelet. It is humble stuff, actually—an assortment of pieces of different origins, from different epochs of industrialization even.

At the bottom the engineers would put an "anchor," a wheel from a railroad car. Attached to it, and stringing all the other pieces together, was quarter-inch line made of Dacron. Eight-thousand-pound test, Milburn joked.

Just up the line would be the unit which released the transponder from the anchor when the research was done. Its release mechanism would be tripped by an incoming acoustic signal of the right frequency.

Above this would be the transponder itself, a small watertight box of electronics.

Finally, at the top, perhaps 100 feet up the line when the transponder array was deployed underwater, would be a couple of hollow balls for flotation. They were seventeen inches in diameter with walls three-quarters of an inch thick. They were made of glass.

Glass is an ideal material deep underwater. Though it can fracture easily at normal atmospheric pressure, under the heightened pressures below sea surface, glass increasingly compresses, which makes it highly resistant to fracturing. The floats will endure 10,000 pounds per square inch, which they encounter only if they go deeper than 6,800 meters. This they rarely do.

When everything goes according to plan, the floats keep the equipment bracelet upright while it is attached to the anchor, and they float the transponder to the surface when the trip is released.

In engineer's heaven, all the instruments would behave as they were designed, and the environment would present no insurmountable challenge. The transponders and the sonar would keep the instrument on track, and then the connection between finding plumes and finding vents would be straightforward.

As the SLEUTH was towed at sea by the research vessel, the data collected by its temperature and particle sensors and by its positioning gear would be constantly transmitted up the coaxial tow cable to computers and displayed on monitors. The displays would show temperature differences from normal at different heights off the bottom.

These graphic displays would provide one indicator of a plume. Light-attenuation data would often give a complementary indication. When these techniques identified a potential plume, water samples would be taken by remote control. Back on ship, the samples would be analyzed chemically to determine if hot springs were likely.

Sometimes, all this work indeed paid off.

It was a long development from the first ocean explorers who had identified the needs for instruments, to the scientists who had discovered the principles to address the needs, to the inventors who had designed the instruments, to the engineers who built and maintained the machines, so that a new generation of scientist-explorers could fulfill the dreams and talents of them all by contributing something to knowledge of the earth.

With tools like Sea Beam, SeaMARC, and SLEUTH, the NOAA researchers gave themselves a decent chance of finding, and thereby coming to learn more about, the hot springs they found so fascinating.

CHAPTER SIX

IN THE HOT SPRINGS OF AXIAL VOLCANO

It was cool inside the *Pisces* and crowded as always, with the three men packed into a space smaller than the inside of a compact car. But Steve Hammond scarcely noticed. A veteran now of submersible dives, Hammond pressed himself close to one Plexiglas port at the bow of the sub, paying attention outside.

"Put it over just a bit, John," he said to the pilot. John Oszust worked the sub's mechanical arm, moving the temperature probe it held into the clear fluid surging out of the vent.

"That's it."

Hammond turned away from the window and resumed counting off the monitor above his head. His voice rose with the numbers.

"Three-ten . . . three-fifteen . . . three-oh-five . . . three-twenty . . . three-twenty-five . . . *three hundred thirty* degrees Celsius!" He stole a look outside.

"Let's look at this vent closely," Bob Embley cut in, alongside him. "We've never seen boiling water down here."

His voice took on a little ironic color. "We may not be seeing it now."

The *Pisces* moved in closer to the source of the hot water. The two researchers watched the small TV screen over the window as Oszust maneuvered the sub in tight alongside the twelve-foot chimney of rock. The picture jumped as the video camera scanned across the rock face.

The pink-and-white bodies of palm worms, looking oddly like fingers, waved at them from their perches in the crannies of the rock. The sub swung around to the other side of the chimney, and a silvery jet of shimmering water passed into view at the bottom of the screen. The camera began to zoom down into the jet. It kept getting closer.

Abruptly, the screen filled with a splash of water.

"*Whoa* . . . "

Hammond and Embley both jerked their heads back, as if they had been hit in the face by a fountain of hot water.

"You can't get much closer than that," Hammond said.

Embley continued to stare at the odd, viscous jet of water, staring as if he were going to dissect it. The question turned over in his mind. Was the water boiling, coming out? Had it boiled below the seafloor?

Water at 330 degrees Celsius—630 degrees Fahrenheit—may be three times hotter than boiling, at sea level. But underwater, pressure keeps the superheated molecules of liquid water from expanding into a gas, and boiling-hot springs were unknown and quite probably very rare. This chimney in the caldera of Axial Volcano was shallow enough—under little enough water—that if the emerging hydrothermal fluids were hot enough, Hammond and Embley might be observing something new to science.

Underwater boiling springs might be a good deal more than a scientific first; one hypothesis suggested that boiling could concentrate precious metals. And if there were silver or gold on Axial in any substantial quantities, that could perhaps change the whole character and development of seafloor hot springs research. The researchers wouldn't know anything until assays were done, however, and that could take months. In a mood of expectation they took some fluid and rock samples from the jet.

It had been a good day. After the *Pisces* had fallen through the sea for nearly three-quarters of a mile, it had come within the ring of cliffs that surrounded the caldera. The sub had continued to slip down for 300 feet beneath the cliffs until it was just above the caldera floor. Then the lights were turned on.

The floor, rough in some places, smooth as glass in others, created an unsettled, eerie feeling. The floor itself was actually a lake of solidified lava, sitting atop a caldron of still-hot magma somewhere below. A caldera forms when a volcanic summit collapses into its own magma chamber after an eruption, so there was probably still the chamber somewhere below, roiling in the dark. The caldera was like the inside of an ancient amphitheater where a spectacle might begin again at any moment.

This general feeling of expectation was not foiled that day. Hammond and Embley saw two large and two small chimneys. The chimneys contained more than a dozen vents, each one different from the others. The fluids they pumped out into the ocean were of various temperatures, colors, and mineral compositions. And they sampled the strange 330-degree vent. Even if it turned out that the caldera was not an actual gold mine, on July 7, 1986, it was showing promise as a scientific one. They felt rewarded—and justified—for their attention on Axial caldera.

Though the discoveries of these vents in 1986 involved pleasant surprises, they owed little to luck. The NOAA researchers had, in fact, stacked the deck in their favor, twice over. Using two separate but complementary lines of reasoning, the scientists had established that the caldera of Axial Volcano would be a good place to look for hot springs.

The process of choosing the caldera had begun five years before. In summer 1981, cruises reconnoitered the length of the Juan de Fuca Ridge from north to south, mapping it with Sea Beam and hunting for signs of hot springs. Steve Hammond was the chief scientist on one of the cruises, and he knew he had found something potentially important when, as he monitored the shipboard plotter, the profile of a large volcano began to materialize. The volcano was not as tall as Mount Hood, the volcano which was about at the same latitude on land in Oregon. But it was about one-third larger. Its base spanned thirty miles at its broadest point. And from the base to the summit the seafloor volcano rose over 3,000 feet.

Arresting as these dimensions were, they were not what caught Hammond's eye. From his measurements it appeared that the volcano was perched directly over the spreading axis of the ridge. The overlap of the ridge and the volcano had been suggested by University of Washington researchers the year before. But seeing the map in front of him made Hammond feel that the overlap would be crucial.

By itself, a seafloor ridge is fed, and moved, by a supply of magma underneath it. But to have a volcano sitting on top of a ridge, Hammond realized, meant that there would be a second source of magma. And since the volcano was big, the magma source could be really quite big. Based solely on its size and location over the ridge, Hammond believed that Axial Volcano would have hot springs.

The following summer, Kathleen Crane of Lamont conducted a temperature survey of the ridge. The SLEUTH instrument package was not yet designed, but Crane used a chain of underwater thermistors towed along the bottom to detect variations from the background ocean temperature in thousandths of a degree Celsius. She discovered five locations along the ridge, about 100 kilometers apart, with temperature plumes. The heat spikes in the water column suggested the presence of hot springs on the ridge below.

The notable feature of the discovery was that each of the sites occurred at a point where the ridge's elevation above the seafloor was higher than anywhere else nearby. This connection between topographic high points on the ridge and the presence there of hot springs was just what a conceptual model newly proposed at the time predicted. It had been developed by Bob Ballard and his colleague Jean Francheteau.

From their studies at the Galapagos Rift and along the East Pacific Rise, Ballard and Francheteau had observed that hot springs were often found at high points along the ridge. Ridges, they knew, are elevated above the seafloor in the first place because of the presence of hot magma below the floor. The magma was believed to collect into pools which heated the crust above it, causing it to rise. A somewhat higher spot on a ridge, then, would suggest the presence of a relatively shallower pool of hot magma. The apparent corollary of this was that a magma chamber close to the surface would make it easier for hot springs to form.

Kathleen Crane's temperature map, showing the relationship between the highs of the ridge and the areas of likely hot springs, not only neatly corresponded to the model of Ballard and Francheteau, it had the practical value of suggesting where to look for hot springs along the Juan de Fuca.

The map pointed to one singularly promising feature. Seen in profile from the side, with the ridge's north-south length compressed and its height emphasized, a particularly steep elevation of the ridge stuck out. It was Axial Volcano.

Hammond's mapping and geophysical interpretation and Crane's thermistor readings were reason enough to devote research attention to Axial, but other factors recommended it as well. For one, Axial rose up high enough underwater so that diving onto it would be comparatively easy. The most likely sites for vents were only about 5,000 feet below the sea surface, which was about one-half the depth of the hot springs sites on the Galapagos Rift and East Pacific Rise. Conveniently, Axial was within reach of some of the shallower-diving submersibles.

The other factor was Axial's closeness to the northwest coast. Approximately a day from either Newport or Seattle, it would be comparatively easy to mount expeditions to the volcano.

Hammond was eager to use Axial to understand hot springs. Yet the first dives onto the volcano were not conducted by NOAA but by an ad hoc group of American and Canadian researchers. The year was 1983.

In the early 1980s, while Americans had been devoting their attention to the southern sections of the Juan de Fuca Ridge, Canadians had been working on the northern Juan de Fuca and on the Explorer, the short ridge that extends beyond it off the west coast of Vancouver Island. By 1983, the Canadians were ready for a submersible expedition to the Juan de Fuca. Moreover, they had a submersible available, the *Pisces IV*. *Alvin*, the only American deep-diving research sub in use at the time, was in use elsewhere.

This first exploration of Axial Volcano built off the reconnaissance data produced the year before. In their planning, the Canadian and American researchers consulted the Sea Beam bathymetric map, the SeaMARC sidescan sonar image, the temperature map, and photographs, and they decided to focus their search for hot springs in a particular part of the caldera floor. Their choice of location was based on an understanding of the origin of calderas.

Since a caldera forms after a volcanic summit collapses into its own magma chamber, the likeliest place to look for hot springs, the researchers reasoned, would be where the caldera would still be in contact with the magma zone. This would occur at major fractures in the caldera, such as the edge between the floor and a wall. Accordingly, when the CASM—Canadian American Sea Mount—researchers arrived over the site that summer, they chose their initial dive targets on the caldera floor where it met the northern wall.

Down on the bottom they had a surprise. The floor of the caldera was generally flat, but it was bisected by a single deep fissure. "Fissure" doesn't quite convey the sense of scale the explorers encountered. The gouge was made up of a series of elongated depressions, some of which were the size of a city lot with a five-story building in it. As the researchers examined this deep crack along nearly 1,000 feet of its extent, they observed the first hot springs to be seen from a submersible in the northeastern Pacific Ocean. These springs weren't chimneys, but rather low-temperature vent holes in the walls of the fissure. Generically, that made them like the first hot springs found at the Galapagos Rift.

Chimneys, however, were also present in the caldera. East of the fissure, the explorers found two that were inactive and a third that was still venting fluids out of its side. On this one, the normal route for flow out the top of the chimney was blocked by a thick cap of mineral deposits. The cap on the stem gave the chimney the appearance of a weird giant mushroom.

Fluids were venting out the stem of the chimney and under the flanges of the cap, and though the waters coming out of the chimney were only 19 degrees C., that was plenty hot enough to qualify as a bona fide seafloor hot spring. The discovery of the mushroom chimney added another site to the small but growing global inventory.

The success of these first 1983 dives onto Axial heightened the interest of the NOAA researchers in going there themselves. Their first dives took place the following year. Steve Hammond and Alex Malahoff were on board the *Alvin* during the first dive, and when they examined another corner of the squarish caldera, they discovered new high-temperature springs. They lingered over the caldera long enough to produce a more detailed map of their location and to collect some rock samples. After that, Malahoff and company continued on up the Juan de Fuca.

At that time, 1984, the government program saw its mission as exploration and broad-scale reconnaissance work. But by 1985 Malahoff had returned to academia, Hammond had been elevated to program manager, and first the scope and then the emphasis of the research had begun to change.

The change in scope was apparent during the 1985 summer research cruises. Fine-scale reconnaissance mapping represented a change in degree, not conceptually a change in kind, over the previous year's work. But the difference between the new fine-scale work and the previous broader studies was substantial. Using the NOAA research ship *Surveyor*, Embley and other Vents scientists conducted three research cruises over the Juan de Fuca. On Axial they mapped the caldera at a much finer scale than they had accomplished before with the Sea Beam, using the deep-towed Sea-MARC.

They also began shooting color slides by remote control with a 35mm camera towed in a camera sled. They hoped the slides would give them the ultimate detail available without going there themselves, what mapmakers call "ground truth." In theory each photo would be classified by the characteristics of the area shown and correlated with the Sea Beam and SeaMARC data for the same location. In practice, matching thousands of nearly similar views of gray lava to their precise location proved hard work. Still, when the process worked to their satisfaction, it gave the researchers a highly detailed geologic map of the caldera and hot springs.

Viewed as a whole, the first striking aspect of this interior floor at the top of Axial volcano was its surface dimensions. Two miles wide by four miles long was a good-sized caldera. The crater left after the 1980 eruption of Mount St. Helens was, by comparison, only about one-third the size, 1.2 by 2.4 miles.

A second striking feature: Within the eight-square-mile caldera, there were at least three vent fields, covering thousands of square meters at their broadest. The CASM field was at the north edge of the caldera. The high-temperature vent field discovered in 1984 was about four miles south. One other identified in the sidescan images lay along the southeastern corner.

By 1985 they knew the rough shape of what they liked to call their "research laboratory," and they had a pretty clear idea of its superficial qualities. The next change in the research program—the change in emphasis from qualitative to quantitative studies—brought more, and deeper, insights.

Hammond talked about this change one summer afternoon in 1987. At different times during the previous three years he had described and explained to me what he and the other Vents scientists were working on. But this time his manner seemed new.

He laughed easily at the suggestion he was working too hard; from the bottom drawer of his desk he produced a bag of chocolate-chip cookies. An old joke: He had a habit of working at his desk through lunch.

I asked him if he missed spending time on his own research, now that he was so involved as the manager of the program. A bit of the folklore that scientists share is that good scientists don't become administrators.

"Sure, I miss it," Hammond said. "But now what I do is organize other people into a research program. I enjoy that."

He leaned back in his chair, and his desk, a big mahogany affair, seemed to get even bigger. Stacks of papers, neatly played out in lines, covered most of the desktop in front of him: memos, letters, reports, telephone messages. They looked like cards waiting to be played. Science as a complex game of risk.

There were plenty of challenges in organizing a research program. "A research program isn't something static that heads forward in some preordained design from the outset," Hammond observed. As a manager he was still involved solving puzzles, one of the activities that made laboratory science satisfying. The way that Hammond saw it, it was just that the size and shape of the puzzle had changed.

He talked about the challenge with enthusiasm. The outset of NOAA's work—the mapping—was all well and good, and necessary, he said. But it was the job of the national ocean agency, he and his superiors felt, to understand the effects of these newly discovered physical features on the ocean. Once it was understood how venting affected the ocean, something could be said about the effect on people. Perhaps the vents warmed the oceans enough to affect climate: That would have implications on society worth knowing about.

Relevance to society—that was the ultimate justification for a government agency.

Understanding the overall effects of the hot springs on the ocean meant a shift away from just locating and describing their occurrence, the earlier qualitative work.

"Yes, we found some vents. But the question then becomes, how do you really study them?

"You need to gather information that's quantitative," he said, answering himself. "You need to make measurements. And to get the measurements, you need to place instruments on the bottom."

He smiled a bit sheepishly. The logic was simple, but the implications, he knew, were not. Where were the instruments to be placed? Which measurements were to be taken?

In the best of all possible worlds, a Vents Program might do everything. It might try to understand the entire global phenomenon of venting. But given the constraints of money, time, and people, Hammond had to shape something manageable.

The NOAA scientists took as givens that venting is global, that the process transfers significant amounts of heat and materials between the earth and the ocean, and that it has been going on during virtually all of geologic time. So the dimensions the Vents scientists needed to comprehend were big.

But bigness was only half the problem. Hammond spread his hands out, palms up, in a gesture of mock despair.

"But look—venting is also local," he said. "It sometimes involves tiny quantities; and it also takes place over minutes and hours."

Considering the spread of the dimensions, getting a grasp on the effects of the hot springs on the ocean could all too easily appear impossible.

He paused for a moment. What were this mere handful of ambitious scientists to do?

Hammond leaned back again into his chair and drew thumb and forefinger through his thick dark mustache. As he leaned back, two charts on the wall behind him came into focus. Over one shoulder was a *National Geographic* map of the ocean floor. Over the other was an irregular-looking red poster with the wacky headline "Stop Continental Drift." They seemed to bracket Hammond figuratively as well as visually: the serious and the but-not-too-serious worldviews.

So what would the Vents scientists do?

They would take on the challenges step by step, adopting an approach that scientists are good at; they would break the problem down into its parts. They would look at the hot springs as a system and try to model it, define it with numbers.

Looked at simplistically, it was a flow-through system; cool seawater was the input, the heated hydrothermal fluid was the output, and the fractured crust, hot magma chamber, and vents made up the conduit between. It could be crudely compared to a household plumbing system with its connections to the incoming water main and the outgoing sewer.

But of course the vents were not as simple as a plumbing system. They weren't just simple flow-through pipes; there wasn't just one motive force, but two: water and heat. The vents were likely to incorporate a net of interrelations, of feedback loops that would regulate the system, turning elements off and on, speeding them up or slowing them down.

And the Vents scientists weren't only interested in knowing the vents in their spatial dimension; they were also interested in knowing how the vents could vary over time.

They had still set themselves a potentially vast and intricate problem. If funding for civilian science had had a higher priority during the Reagan administration the Vents Program might have done more themselves. But under the circumstances, they set up a plan to make their studies manageable. The NOAA scientists limited the size of the puzzle they themselves tackled. They got help in analyzing the complexities of the system by working with scientists from other institutions and programs. Together they all focused on a representative example of a seafloor hot springs system and concentrated their attention, at least initially, on local and nearby effects.

For all these purposes Axial caldera was ideal. From 1985 to 1988 the Vents Program spent about half of its total resources, $1 million per year, on studies of venting at Axial.

The NOAA scientists were, obviously, not the only ocean scientists doing vent research. Scientists from the Geological Survey and from institutions including Oregon State, the University of Washington, Woods Hole, Scripps, and Lamont continued their own research on other ridges, including the Mid-Atlantic and the East Pacific Rise. These other research efforts had their own trajectories and progressed in their own ways. What made the Vents effort unique was that it was a continuous program and that it focused much of its attention on one location, seeking to develop a comprehensive understanding of that place.

In their study of Axial, the NOAA scientists and their colleagues began at the nozzles of the vents themselves. But their desire to understand the oceanic effects ultimately got them looking down into the crust, and far away from the ridge, and back in time.

*   *   *

In the *Alvin* and the *Pisces* subs the researchers took direct measurements at the nozzles of the chimneys and the openings of the vents. The temperatures of the hot springs that they sampled ranged from less than 10 degrees C. to more than 330 degrees C. The volume of an average vent, some three inches in diameter, ranged from one quart per second to as much as an astonishing ten quarts *per second*. The velocity of the flow coming out of these vents was similar to rates calculated in other locations, on the average of three feet per second and as much as about eight feet per second at the nozzle. The velocity decreased rapidly as the plumes rose.

From estimates of the volume and heat of large plumes, the Vents researchers calculated the first tentative estimates of heat flux for two short sections of the Juan de Fuca Ridge. The flux was on the order of 1,000 megawatts—that is, 1 billion watts—over areas of five to ten kilometers, about three to five miles. This energy output is equal to the normal power usage of Seattle, Washington.

This amount of energy could seem large if it weren't something as big as the earth that was losing the heat. That the earth has heat to lose is a legacy of its origins.

When the planet accreted from space dust and gas it trapped unstable isotopes of some elements inside itself. These radioactive isotopes give off atomic particles as they decay, and those energetic particles heat up the planet's interior. Some of this inner heat comes out through the crust in a regular way, at minute levels not detectable without instruments. Some of it also comes out in intermittent and even violent ways, such as at hot springs and eruptive volcanoes. In a sense the seafloor vents are a safety valve for the inner heat of the earth.

Although measurements based on a few close observations along one section of ridge were useful in putting some frame on the size of the local phenomena, after only a few years of research these numbers were by no means final. It was a common observation that the vents could be highly variable in their activity; from one week to another, vents could turn on and off. This was a critical fact, for it put a crimp into the system at the output pipe. The flow through the system clearly was not a constant.

But what factors influenced it?

Surface influences on individual vents were easy enough to see and appreciate. As the Canadian-American exploring party observed at the mushroom-capped chimney in 1983, vent openings could get plugged up by the minerals in the fluids they were venting. But what of the sub-seafloor influences on the system? The cracked and fractured rock layers, the underground channels through which the seawater descended and ascended, were a plumber's nightmare. It seemed reasonable that this plumbing might well be the key to the output flow. But getting down to examine it posed a major challenge.

As the seafloor itself had been the unknown realm for scientists of the previous generation, so the sub-seafloor was the new invisible world to the hot springs explorers of the 1980s. Nevertheless, though their quarry was invisible, the ocean explorers had an ally. It was a familiar one: sound, invisible itself, and invasive.

Sound waves that produce a profile of the subfloor need to penetrate a different medium from sound waves that profile the floor itself. Sea Beam, for example, uses sound waves with a frequency of 12,000 cycles per second, or twelve kilohertz. (This is outside the range that humans can produce; it's about the highest squeak a robin can make.) Such high-frequency waves are appropriate for measuring depths to objects close together, because their wavelengths are short, on the order of four inches. Short wavelengths can provide a tight fit to an object. This is what "high resolution" is about. For sub-bottom profiling, however, high frequencies and short wavelengths are not so desirable.

What happens to sound frequencies in the rock of the seabed is comparable to what happens when you put your hands over your ears: the treble sounds are muffled, while the lower tones come through. Layers of rock, naturally, dampen sound more than hands do. To create an image of the sub-bottom, geophysicists shoot sound waves of low frequency, whose long wavelengths, on the order of a few tens of meters (dozens to a few hundred feet), snake through the subfloor. As they hit the layers of rock the waves are reflected on an angle back to the surface of the sea.

By interpreting the time, strength, and angle of arrival of these reflected seismic waves, researchers can map the depth and position of the important rock boundaries beneath the seafloor. Or at least that's the way it works in principle. The art of interpretation plays a critical supporting role in the science of seismic profiling.

By the early 1980s, academic and agency scientists were using the most sophisticated sort of profiler available, the multichannel seismic reflection systems, which had been more commonly used by offshore oil and gas exploration companies. The multichannel systems were a big advance on the systems used by the first generation of seafloor explorers. They were more powerful and much more flexible.

The depth to which the low-frequency waves can penetrate into the rock is strongly dependent on the intensity of the incoming sound wave. In the 1950s, when Maurice Ewing was directing the first comprehensive ocean seismic surveys, the sound source of choice was TNT, in half-pound packages. One backpack of TNT over the side of the ship and into the water every three minutes produced enough reflections to permit a continuous profile.

In the 1980s a researcher interested in producing seismic profiles had a selection of electronically triggered sound sources capable of producing powerful sound waves of different frequencies. "Airgun," "sparker," and "boomer" were the names of some of them, and the names were appropriate. A typical high-pressure airgun could pack a wallop equal to two pounds of TNT. By using an ensemble of such chamber instruments, geophysicists could orchestrate the effects they desired.

Janet Morton, of the U.S. Geological Survey's Pacific Marine Geology branch, was one of the group of academic and government scientists to begin using the multichannel seismic ensemble in the mid-1980s. Typically, she ran profiles from the Survey's research vessel, the *S. P. Lee*, shooting five airguns beneath the sea surface and recording the incoming reflections on hydrophones towed behind the ship. The shots occurred every seventeen seconds, the recordings lasted ten seconds, and the result, over an eight-hour survey, was a barrage of data: one data point every two milliseconds. However, once she had massaged the data with numerous computerized manipulations, they could begin to show a body of useful information about the profile of the subfloor under the ridges.

Morton devoted a good deal of attention to producing seismic profiles of seafloor ridge areas. In 1984 she made one of the first profiles that showed persuasively the position of a magma chamber under a spreading ridge. Since magma chambers are the engines of the hydrothermal system, she believed it was critical to understand the location, size, and shape of chambers below the vents.

Her 1984 profile was of the Lau Basin in the southwestern Pacific. As printed by a computer plotter, the profile showed a dark horizontal line beneath the seafloor at a depth of 3.5 kilometers, a little over two miles. Based on the nature of the reflection signal, she was convinced that the line marked the top of a magma chamber.

Her reasoning was straightforward. Sound waves travel more slowly in molten magma than they do through the rigid rocks of the seafloor crust. When the incoming sound wave hits the magma chamber this slowdown is seen as an inversion in the returning wave. Such an inversion occurred in the seismic reflections in the Lau Basin.

She attempted to apply essentially the same methods to a seismic survey of the Juan de Fuca Ridge, also in 1984. But the results were disappointing. Only a weak reflection was seen, approximately 2.5 kilometers below the ocean crust, and Morton came away feeling that it was going to be hard to demonstrate conclusively the position of a crustal magma chamber on the Juan de Fuca.

Other seismologists agreed, though the reason for their agreement might have seemed to Morton more unsettling than reassuring. One straightforward argument suggested that the reason magma chambers were difficult to find in the crust along the ridge was that they weren't there. They were not so close to the seafloor, but were instead deeper, in the mantle, the next layer down in the earth.

The ocean crust is, on average, some six kilometers deep, about 3.6 miles. Some seismologists believed that the main magma reservoir of the Juan de Fuca resided in the mantle at depths of ten to fifteen kilometers, and not in the crust at all. At this depth the chamber wouldn't normally be detected by multichannel seismic systems, which penetrate less than ten kilometers. Over geologic time, in different places, flows of magma do stream up from the reservoir to create pools in the crust, but—argued proponents of this point of view—crustal chambers were fairly limited in size, relatively short-lived, and therefore likely, as Morton felt, to be hard to find.

If the larger picture of the magma system underlying the Axial hot springs remained temporarily obscure, the Vents researchers were determined to get at least a snapshot of the plumbing system under the Axial caldera itself. For this task they engaged the services of seismologists from Oregon State University.

In seismic profiles down to 1.4 kilometers below the caldera floor, the researchers found no evidence of a magma chamber.

They did, however, find out something else about the structure of this near-surface layer of crust. A good deal of it was cracked. They calculated that near the caldera floor the rock was 30 percent porous, with numerous pathways through which the seawater could circulate. This was striking, and they wondered what had caused the near-surface crust to be so broken.

Steve Hammond had a theory. He thought of it when he saw the outlines of the caldera coming up in the bathymetry the first time, in 1981. The spacing and the elevation of the contour lines being printed on the shipboard plotter told him that a volcano was under the ship. He saw that it was big and that it sat on the ridge, the first significant facts. He expected to see a circular crater or caldera at the top of this big volcano. But he was surprised at the image on the plotter.

"It hit you in the face," he recalled. "You didn't have to be a geologist to notice that *there* was something really weird on the seafloor."

The caldera was rectangular. Hammond had a notion that the odd shape would be the key to both the evolution of the volcano and its recent geologic history, right up to the cracking in the crust. The clue to the meaning of the odd shape, Hammond came to believe, was off the ridge to the west of Axial. There a group of underwater seamounts ran in a line, away from Axial Volcano.

In 1963 Tuzo Wilson had explained the significance of such chains of seamounts. Wilson noticed that the Hawaiian islands trend in a line off to the northwest. He also knew, from the dating of magnetic anomalies, that the Pacific plate was spreading in a northwesterly direction. He suggested a connection: the Hawaiian islands were extruded by a source of magma beneath them, and over time, the moving plate rafted them away. He called this kind of magma source a hot spot.

The seamounts that extended off to the northwest of the Juan de Fuca Ridge on the Pacific plate were identified in 1974 as composing another chain formed by a hot spot. In 1985, Hammond and John Delaney of the University of Washington proposed that Axial was the youngest in the chain formed by the Cobb hot spot. The unusual size of Axial, they formally proposed, was the result of two supplies of magma, one that fed the ridge, the other that came from this hot spot.

The contorted shape and square caldera of Axial was the result of the interaction between these two primal forces, Hammond and Delaney believed. The hot spot, the fixed, potent source of new ocean crust, was producing the volcano; the spreading seafloor, the relentless conveyor belt, was pulling it apart. The spreading activity cut through the caldera in two distinct rift zones. The existence of these two zones could explain the large amount of rock fracturing in the caldera.

After a couple of years examining the hot springs plumbing system, the Vents researchers and their colleagues knew something about how it worked. They had gained a good deal of knowledge about local conditions at Axial Volcano, their chosen seafloor laboratory. They knew roughly about how fast water flowed through its vents, about how hot the water was when it emerged, and a bit about the hidden piping under the seafloor. But the overall picture of the system was still far from clear.

Knowing the effects of the vents on the chemistry of the ocean was still one main goal, and here the researchers built on the original work of John Edmond of MIT, who had participated in the 1977 Galapagos expedition.

The MIT geochemist had described the chemical reactions which occur at each main point of contact between the water and the subfloor rock. These reactions transform the incoming seawater into outgoing hydrothermal fluid. A number of reactions between several elements happen simultaneously, and the whole affair is complex, but the gist of the process can be gleaned from following a key element through its transformations.

Sulfur is important as a partner in the major vents reactions. But sulfur is only a small part of the volume of seawater; most salt water, 96.5 percent, is pure water. Four elements, sodium, chloride, magnesium, and sulfur, make up much of the rest. They are present in solution as charged ions.

In the incoming seawater, sulfur is part of sulfate, a negatively charged molecule. As the seawater comes into contact with the basalt rock below the crust, it is changed into an acidic solution, containing hydrogen. The sulfate bonds with the hydrogen, creating hydrogen sulfide.

Heated, the hydrogen sulfide begins to rise up to the sea surface, and as it does, the sulfur may change partners again. Iron in the basalt, for example, has a stronger attraction for the sulfide than does the smaller hydrogen ion, so iron sulfide may be formed and some of it may precipitate below the seafloor.

Some of the heated iron sulfide, alternatively, may continue to rise until it emerges into the cold seawater above the seafloor. There a couple of new reactions are likely to occur. The iron sulfide may either precipitate as part of a vent chimney or may escape temporarily, forming a hot chimney's characteristic black smoke. Eventually, the iron will itself make another new alliance, this one with the abundantly available oxygen of the seawater, and it will fall to the ocean floor as iron oxide, there to become a brownish or yellow sediment. Meanwhile, the sulfur, loosed from the iron, will come full circle in its reactions; it will bond with oxygen in the seawater and return to solution as sulfate.

Understanding these sorts of transformations began with the work of Edmond and his colleagues. They not only described the chemical reactions that the hot springs fluids went through, they also calculated their effect on the concentrations of elements in the ocean. Projecting their data from the 1977 Galapagos expedition, they proposed that the spreading axes of the global ridge system consume most of the magnesium and sulfate that are introduced into the sea by rivers. The springs also release into the ocean concentrations of a number of elements in amounts that are comparable to or greater than the amounts that come off the land. These elements include potassium, calcium, silica, rubidium, and lithium. The vents are both a source and a sink for chemical elements.

NOAA's Ed Baker drew upon Edmond's work in continuing with his efforts to understand a crucial effect of the hot springs system, the dispersion of the hydrothermal plumes through the water column. Baker thought that by examining the plumes coming from ridge segments, he could find the key to understanding the effects of venting on the nearby ocean. But also he thought it might be possible to develop a general model for the oceanic effects of hydrothermal emissions by comparing venting on geologically different segments.

Any notion that this model would be easy to develop was dispelled by two discoveries made in 1986.

In August, Baker was doing plume surveys along the southern Juan de Fuca, on a well-studied part of the ridge. On this cruise the work of minding the SLEUTH probe had settled into its routine. After the crew had gotten the instrument in the water, Baker would watch the monitors to see what information it was picking up. At the same time he would direct the "tow-yoing" as the instrument was gingerly towed behind the research ship, up and down underwater.

Baker's own watch in the monitoring room would go on for hours. Sometimes the work of keeping the tow out of trouble was nerve-racking, sometimes just plain tiring. But one particular August evening something different occurred, something more characteristic of a grade-B science fiction movie than of a science cruise.

There was Baker, bleary-eyed, staring at the video monitor. Slowly the numbers on the screen began to go way outside their normal ranges.

No, he thought. It can't be.

An idea crossed his mind: Too much coffee.

He gave another look. No, this actually is happening.

Then he thought perhaps something was wrong with the instruments. He checked.

Nothing was wrong with the instruments.

Baker knew quite well that hydrothermal plumes are measured in tens or hundreds of feet. But the numbers on the monitor indicated the plume was vastly larger.

Then Baker really couldn't take his eyes off the screen.

When the giant plume was fully mapped, after five days, it measured twelve miles in diameter and 2,000 feet thick at its thickest point. Roughly oval in shape, it tapered out toward the edges, like a huge discus, or a small floating island.

Baker's astonishment at encountering this giant plume was surpassed when he began taking measurements and computing. He calculated that the heat energy in the mass of submerged water was the equivalent of 10 billion kilowatt-hours of energy, about four times the annual production of an entire large vent field on the Juan de Fuca. When he sat down and worked it out, he realized this was also equal to two years of hydroelectric energy production at the giant Bonneville Dam on the Columbia River near Portland. And its particulate matter was twenty times greater than normal for the deep ocean. It contained 6,000 tons of particles, much of it minerals.

"Megaplume," the phenomenon was quickly dubbed. What gave birth to it?—the obvious question. So much energy concentrated into a single, symmetric plume likely resulted from one brief event that lasted no more than a few days, Baker believed. It was certainly transitory; its local effects appeared to vanish quickly. When a later cruise returned to the area a few months later, no trace of the megaplume was found at all.

As to what caused it, Baker and his colleagues came to propose a rather daring hypothesis. The first indication came from the composition of the plume itself.

Anhydrite—calcium sulfate—originates beneath the seafloor and is usually dissolved within days in the ocean. Anhydrite was found in the plume.

The plume also was located much higher up in the ocean above the ridge than normal, suggesting that it had been propelled by much larger than normal forces.

And its mineral composition indicated that the expulsion, or eruption, had involved superheated water, at least 300 degrees C.

From these observations, Baker, Richard Feely, and Gary Massoth reasonably argued that the megaplume was the result of some recent, catastrophic release of heated water from the seabed.

The NOAA scientists and their university colleagues began suggesting tantalizing interpretations. Perhaps the megaplume was caused by a volcanic eruption on the ridge. Or perhaps it was caused by the main event of earth-building, the spreading of the seafloor itself. Neither process had ever been witnessed.

Whatever else it meant, the discovery of the megaplume punched a gaping hole into the theory that a model of venting could come from examining the regular output of local ridge vent fields. There were simply larger, irregular contributions, and somehow they needed to be included into the model.

The frame of reference for the vent system was enlarged again in 1986, when the NOAA researchers learned of another curious discovery, this time made by a university oceanographer. Lynne Talley of Scripps conducted a major cruise that year in the Pacific to sample the water vertically at many locations. The sampling continued west of the Juan de Fuca along the 47th Parallel two-thirds of the way across the Pacific. Virtually everywhere Talley sampled the water, she discovered enrichments in silicate at a depth of 2,000 meters.

Silica, a glassy mineral, is derived from basalt rocks of the ocean crust during hydrothermal reactions. When it is vented to the sea-water in plumes, it combines with oxygen to form silicate. Since 2,000 meters, the depth of the silicate signal, is also the depth of the Juan de Fuca ridge crest, and other studies had shown the ridge to be enriched in silicate a hundredfold, it seemed reasonable to theorize that the silicate might represent, at least in part, the residue of Juan de Fuca venting. It was dispersed through the ocean as far as the Scripps cruise sampled, 3,500 miles away. Considering patterns of ocean circulation, that distance probably represented dispersal in the ocean over a few hundred years. Although the enrichment was small, on the order of 2 to 3 percent above normal, it helped confirm the significance of hot springs as a source of silica.

About one-third of the ocean's silica comes from hot springs. The rest comes from rivers on land.

The discovery of the silicate signal far beyond the ridge itself claimed importance for two reasons. First, it told the Vents researchers that as they developed a model for oceanic effects of venting, not only did they need to account for large hydrothermal emissions like the megaplume, they also needed to account for the transport across the ocean of at least some hydrothermal emissions.

And this broad-scale transport might have some wide-ranging oceanic effects. Abundant plankton known as radiolarians make their skeletons out of silica. The radiolarians are one of the foundations of the ocean food chain. Therefore the widespread dissemination of silica, which is available generally only in limited quantities in the ocean, might suggest very large, even global biological implications for the vents.

The investigations of Baker, above the ridge, and of Talley, far from the ridge, added new dimensions to the inquiry about hot springs chemistry and its significance. Investigations of the effluent of some springs on Axial added another.

The geochemical model described by John Edmond was broadly valid. But it became clear, as scientists analyzed hot springs in different locations, that the composition of the minerals precipitated from hot springs plumes differed from one geologic setting to another. The factors that caused the variation were initially unclear, so deposits were analyzed to determine their mineral composition. The composition might offer clues to their formation. Special attention came to be focused on Axial because the payoff of this line of research might prove to be more than scientifically valuable. It seemed quite possible that Axial's deposits might be enriched in gold.

"Enriched in gold"—the words assume an almost mythic proportion. The value of gold is at least partly linked to its rarity; and gold is an extremely rare element, making up only about one to two parts per billion of the earth's crust. So rare is it that despite all the human toil brought to the task, the total quantity of gold that has been won from the earth throughout history is estimated to amount to a cube sixty feet on a side. Its rarity is in turn linked to a tantalizing promiscuousness; the metal is widely dispersed and found in no less than nine principal types of deposits, in a great variety of geological settings.

Given the difficulty of finding it and its value when found, it is perhaps not surprising that beliefs about how gold forms always provoke controversy. The medieval alchemists, who believed they could transform base metals to gold through the agency of some secret ingredient, were not the first, or the last, to be persecuted. During the last century, it has been the common lot of economic geologists who advanced new interpretations to have those ideas ridiculed and vehemently challenged by one or another faction of opposing scientists.

An article written in 1975 for one professional journal summed up the situation nicely. Writing on the history of the theories explaining the largest of the world's gold deposits, the Rand conglomerates in South Africa, D. A. Pretorius observed that in the week following their discovery on a Sunday morning, "there was general agreement by the Wednesday afternoon as to the discovery's significance, and . . . by the Saturday evening a violent controversy was well under way as to what had been found."

Pretorius added, "To this day eighty-nine years later, no one single explanation of what the conglomerates really are has received universal acceptance." Given these kinds of controversies, new insights that could clearly explain how at least some gold deposits form would be worth a good deal, both to scientists and to the mining industry.

Although disagreements persist over how gold is formed, general agreement exists that the numerous types of gold deposits belong to three basic categories. A placer deposit is put into place by the sorting action of water currents, typically rivers. A vein or lode deposit concentrates gold in a rock fracture. (Most veins are associated with major structural breaks, where slices of continent come together.) And an epithermal deposit is formed by an intrusion into a continent.

The different kinds of deposits are not necessarily physically distant from each other. The gold rush of the 1850s in California, for example, began when miners, panning for gold in the rivers of the Sierra Nevada, discovered gold placers. Soon the source of the gold was traced back to the Mother Lode, a network of veins in the Sierras themselves.

As to the origin of deposits, some general points of agreement exist. Since about 1850, geologists have recognized that veins of gold deposits can be formed when water circulates through hot rock, reacting with it and selectively leaching out minerals. Although they knew that veins were hydrothermal, the nineteenth-century geologists had no unified theory to help them coordinate the search for such deposits. The best they could do was to know that gold might be present when they found a hydrothermal deposit.

Geologists have also known since the early part of this century that gold is found in another kind of hydrothermal deposit, the massive polymetallic sulfide deposit, in quantities averaging six-tenths of one part per million.

When the 1978 and 1979 expeditions to the East Pacific Rise and Galapagos Rift made it clear that massive sulfides formed along seafloor spreading ridges, it became reasonable to ask whether any such deposits were enriched in gold. Since it would be impractical to go about sampling along the more than 33,000 miles of the global ridge system, an exploration hypothesis was needed.

In 1982, John Delaney and Barbara Cosens of the University of Washington suggested that deposits enriched in gold and silver were more likely to be found in undersea volcanic and hydrothermal systems that were in shallower ocean waters. The researchers proposed that the seamounts associated with the Cobb hot spot and closest to the Juan de Fuca Ridge would be settings of the appropriate kind.

Delaney and Cosens proposed these seamounts, including Axial Volcano, based on the notion that boiling could take place there. Such seamounts rise up rather high in the water; the top of Axial is less than a mile below the surface. At this depth, the pressure of the overlying ocean would not be as great as on deeper ridge areas, and hydrothermal fluids of sufficient temperature might actually boil. Boiling was important, the Washington geologists pointed out, because other studies had suggested that precious metals would concentrate when the hydrothermal fluid separated into vapor and liquid phases.

In the next several years, samples were taken from the volcano, and the prediction was put to the test. Delaney himself took some samples in 1983 during the first Canadian-American expedition to the caldera. The Canadians became increasingly involved. Metals account for approximately 5 percent of Canada's gross national product and from 20 to 30 percent of its exports, so Canadian researchers came to the investigations with motivations and skills. The Vents Program formed cooperative agreements with the Geological Survey of Canada in looking for the mechanism of gold formation. The potential value of a major breakthrough on the subject was not lost on anyone.

One of the priorities of the 1986 American-Canadian dives, then, was to obtain accurate vent fluid temperature measurements that would determine whether boiling might have occurred. That was why Hammond and Embley were intent on observing the vent that produced the 330-degree fluids—so intent that they scorched the lens of the videocamera. Three hundred thirty degrees was very close to the temperature at which separation into liquid and vapor was believed to occur at Axial's depth. Hammond and Embley's vent showed that temperatures existed in the right range, but there was no immediate evidence of boiling.

Another dive, however, showed something more. Bob Embley and Jim Franklin of the Geological Survey of Canada came upon an unusual chimney in the southeast corner of the caldera.

Most hot springs chimneys are made of dark rocks and are thick, but this chimney was pure white and slender, almost statuesque. "Virgin mound," it had been named. The water shooting out of it, moreover, looked clear. The pilot took a temperature measurement; it was more than 300 degrees C. Samples of the fluid and the rock of the mound were collected. Franklin, who was the coordinator of the seafloor minerals program in the Canadian Department of Energy, Mines and Resources, took the rock samples and some fluid samples back to Ottawa.

Subsequent examination of the fluid and rocks revealed that the mineral samples from Virgin mound and the "Inferno" chimney, nearby it, were enriched in gold. Some of Franklin's samples contained four parts per million, two thousand times more than the average in the crust. Four parts per million is four grams per ton; deposits of four grams per ton are mined on land.

Studying the fluid and mineral evidence, Franklin developed some ideas about how the Axial gold enrichments occurred. He knew that gold is carried in solution as part either of a chloride or a bisulfide mineral complex. And when bisulfide-complex gold is exposed to oxygen, the bisulfide is destroyed and gold is precipitated. Why boiling hot springs are important, Franklin saw, is that first, boiling of hydrothermal fluids would lead to formation of bisulfide-complex gold; and second, these boiled fluids would be put into contact with oxygen in seawater at or near the seafloor. Gold would precipitate.

Franklin was pleased with the discovery of gold on Axial and with his hypothesis of the mechanism of its precipitation. But he was also cautious to see around the corners of the idea. Some might argue, he realized, that the boiling explanation was unnecessarily complicated. Perhaps the reason that gold was deposited at some submarine hydrothermal locations more than at others was that there was simply more gold in the source rock. Other Canadian researchers from the University of Toronto had, however, already addressed that objection in 1986.

They chemically analyzed sulfide deposits from various ridge sites in the eastern Pacific. They found that the percentage of gold in the rocks from the seven sites varied only slightly, while the enrichments in the precipitates varied by an order of magnitude. Most of the sites had normal gold content, but two sites were enriched in gold. One of these was the southern part of the Explorer Ridge, the ridge just to the north of the Juan de Fuca. The other was Axial Volcano.

Franklin was eager to go back to the ridges to learn more about their gold deposits. But, initially at least, he had no illusions about any big economic payoff. He figured the total quantity of sulfides at Axial amounted to perhaps twenty minutes of mining, measured by the operation of a major sulfide mine on land.

Still, he could envision a big payoff in the future, perhaps on the seafloor, perhaps on land. In this he was not alone. There were tantalizing indications.

CHAPTER SEVEN

OUT OF THE
SEAFLOOR CALDRON

Driving north on Interstate 5 out of Grants Pass, Oregon, Len Ramp pointed toward a large hill that rose ahead alongside the road. The right half of the hill was heavily timbered, but the left half had only a few trees. Around this part of southwestern Oregon the hill's appearance usually would be the result of logging. But there was no sign of it.

"That's Sexton Mountain," said Ramp, over the noise of the pickup's engine and the wind. "It's an interesting case.

"The part of Sexton that doesn't have the timber on it is made of a rock called serpentinite," Ramp said as the pickup passed close to the hill. "It's very high in magnesium and relatively low in calcium. So it doesn't support vegetation very well." The soil was an odd reddish brown, deepening to black.

He leaned over the steering wheel and pointed again. "Now, the part of the hill directly adjacent to it is made up of another kind of rock—not serpentinite.

"There you get the trees."

In the bright sun, pine and fir stood out starkly against common brown soil.

Ramp started out as the resident state geologist in Josephine County in 1952. Over the years he learned to read the land fluently, recognizing its grammar in soils and rocks, its syntax in riverbanks and roadcuts, its major themes in the placement and succession of mountains, valleys, and streams. He demurred at the suggestion, though, that he had any specialized knowledge of botany.

"No, what I've picked up is just to help understand the geology around here. You appreciate any help you can get."

The enjambment of serpentinite in Sexton Mountain was the first indication that the Klamath Mountains are geologically complex. They contain some striking juxtapositions. Ramp had promised to show some of these odd assemblages, and not just any odd assemblages; he was taking me on an impromptu tour of old mines. It was a sunny afternoon, and, dressed in sturdy cotton twill pants and hiking boots, he looked happy to be out of the office and, as he put it, "in the field."

Off the interstate, the road quickly became a backcountry affair, following the twists and turns of the Rogue River through public forest land. Fringing the road the forest was dense and green, but it looked parched already in the early summer. Now and then a clear-cut hillside, tan and scarred, was visible above the road. Down below, the white-flecked river passed in and out of view.

Ramp resumed talking a bit about serpentinite. It is altogether an oddball rock. Greenish, it resists weathering but gradually takes on a color that resembles buckskin. When it is broken up, its sheared surfaces are shiny and have a greasy feel. It is soft. In fact, one altered form of it, commonly known as soapstone, is soft enough to carve with a pocketknife. This soapy, greasy, soft character is partly the result of the rock's water content.

That rocks with water inside them are found in the dry mountain country of southwestern Oregon might well surprise some people. There was a good explanation, though, Ramp said. He let it go at that for a moment.

After crossing a bridge, Ramp pulled the truck over on a narrow shoulder, parked, grabbed his rock hammer, and quickly made his way down a rocky bank. At the bottom he walked out to the edge of the Rogue River and pointed out a spot on the opposite shore. Some wooden timbers and a large pile of rock rubble were signs of human activity, abandoned some time before.

"That's what's left of the Almeda Mine," said Ramp. "It had a heyday, from 1911 to 1916. Produced more than sixteen thousand tons of ore."

A smelter, propped up on those timbers, had yielded some 260,000 pounds of copper and 7,000 pounds of lead. It also had rendered 48,000 ounces of silver and 1,500 ounces of gold. But what had formed this mineral deposit was a matter mainly for speculation, if that, to the miners of the turn of the century.

To the untutored eye, the rocks were as mute as ever.

Ramp leaned over and quickly chipped out a piece of grayish rock from a boulder at the river's edge. He held it familiarly in his hands.

"Barite," he said. "Look—it's soft but quite heavy for its size."

Barite is a sulfate of the metal barium. As a sulfate, barite typically is found on top of metallic massive sulfides. True to form, underneath the barite in the Big Yank Lode was a zone of minerals about 300 feet thick. The zone, tilted on an angle under the river-bed, yielded the mine's copper, lead, silver, and gold.

"They did have one big clue about the formation here," said Ramp, gesturing upriver. "But they weren't quite sure what to make of it."

J. S. Diller, the pioneer geologist of the region, found fossils of a little clam that lived during the Jurassic period, about 150 million years ago. The clam was a marine organism in a marine sediment. That much was clear enough to Diller. What wasn't clear was the sequence of events explaining how this ocean creature had landed forty-five miles from the Pacific Ocean.

"You can imagine how they puzzled over this," Ramp said. What were they supposed to make of the ocean in the mountains?

Back in the pickup, Ramp drove toward another abandoned mine, this one up in the hills themselves. There, he said, the presence of the ocean would be unmistakable.

He had unfolded a geologic map of the area onto the seat of the truck. A geologic map can seem like the worst sort of intellectual rank-pulling. There, superimposed on hills, valleys, and streams, one may think one knows quite well enough, are odd patches of color, representing interpretations that carry unfamiliar names, like "Mesozoic sedimentary and volcanic rocks older than Kimmeridgian (pre-Nevadan orogeny)."

But with this map of southwestern Oregon, one thing was clear at a glance. Two main belts of color signified clearly that the Klamaths were not always as they look today. From their different colors, representing different times, the rock belts of the Klamaths appeared to have arrived in waves.

Turning off the highway onto a dirt-and-gravel road, Ramp dropped the pickup into low gear to climb an incline. At about 2,000 feet, honeysuckle, ceanothus, rhododendron, and red-barked California madrone crowded the road. Turning a corner onto level ground, the truck passed in front of a small hillside with a rocky face.

Ramp backed up. A hole in the slope became visible. We got out and a few moments later were standing in front of the fallen-down wood-frame entrance to a mine. Ramp checked the passageway with a flashlight, and not seeing any rattlesnakes lounging in the shade, he led the way in.

Inside, only some spiderwebs and a couple of puddles needed to be avoided. Still, we breathed easier when the narrow passage opened abruptly into a room. It was almost completely dark. As Ramp scanned with his light it became clear we were inside a high-ceilinged dome. The walls were composed of different-colored rocks in distinct but irregularly spaced bands of blue, brown, and black. In some places the rock was flecked with bronze.

"This," said Ramp, "is a massive sulfide deposit." The geologist's normal speaking voice resonated in the dome.

"We believe now it was formed on the ocean floor, sometime between about two hundred and twenty million and one hundred and fifty-five million years ago."

When he said that, the gulf of time and space seemed to collapse, leaving us under a murky sea, caught in some strange gestation.

A gleam of light played over the wall.

"For years and years," Ramp said, pointing with his flashlight, "we didn't know that this came from the ocean floor. But for one thing—it's layered; it looks like material that's been precipitated and deposited on a flat surface. You can imagine the black-smoker hot springs. As the black smokers continued they deposited minerals in layers."

A gnarled limb of rock jutted out from the wall. Ramp chipped away at it with his hammer, making sparks.

He held out some broken pieces. The blue chunks were copper sulfate, the shiny brown masses iron oxide, the bronze flecks iron and copper sulfides. And, although it could not be seen, there was gold, he said. It was gold for which the mine was worked earlier in the century.

The semidark vault, its air cool but stale, brought to mind an ancient tomb—a tomb encrusted with jewels left behind from an unknown dynasty.

Outside in the sun again, Ramp talked about the seeming incongruity of the ocean in the mountains. To him it made a good deal of sense.

"When I graduated from the University of Oregon in 1950 there wasn't any such thing as plate tectonics. As a matter of fact, they had a theory called continental drift, which most geologists laughed at. They said it couldn't be." Ramp smiled.

"Oh, they talked about hydrothermal deposits and recognized that you had to have heat and aqueous solutions to form these deposits here. But the environment of the formation, they thought, was just where they are now. They didn't know that these things were happening on the bottom of the ocean, because they hadn't been down there to see them."

Ramp talked more about the changes he had seen in geology as he began the drive back to town.

Through the 1950s and 1960s he recalled feeling often frustrated in his understanding of the Klamath Mountains. He would see assemblages of rocks that "just didn't make sense." Then in the 1970s the idea of ophiolites became respectable.

An ophiolite is an assemblage, or as geologists like to say, a suite of rocks which make up the ocean crust and extend down into the upper mantle. Massive sulfides are found in ophiolites usually just on or below the seafloor crust. In the light of plate tectonics and ophiolites the structure of the Klamaths become much clearer.

Around 200 million years ago the shore of the Pacific Ocean was far inland with respect to the modern southern Oregon coast. Eastward-moving Pacific seafloor collided with westward-moving North America, and pieces of the seafloor were jammed into and shoved under the continent along at least three separate zones. Each successive zone of oceanic crust is younger to the west. As the seafloor collided with the land, sections of ridge hydrothermal systems were subducted beneath the older continental crust. Gradually, they were deformed and uplifted, the overlying rock eroded away, and they became exposed, as ophiolites. The mines of the modern Klamaths are the outcome of these processes.

Beginning in the late 1960s, Ramp said, he tried to apply what plate tectonics theory had to offer, and he found it useful. It helped him understand how geologic features got to where they were. And it helped him visualize what was probably adjoining a visible layer of rock, out of sight.

"When you find what you expect, it reinforces your confidence in the theory," he said.

"It's been a good time to be in geology," said the geologist as he guided the truck off the interstate back toward his office. "There's been a lot of change. People talk about a revolution, you know?"

Ophiolites have been mined in numerous places on land for hundreds, even thousands, of years. The Troodos Massif on Cyprus has been mined for copper since the era of the Greek city-states. The word "copper," in fact, comes from Kypros, an old spelling of the island's name.

Recognition of the origin of ophiolites in the 1970s suggested a potential economic payoff. These formations could be profitable when they wound up deposited onto land, but the deposition often broke them up and made them hard to exploit. It was believed that if the original deposits were found intact on the seafloor and were large enough, it might be more profitable just to mine the seafloor.

This was a notion that members of the Reagan administration came to espouse in the early 1980s. The interest in the potential of seabed mining wasn't merely economic, but also strategic, ideological, geopolitical. It was tied up with the United Nations' effort to establish an international Law of the Sea Treaty, and it played a role in the downfall of the treaty at the hands of the Reaganites.

As part of his 1980 campaign theme of "making America strong again," Ronald Reagan called attention to America's supplies of strategic minerals. These are the minerals needed for industry and for national defense, including aluminum, chromium, and cobalt; and Reagan's concern was the United States was vulnerable because it was dependent on other countries—sometimes not very friendly or stable countries—for its supplies.

Developing new domestic sources of such minerals was called for by the National Minerals Policy Research and Development Act of 1980, and when the Reagan administration took office in 1981 such development became a priority. Secretary of the Interior James Watt, early in his stormy term of office, announced that implementation of a national minerals development policy would be a top goal. A coalition of major U.S. environmental groups responded in October 1981 with a report which noted that although four of the ten major strategic minerals came from "nations considered unstable or unfriendly" to the United States, "being dependent is not the same as being vulnerable." The coalition of groups suggested practical alternatives to new mining efforts. For example, they wrote that "many of the innumerable tons of valuable metals lost to landfills and scrap piles can be recycled."

Such arguments probably sounded unrealistic to the administration as it developed its natural resources policies. Watt was also head of the cabinet-level Council on Natural Resources and the Environment. So it was not much of a surprise when the administration brought a new emphasis and scrutiny to a pending international agreement that had an important bearing on strategic minerals.

The international agreement was the Law of the Sea Treaty, a monumental effort developed under United Nations auspices at a nine-year-long conference that began in 1973. It was described by Elliot Richardson, who served as head of the U.S. delegation for several years, as "the most significant event in the history of law and peaceful cooperation among nations since the creation of the United Nations."

Begun during the Nixon administration, the complex negotiation of the treaty wound its way through the rest of the decade. At first, the primary interests of the United States were preserving its navigation rights. When the Reagan administration took office it focused attention as well on another element of the proposed treaty. This element was a radical plan to exploit the minerals of the deep seabed, including major untapped sources of cobalt and manganese. These minerals of the deep seabed lay outside national jurisdictions and under several miles of ocean.

The plan had been developed by a number of Third World countries known as the Group of 77. It reflected their political worldview and carried their aspirations, as James Malone recognized. Malone was appointed in March 1981 as the chief U.S. negotiator to the treaty conference and the President's special representative.

"It was the feeling of these countries," Malone observed, "that the wealth of the earth hadn't been very well distributed. The northern industrialized states had their hands on all of the productive resources. They controlled the economic systems and so forth, and the Third World, especially the South, was going to be sort of in penury to the North."

The Group of 77 accordingly had developed a concept, called the New International Economic Order, which they believed would produce a more equitable distribution of the wealth of the world. They conceived of the deep seabed and its resources beyond national jurisdictions as "the common heritage of mankind." They believed that the wealth of the deep seabed should belong to all nations, regardless of whether they were maritime countries or whether they were involved in extracting these resources. The Group of 77 developed a plan that would share the revenue from the exploitation of deep seabed minerals among all countries, and would put the balance of control of the development process in the hands of the Third World.

To Ambassador Malone "the plan was a sort of socialization or collectivization of the seabeds to be run by an international organization on a kind of planned-economy, totally controlled basis." He took a dim view of it.

The Group of 77's plan "was not to be a situation where free market forces would essentially be the determining factors of whether you mined or didn't."

The Reagan administration deemed the plan unacceptable. Malone explained, "The United States is fundamentally opposed to the concept of the redistribution of world wealth on a nonproducing basis." He believed that if the New International Economic Order became instituted with ocean resources, it might later extend to other untapped domains, such as Antarctica and outer space.

The objections of the administration were not merely ideological but practical. Development wouldn't occur at all under the Group of 77's regime, the Reaganites believed, and that, too, was unacceptable as a premise. Malone was given the task of attempting to negotiate changes to the deep-seabed-mining provisions which would be acceptable to the administration and to the mining indus-

try. Negotiations continued right until the deadline for completion
of the treaty in April 1982.

At stake were supposedly vast quantities of manganese nodules.
In the 1960s the nodules, small, potato-shaped mineral deposits,
were dredged from numerous sites in the Pacific, and estimates
were made that they might be recovered with substantial profits.
An influential book on the nodules suggested that they held enough
titanium, nickel, manganese, and aluminum to last miners for hundreds of thousands of years.

At the last, however, the concessions offered the United States
ultimately didn't allay the administration's basic concerns. The
U.S. delegation recommended to the President that he not sign the
treaty, and when the treaty was presented for signature in December 1982, 119 countries signed it, but the United States did not.
The Reagan administration simply didn't see the need to. It believed that the disputed mining of deep seabed minerals was a
freedom of the seas, like high-seas fishing, and was covered by
customary international law.

Without U.S. participation in the treaty, ratification was expected to encounter rough sailing. In this international context,
while legal scholars and government officials around the world de-
bated whether the provisions of the treaty would take effect, the
Reagan administration went ahead proclaiming its own national
version of a law of the sea.

On March 10, 1983, the President issued the Exclusive Economic Zone Proclamation, declaring U.S. sovereignty over natural
resources to 200 nautical miles offshore of U.S. territory. The
Exclusive Economic Zone, or EEZ, added a huge quantity of new
territory to the nation, some 3 billion acres, an amount one-third
larger than existing U.S. territory on land. The acquisition, the
President's admirers said, rivaled the Louisiana Purchase, not only
in scale, but in significance to the nation. There was one small
hitch. Like the region west of the Mississippi in 1803, most of the
new offshore region in 1983 was a vast unknown.

Most of the resources of the EEZ, however, were already addressed in other national laws. The main new element of the proclamation was its assertion of sovereignty over seabed minerals.

Among the supposedly hot prospects that had captured the administration's attention in 1981 and 1982 were the then little-known
polymetallic sulfides. One of the key pieces of information was

Alex Malahoff's dives on the Galapagos Rift and his assertion of the $2 billion value of the copper in the sulfides he found there. The idea quickly arose that other ridge sites might also contain potentially lucrative deposits, and attention turned to the new 200-mile zone. The Gorda Ridge was the only seafloor ridge within the U.S. zone.

Two weeks after the President's EEZ Proclamation, the Minerals Management Service of Watt's Interior Department announced that it intended to develop an environmental impact statement for a proposed lease sale of sulfides on the Gorda Ridge. The leasing program was described by the Minerals Management Service as "an important element of the Administration's national strategic and critical minerals policy."

Gorda Ridge development would potentially "decrease America's vulnerability to mineral supply disruptions and political pressures from other nations possessing those [mineral] resources," said the service. But the same document showed that the United States was not really alarmingly dependent on imports for the most common minerals of polymetallic sulfides. While, as of 1984, the U.S. was 67 percent dependent on imports for zinc, the minerals service said, the nation needed to import only 21 percent of copper and 18 percent of lead. The agency identified that the supplying countries for these minerals in 1984 were Canada, Chile, Peru, Mexico, and Australia; these were not exactly countries from which the United States generally needed to fear "political pressure."

The agency directly conceded as much in the draft environmental impact statement for the lease sale, but made the argument that metals from the lease were not expected until the year 2000, "at which time the domestic sources of these three minerals may not be of sufficient quantity and quality to preclude United States reliance on foreign sources of these metals."

Its arguments may have satisfied itself, but the agency's exertions on behalf of mining the Gorda were conducted at the edge of an abyss. In 1984, before the NOAA dives, the Gorda, like much else of the EEZ, was largely an information void. Although it has been there for a very long time, at least 200 million years, the Gorda Ridge was still little more than a name to even most ocean scientists.

H. W. Menard of Scripps had mapped the Gorda in the 1950s, but his detailed maps were classified by the Navy, and since detailed maps are necessary for exploration, Malahoff, Hammond, Embley, and other NOAA scientists went over the ridge again with the Sea Beam system. In their first survey they found that the Gorda was about 180 miles long and was cut by a deep central valley as much as ten miles wide and 12,000 feet beneath the surface. Above this undersea valley floor, craggy peaks rose up from 2,500 feet to more than 6,000 feet. The general topography of the Gorda was known, but that was about all that could be said when Watt proposed that the Gorda be opened for mineral-mining activities.

The consternation over the Watt proposal was immediate. The plan initially called for leasing some 108,000 square miles of seafloor adjacent to and including the ridge itself. That was an area a bit larger than Oregon itself, or, for another comparison, twice as large as the state of New York. The scheme envisioned low-cost leases, yet from the first it appeared to attract little interest from the mining industry. Few people, in fact, could see what the rush was all about.

In Oregon, reactions to the leasing plan ran from incredulity to outrage. Environmental groups were, generally, outraged; the reaction of the Oregon Shores Conservation Council to the Interior plan was typical. Under the headline "Stripmining on the Coast," the council's newsletter worried about "undersea bulldozers as large as your corner Safeway supermarket ripping up the seafloor." And the giant bulldozer wasn't the only thing about the mining plan to get an environmentalist's blood pressure up.

Under one scenario described in Interior's environmental impact statement, 15,000 metric tons, about 33 million pounds, of ore would be bulldozed daily on the seafloor and pumped to the sea surface in a watery slurry. There a giant platform would receive the slurry, expel its excess water back into the ocean, and load the remainder onto barges for a voyage to a coastal processing plant. In the course of its business, the processing plant would generate about 4,500 metric tons, nearly 10 million pounds, of mine tailings per day.

Such a vision prompted questions. What would happen to organisms living near the seafloor? What would be the consequence to fish and other marine life of dumping mineral-laced slurry back into the sea? And what would happen to the tailings?

Oregon state officials were thrown into their own paroxysm of anxiety over the mining. Was the state ready to deal with new kinds of activities that would affect its coastal towns and environment? Were regulations on the books? Would the state wind up absorbing the costs of development and not share in the profits?

At Oregon State University the oceanography faculty took a special interest in the Gorda plan. University researchers had been studying the seafloor and the sea off Oregon since the early 1960s, and quite a few had been involved since then in ridge research. They were better equipped than most others to make some kind of assessment of the plan.

G. Ross Heath was dean of oceanography in 1983. He was also a government policy analyst with the National Research Council. A transplanted Australian, he was the sort of academic who didn't mind plain talk about complicated subjects. That fall he had listened to a variety of points of view on the Gorda, and come, he thought, to an accurate evaluation of the Interior venture. "Premature" was his word for it.

The metals markets were in "terrible shape," the dean said. Mining companies didn't have enough information about the Gorda to "engage in a speculative venture like this." And, Heath said, "We don't have a clue to the effects of disturbances on the living environment in these areas."

When or where to mine wasn't the issue. Given the unknowns, Heath believed it was essential not just to bumble headlong into mining, but to anticipate problems and get answers. He advocated a moratorium of from two to five years on the lease while scientific research began to address the most obvious questions: Were there indeed mineral deposits on the Gorda? If mining occurred, what would be the environmental consequences?

One didn't need to be flatly opposed to mining to take a cautious view of the proposed lease. The few major companies who had the expertise and the interest to mount an ocean mining venture had been burned once by such a promotion and were wary. Manganese nodules, the prize in the 1960s Cracker Jack box of the ocean, had proved rather a disappointment to the mining community. Not only were there the protracted struggles over the Law of the Sea Treaty, the nodules themselves turned out to be not such a great deal. When exploratory work began on them, there were fewer nodules and their ore content was lower than expected. It was not surprising that companies were not eager to lead the charge onto the

Gorda. No one was eager, apparently, except the Department of the Interior.

In February 1984, the governor of Oregon and a new Secretary of the Interior, William Clark, announced that the federal department would back off the Gorda leasing plan indefinitely and would contribute significant funds for research into the ridge. As Heath had urged, scientists would be given the opportunity to answer the questions that Watt had tried to finesse.

The task was substantial, and, auspiciously, it began in a spirit of cooperation. A fifteen-person task force was set up to coordinate activity between the state and federal governments and research institutions. Oregon, California, and Interior's Minerals Management Service shared direction of the task force, while a panel of scientists from Oregon State and other institutions was established to guide and coordinate the research. The Geological Survey and NOAA participated in the planning and brought separate budgets to bear on the effort.

This was the first time a research program had been assembled to explore an entire ridge for mineral resources. It was sure to stretch the capabilities of the researchers.

At the outset, however, the challenge was in simply knowing how and where to begin.

The Vents researchers took the first crack at it with a straightforward approach. Get a theory, they reasoned, that tells you where the minerals should be, find that place on a map, and go there. Their guiding theory was essentially the one developed by Ballard and Francheteau after their work on the Galapagos Rift and East Pacific Rise. To find mineral deposits, look for vents, the theory said. And the most likely place to find vents along the ridge would be in the rift valley between ridge crests, where the spreading was actually taking place. In that central valley the best place to look would be at the highest elevations, above where the youngest, hottest magma reservoir would be.

The first strategy to find mineral deposits on the Gorda involved finding the ridge's topographic high points. Fortunately for their ambitions, the NOAA researchers had their detailed Sea Beam maps. So with maps in hand, they selected five sites where the theory suggested they should find some vents. And in July 1984 they dove on the sites in *Alvin*.

But no vents showed. The NOAA researchers thought about that quite a bit.

At the time Steve Hammond was only one of the scientific party, not the program manager; those Gorda dives were his first. Looking back on it later, he admitted that, like himself, the research effort in 1984 was learning about the realities of ridge exploration.

"It's not that the theory of venting at topographic highs is a bad one," Hammond mused. "But vents are very small features, on the order of a few feet in diameter. The Gorda Ridge, on the other hand, is one hundred and eighty miles long, and we dove on five small areas.

"We didn't find vents." He allowed himself a smile. "It wasn't that surprising."

Coming up empty-handed was a little sobering, however, and it suggested that there might be a better way. For the summer research season of the next year, 1985, the Gorda Ridge task force members put heads together and decided on a couple of new approaches. NOAA and Oregon State University scientists would be primarily involved in one; other university scientists and Geological Survey researchers would be involved in the other.

Where NOAA's 1984 initial effort had examined the first dimension, the surface of the seafloor ridge, their cooperative effort with the university scientists in 1985 would look upward to a second dimension, the water column above the ridge. Again starting with the Sea Beam map, the researchers selected locations where they would look for mineral plumes in the water.

The cruise was in May 1985. For his plume investigations, Ed Baker used a CTD with a transmissometer. The former would measure the seawater conductivity, temperature, and depth, the latter the particle concentrations.

Again the working hypothesis was good, the hardware was top-notch, but the cruise was the kind of experience that made Baker wonder why sensible people, himself for instance, became oceanographers.

On a reconnaissance cruise like this the idea is to get as much data as possible, so Baker and his colleagues on board the NOAA *Surveyor* tried to keep the instruments working essentially around the clock. Sometimes they would arrive at a deployment station at midnight. It would be pitch-black, the wind might be blowing salt spray cold in their faces or the boat might be lurching; but whatever

A JOURNEY TO SEAFLOOR HOT SPRINGS

Steve Hammond describes how maps are made for seafloor exploration. Behind him is part of a large-scale contour map of the Juan de Fuca Ridge, off the Oregon coast. Such maps are the result of sophisticated echo-sounding technology and computer processing; they provide information about the earth that was never available before.

A three-dimensional map view of part of Axial Volcano, on the Juan de Fuca Ridge. This computer image was developed by Vents researchers to aid their investigations of the large underwater volcano, which has been a major research location for U.S. and Canadian scientists since 1983. Numerous hot springs have been observed in the volcano's caldera.

The submersible Alvin *is launched from the rear deck of the* Atlantis II. *Dives to the seafloor are scheduled to begin in the early morning and end before nightfall, when recovering the sub becomes much more hazardous. Swimmers ride out on the sub to release the cable that connects it to the mother ship.*

A swimmer makes a final inspection of the Alvin *as it prepares to dive. When the sea is brilliantly lit and calm, this pause can be a fine moment for the pilot and two observers inside the sub. When the sea is rough, it can be torture. Once the* Alvin *begins its descent, sunlight will fade within several hundred feet of the surface and the sub will enter a perpetually dark and potentially very dangerous world. To maneuver on the seafloor the sub has six small electric thrusters which can turn it in any direction.*

Unusual rock formations are encountered on seafloor ridges, and exploration is so new that the origin of some formations is not always clear. Scientists think that these structures, along the Juan de Fuca Ridge, are all that remains of what was once a lake of lava that drained back into the seafloor.

A seafloor hot spring, in this case a "black smoker." "Smoke" can also be white, gray, or clear, depending on the minerals being carried in the hot fluids. The minerals are leached out of the rock beneath the seafloor by ocean water descending through cracks in the floor and becoming superheated. This relatively small, though vigorous, smoker was found during the Galapagos Rift expedition of 1979.

A hot springs "chimney," smoking away. The minerals that precipitate out of the vent fluids form the chimneys. In different locations those minerals include copper and zinc, and sometimes silver or gold. Mining of some seafloor deposits in the Gorda and Juan de Fuca ridges has been discussed.

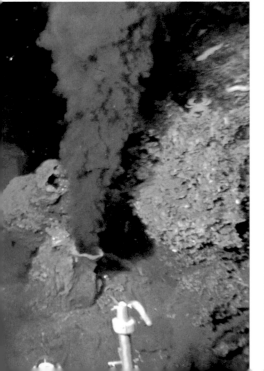

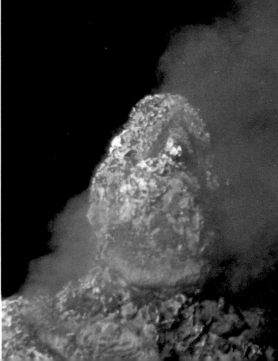

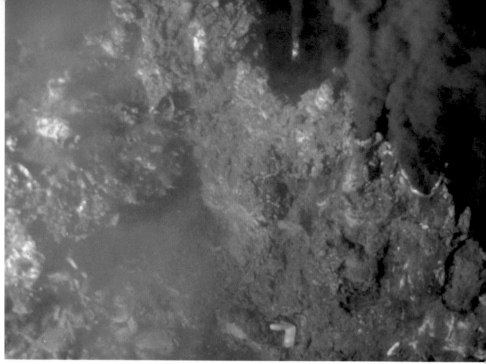

Numerous hot vents spew smoke from a sulfide mound. Venting not only heats the surrounding seawater but is known to affect the chemical compositions of the ocean far from the vents. The global effects of this transfer of heat and chemicals from inside the earth to the biosphere is a focus of research.

Life on the seafloor is generally sparse. Some brittle stars find a perch among pillow lavas on the Galapagos Rift. The pillows formed when lava squeezed out of the seafloor and was congealed quickly by icy seawater under pressure of two tons per square inch.

Nothing on earth quite like this had ever been seen in 1977. When John Edmond looked out his Alvin port on the Galapagos Rift, a mile and a half beneath the ocean surface, he saw an oasis of life. The animals, most previously unknown, included tube worms, blind white crabs, and a pink fish, which hovers above the warm vent.

The giant tube worms of the Galapagos Rift. Their discoverers noted that the worms bear a certain eerie resemblance to lipstick coming out of a tube. The worms grow to five feet, and for several years it was a great puzzle how such large organisms could be thriving at the bottom of the sea.

Another species of tube worm, found along the Juan de Fuca Ridge. This close-up photograph also shows another variety of worm, commonly known as a palm worm because of its shape and the way it sways in the current.

What was the reason that so many of the organisms found at the hot springs were new to science? And not only were they new species, many appeared to be throwbacks to much earlier forms of organisms. Were the hot springs a glimpse of the ancient earth?

At the end of a dive, the Alvin rejoins its
mother ship. There the three people who have
dived for perhaps eight hours in the tiny sub
will extract themselves from the cramped cabin.
The sub's batteries will be charged up for
another dive. Until 1983, the sub's mother ship
was Lulu, a makeshift catamaran seen in the
background.

Jack Corliss with a giant clam from the
Galapagos Rift. This variety has red blood and
smells powerfully of hydrogen sulfide. The
strangeness of the vent organisms prompted
Corliss and other scientists to wonder about the
evolutionary meaning of the hot springs and to
develop ideas about the origin of life at them.

The moment of truth after a dive.
Biologist Verena Tunnicliffe has
rushed up to examine the contents of
the sampling basket, only to be
greeted by a tangle of smelly worms.
(Actually it was about what she
expected—even hoped for. The
samples would allow her to advance
her studies.)

Close-up photographs don't do justice to the reality of an ocean expedition. Nothing compares to the solitude felt at sea, the sense of human smallness, which is perhaps why the feeling of community among mariners can be so strong. The NOAA ship Discoverer *waits in the early morning while a motor launch returns to it following a transfer of scientists to the* Atlantis II.

Seafloor research doesn't require that people actually go to the seafloor themselves. Bob Ballard, discoverer of the Titanic, *has championed the idea of "telepresence"—using remote-controlled vehicles to explore the seafloor with video cameras. He used such robots to explore hot springs sites in the Mediterranean Sea in 1989.*

the conditions, four of them would try to muscle a piece of gear that was bulky, cost $50,000, and was easily damaged, into the water. After two weeks of this sort of thing, with only two days before the end of the cruise, Baker and company had found no plumes.

On the evening of May 20, Baker had stepped out on deck to watch the sun set into the Pacific. Then he had gone back inside, where he sat watching the needle of a chart recorder draw a straight line, telling him that the water under the ship was pretty much all the same. No plumes. Baker sipped his coffee deliberately, reminding himself that he was essentially a low-key guy, that waiting was okay, and besides, in scientific research sometimes things didn't work out the way you planned.

Suddenly the needle jumped.

"Bingo," Baker said out loud. He moved closer to the paper to watch. The needle jumped again. Baker noted the depth of the signal—300 meters above the floor. The particle signal was not likely to be caused by some erosion of the ridge, he figured, not at that height. He rushed off to talk to the scientists who had their sample bottles attached to the CTD.

In a few minutes, they had agreed on a plan; in a few more minutes, the bottles 300 meters off the seafloor were being opened by remote control. A few hours later, working rapidly in the shipboard laboratory, Bob Collier of Oregon State measured the concentrations of manganese. Manganese is the indicator of choice for hydrothermal plumes, and the concentrations were high. Collier was convinced a hot vent would be located below the plume. The resignation of the first two weeks of the cruise turned to optimism.

Hopeful researchers on two later cruises that summer tried to get more information about the hot spring that had waved its little finger. But no luck. The finger did not seem to be clearly attached to any body of hot rock below.

The explanation, while not very comforting, was straightforward enough. Plumes drift in the water away from their source vent. Vents turn on and off.

While this examination of the water was going on, the other strategy that might find minerals was put into action. The Geological Survey and university scientists went to sea to examine the unexplored third dimension of the Gorda, the composition and structure of the rock on and below the seafloor crust. The notion here was that by looking at sediments, listening for earthquakes, probing for unusual hot areas, and shooting profiles of the sub-bottom structure, they might be able to find the most likely geo-logic setting for deposits.

Up until this point in 1985 most of the research on the Gorda had concentrated on the northern part of the ridge. That portion of the ridge was spreading more rapidly than the southern part, and the-ory, as well as most of the evidence to that time, suggested mineral deposits would more likely be found at faster-spreading ridges, where the crust is presumably hotter.

Little attention had been given to the southern part of the Gorda, the Escanaba Trough. There the conventional wisdom was that even if the standard sort of chimney-shaped deposits existed they would almost surely be buried under a heavy blanket of sediments. Sediments from off California and the continental shelf had accu-mulated in the trough in some places to a depth of 1,500 feet.

In 1983, though, the Geological Survey had made some geolog-ical and geophysical surveys of the ridge and had come to the conclusion that the southernmost section was worth a look. Janet Morton took the assignment of getting to the bottom of the Escan-aba sediments, and in August 1985, she was on board the USGS research vessel *S. P. Lee*, shooting heavy-duty airguns into the trough. One day the reflection picture began to show something quite unexpected. Under the cover of sediments in the trough were the outlines of domes that rose up under the sediments as much as 1,500 feet high.

Moving the *Lee* in close to two of these sediment-covered domes, the researchers lowered a probe to take heat measurements. The readings were frequently high, sometimes off the instrument's scale. They took photos with a bottom camera. It showed fresh lava flows in the vicinity of the uplifted domes.

Intrigued and wanting to know more about the sediments, the researchers dropped a dredge basket to the floor and hauled up some of the bottom. They were finishing sorting and labeling sam-ples of the sediment when they looked down and saw some black rocks, sparkling a bit. Everyone stared, not knowing quite what they were. None of the scientists was a mineralogist. Mark Holmes, a marine geologist from the Survey, picked one of the rocks up.

"Hmm, not a standard basalt, is it?" he said playfully. "Rather too heavy."

He handed the rock to Morton. At the same moment, they both laughed.

Sometimes you can pay too much attention to the familiar, not enough to the unfamiliar, she thought.

"They're sulfides," they both exclaimed. This was what they were looking for. Everyone laughed then, charmed by the offhand way the Gorda had finally revealed its secret.

Scientists knew then that polymetallic sulfides could be found on the southern Gorda Ridge. But the Geological Survey cruise recovered only five pounds of sulfides. This was not the sort of haul to send potential miners running for their scuba gear and pickaxes. Obviously, the next step was to go down for a better look and find out how much polymetallic sulfide was down there.

That step was taken in the summer of 1986. First NOAA made detailed bathymetric maps of the trough; then the Navy towed its sidescan sonar system to get a closer view of some potential dive targets. Meanwhile USGS scientists took underwater photographs, dredged up some more samples, and ultimately selected some promising dive sites about 150 miles west of Eureka, California. In August, with the planning completed, a Navy deep-diving submersible, the *Sea Cliff*, was brought to the scene. Scientists who had studied this unusual slice of the Pacific from the surface were going to get a chance to immerse themselves in it.

It had been named well, the Escanaba Trough. The descent in the *Sea Cliff* took two hours—at a rate of about 100 feet per minute—before the scientists were all the way down. Eight thousand feet they fell below the surface of the Pacific before they were within the ridge. Then for nearly 3,000 feet more they slipped down between the steep rocky flanks of the trough. Two miles down, at the trough's bottom, the lights of the *Sea Cliff* came on, revealing the domes. They were like nuggets settled to the bottom of a gigantic prospecting pan.

The explorers found some mineral chimneys sticking out of the domes, but, unlike chimney sites on other ridges, the site held no active hot springs. Instead, most of the Escanaba deposits were found in layers, either on top of the sediment-filled domes or within faults along their sides. From the submersible they counted some dozen sulfide deposits; one large field of sulfides was 300 feet across. In eight dives on two of the domes, the scientists took thousands of frames of photographs, dozens of hours of videotape, and copious notes, and, using the sub's mechanical arm, they grabbed more than fifty pounds of sulfide samples.

When the samples were analyzed back on land, the results were encouraging. Using a combination of techniques including scanning electron microscopy and X-ray diffraction, U.S. Bureau of Mines researchers identified the samples as having "significant concentrations" of copper, zinc, lead, and cobalt. A bonus was silver. The precious metal was found in higher concentrations than had been described in any other seafloor deposits.

There was a certain air of satisfaction in the gathering of some ninety scientists who participated in a symposium about the Gorda in Portland, Oregon, the following May. In the course of just three summers of research, a comparatively small group of scientists had accomplished the initial mission of finding minerals on the Gorda.

Although the quantity of sulfides that had been recovered was small, the volcanic domes, which appeared to hold varying quantities and formations of deposits, were as much as four miles in diameter and 1,500 feet high. Several deposits were reported to be approximately 600 feet across and 100 feet thick. A number of specialists at the 1987 symposium believed that the signs pointed to the Escanaba deposits being very big indeed.

Peter Rona, for example, a senior researcher and minerals expert with NOAA, thought that the deposits had "the potential to build to hundreds of millions of tons of sulfides, with concentrated copper, zinc and lead, and significant quantities of silver and gold." Jim Franklin of the Geological Survey of Canada said that the deposits were "an order of magnitude larger than any that have been previously found on ridge crests." He estimated that their overall size might run 100 million, even a billion tons.

The main reason for this speculation of greatness was that the Escanaba deposits are generated within sediments, and the sediments efficiently trap and conserve the minerals as they are produced by volcanic and hydrothermal forces under and within them. Concentrated, enriched deposits can result.

The consensus, however, was that a great deal more remained to be learned about the deposits. While there was little question that they might be huge, no detailed information about their size and overall grade was available. To gather this information, the preferred technique was to drill deep into the domes in a number of places and analyze the resulting cores. Such work was done in deep water only by the Ocean Drilling Program, and the soonest that this international program might get to the Gorda would be the early 1990s.

In the meantime, barring some unusual development—discovery of highly enriched veins of gold or silver, for example—most of those at the 1987 symposium who were familiar with the mining industry felt that mining the Gorda would not be economically feasible until at least the turn of the century. The additional costs of underwater mining operations and the likelihood of meager return on investments, owing to depressed prices for metals, discouraged prospective miners. Moreover, current world supplies of metals were perceived as adequate, and the development in the 1980s of substitute materials for metals, such as polymers and ceramics, made costly seabed mining only more marginal.

Ultimately, the sense that there was no great urgency to the development of the Gorda became assimilated at the Department of the Interior and translated into a new policy position. In a Federal Register notice in March 1988, the Minerals Management Service announced that the agency had suspended plans for a lease offer because of the mining industry's "lack of interest." No further efforts, the agency said, were to be undertaken to prepare a final environmental impact statement.

If and when the leasing process was reopened, it would start again at the beginning with a new draft environmental impact statement. This provision was significant for those people concerned with the inadequacies of the 1983 draft plan. The intention to produce a new draft meant that corrections to the biases of organization and to the limitations of the knowledge of the first draft could be part of a new plan, rather than tacked on to an old one.

Indeed, the second major question posed to the Gorda Ridge task force in 1984, about the environment and living resources of the Gorda, had never received the attention that mineral discovery did. What attention had been given it was devoted primarily to establishing baseline information about the organisms found in the Gorda area. But the state of knowledge about what would happen to the organisms and the environment if the giant bulldozers arrived was hardly more advanced in 1988 than it was four years before.

At the 1987 Gorda symposium, Jack Dymond of Oregon State

was listening and thinking about this whole matter of the state of knowledge about the ridge and the approach being taken to studying it. Dymond, a member of the 1977 Galapagos expedition and a specialist in the chemistry of hydrothermal systems, was also one of the members of the Gorda Ridge task force, so he might be expected to think about these things.

"All the discussion about the Gorda has focused on a payoff in terms of seafloor mining in the relatively near term," said Dymond. "But the mining industry says they're unlikely to be interested in mining the Gorda for twenty years at least. More research, sustained researched, is just what they say is needed.

"So why not close the Gorda to mining for a period of years and set it aside, or at least large portions of it, as a research area?"

Research would concentrate on two items of potential economic significance, Dymond suggested. One would be the process of mineral formation at the seafloor. If that process was understood, the exploration for related ore bodies on land, the ophiolites, could be made more efficient.

This was a popular position, one that seasoned academic and agency scientists had had all along. In July 1983, for instance, Alex Malahoff had written an article titled "New Horizons for Deep Ocean Minerals," which concluded that "it is safe to speculate that long before the ocean floor polymetallic sulfides become a commercial proposition, the research knowledge gained from studies [of sulfides and venting] will be used to successfully search for fossil ocean floor polymetallic sulfide bodies on land."

Dymond saw another economic benefit of both a research preserve and a sustained program. This benefit went beyond what most geological scientists would likely be thinking about; it would have nothing to do with mining. Dymond was impressed by what he knew about the living organisms of the hot springs. He saw them as a source of potentially important genetic material and biochemical products. What these organisms might have to offer could have much greater value than the minerals, he believed.

The Oregon geochemist was only one of many people fascinated by the hot springs organisms.

CHAPTER EIGHT

EXOTIC LIFE

The world of living things grew and took a weird twist with the 1977 Galapagos Hydrothermal Expedition.

It was perhaps no more than a coincidence. But for the second time in a little more than a century, a major discovery about the nature of life had occurred in the vicinity of the Galapagos Islands. While Charles Darwin had made observations there that led to an understanding of the origin of species, Jack Corliss, Jerry van Andel, Bob Ballard, and the others on the Galapagos expedition had come upon new species that ignored the old rules about the conditions under which life could survive. The vents were more than just a different, previously unknown terrain. They were a previously unknown ecosystem, an environment with inhabitants both new and puzzling.

In the decade following the Galapagos Rift discoveries, no end appeared in sight to the identification of new hot springs species. The first comprehensive list published, in 1985, identified more than fifty new species of invertebrate animals alone. The sheer number of new organisms, significant and arresting in itself, loomed even more significant as a sign of the unprecedented nature of these isolated ecosystems at the bottom of the sea.

They were called oases. In the sense that the springs offered a warm place for life within the cold desert of the deep sea, the term was apt. But in that it might suggest comfort or ease, "oasis" had a connotation that slid rather askew from the terms of life at the hot springs. Dark, sporadically hot, bedeviled with poison gases, crushed by pressures hundreds of times greater than that at sea level, these environments were more inferno than oasis. And yet the organisms, the big ones like the tube worms, giant clams, and mussels, and the microscopic ones like the bacteria, thrived in them. How was this possible?

What were their adaptations? the biologists wanted to know. But this question begged another, deeper one. What did their adaptations to this harsh world say about the possibilities of life itself?

In the search for the explanation to the first question, how the animals were able to survive, research on the larger animals and the microorganisms proceeded in tandem.

The tube worms, as the strangest of the animals, drew the most attention. With their shiny white tubes and protruding red tips they looked like clusters of huge lipstick tubes on the ocean bottom. When members of the Galapagos expedition brought the first ones up to the laboratory on the *Knorr*, they recognized right away that they had found something extraordinary. Not only did the animals smell of the obnoxious hydrogen sulfide, a metabolic poison which should have killed them, but their bodies appeared to be singularly incomplete. They apparently lacked a mouth, a gut, and an anus. It was almost preposterous: How could they survive without them?

Looking inside the body cavity, the researchers had another rude shock: blood. The worms had red blood. It was all very queer. The worms were more like something from a science fiction story, something out of this world, than like anything anyone on the expedition had encountered before.

One of the few people for whom the worms would not have seemed so extraordinary was Meredith Jones. A specialist in the classification of worms at the Smithsonian Institution, Jones agreed to work on the Galapagos samples when Jack Corliss offered them

to him after the voyage. As Jones examined them and other specimens that he obtained on the Galapagos in 1979, he began to
understand the worms' anatomy. Initially he concentrated his efforts on what came to be referred to as the "giant" tube worms of
the Galapagos.

The worm proper was housed in a tube made of protein and
chitin, a substance that it extruded for the purpose. In this production of a chitin-protein protective structure, the worms were
similar to beetles and crabs. Observations of the worms living in the
hot springs showed that they withdrew themselves into the tubes
when their environment was disturbed.

The tube was interesting as an adaptation, but the body of the
worm was where the animal became intriguing. Certain individual
worms grew to be quite large; the biggest one collected measured
nearly five feet long and an inch and a half in diameter. The large
size only made the puzzle of how they were nourishing themselves
more provocative.

Jones dissected the bodies and examined them, section by section, to try to find out.

He found the body to be made up of four distinct regions. At the
anterior or head end was the red-colored tip that in the living
creature extends and withdraws into the tube. In nature, as the
currents of the hot springs flow past the worm, the tip looks like a
thick red feather. This suggested to Jones an appropriate scientific
name for the animal. He called it *Riftia pachyptila*, the thick-plumed
rift worm.

Examining *Riftia* closely, the biologist saw that the comparison
to a feather was more than superficially appropriate. Like a feather,
the plume had separate filaments that projected at an angle from a
midline which ran the length of the plume. Each filament contained
a pair of blood vessels. One carried blood from the plume into the
rest of the worm's body; the other carried blood back out to the
filament. The plume was a kind of gill through which the worm
might exchange nutrients and waste products with the outside
world.

Jones observed that in the second region, below the gill, *Riftia*'s
cylindrical body swelled into a collarlike bulge, the vestimentum.
This collar held the worm at the opening of the tube, with the
plume extending from it. At the opposite end of the tube, a fleshy
anchor held the worm to the tube.

In between these points, and filling the tube's length, was the third main section, a mass of spongy brown tissue. Some European biologists had labeled this area the "trophosome" in describing a tube worm they collected. The word derived from *trophe*, the Greek word for nutrition, though at the time they coined the word none of the scientists knew whether the function of the trophosome was nutrition or something else. Jones agreed with the European biologists that the trophosome might be involved in detoxifying the worm, preventing it from being poisoned by the gases of the hydrothermal emissions.

Although specific questions remained about structure and function, it was clear to Jones by 1979 that tube worms from various seafloor locations qualified, at the least, as a few different species. But they also shared features in common which united them at a higher taxonomic level, as animals significantly different from all others. In 1979 Jones didn't know what that proper classification should be, but the identification of such interesting species was exciting news by itself in the world of biology.

In March 1980, Jones was invited to Harvard University to discuss his findings with biology classes. His was one of a series of talks given during the course of the term on the newfound vent animals. Jones, who was talking about a larger organism, followed a presentation about microorganisms at the vent sites given by Holger Jannasch, a researcher at Woods Hole.

The world of marine animals was indeed growing larger before the students' eyes, which was very exciting to Colleen Cavanaugh. Cavanaugh was a first-year graduate student in biology at the time, but she had worked for several years at Woods Hole as a research assistant. She was keenly attuned to the changes she was hearing about in marine biology.

The discussion about the nutrition of these organisms fascinated her. In the presentations she heard two lines of reasoning. Clearly, in the ocean depths the light of the sun, the dominant source of energy for life on earth, did not operate directly. Still, the conservative line of reasoning sought to link the new hot springs communities to sunlight and photosynthesis. The argument went something like this: Organic carbon compounds produced by photosynthesis, either in surface waters or passing through them from land, would sink down to the hot springs on cool oceanic currents. The cool currents would be drawn by convection toward the hot springs as hot vent water rose up and out of the way. The hot springs animals would consume this "photosynthetic" carbon.

The second line of reasoning, apparently the more radical, was that the main source of energy for the animal communities was coming out of the seafloor itself. Initial evidence for this idea came from the 1977 Galapagos cruise. Hydrogen sulfide was streaming out of the vents, and the vent waters showed very high concentrations of bacteria. One suggestion, made at the time by microbiologist Jannasch of Woods Hole, and developed in his talk to Cavanaugh's class, was that the bacteria were living on the sulfide, and the higher organisms were living on the bacteria.

This second hypothesis was new, and she didn't know all its implications, but Cavanaugh was struck by how much more plausible it sounded than the photosynthesis argument. She mulled these ideas over as she listened to the curator from the Smithsonian describe the anatomy of *Riftia*.

It was an informal session for the graduate students, and Meredith Jones was showing slides. He paused on one that showed yellow-white spots in a lumpy brown mass of trophosome tissue. When these spots were analyzed, he explained, they were found to be sulfur crystals.

Something clicked in Cavanaugh's head. She raised her hand to speak, and then rose to her feet.

"Really, it's clear," she said. "These worms must have bacteria inside them, just as there are bacteria outside them, in the vent fluids." The other students in the room turned around in their chairs. Jones, up in front, watched her closely.

"The bacteria must be living inside the worms," she said. "Symbiotically."

The effect in the classroom was as if Cavanaugh had launched a dirigible. The idea of symbiosis was something odd, magnetic; it drew thoughts to it. She continued to stand for a moment, a little surprised by it herself.

The guest lecturer sized up the first-year graduate student. "Well," he said, "the trophosome is thought to be involved in preventing the worm from being poisoned by sulfur."

Cavanaugh sat down. Just the same, she had a strong hunch that she was right, and after the session was over, she made her case to the visitor.

She told him that Dr. Jannasch had described how certain kinds of novel bacteria could produce unusual products in the course of their metabolic activities. The sulfur crystal in the trophosome could be such an intermediate product. And though, as far as she knew, there were no examples of symbiotic relationships between such bacteria and worms, she felt that other examples of symbiosis suggested the possibility.

When she was an undergraduate at Michigan, she told Jones, her adviser was a specialist in reef-building coral animals, and she had become familiar with the symbiotic relationships of the algae that nourish corals. Why couldn't such a relationship, she said, operate here as well? Jones nodded thoughtfully.

Then Cavanaugh took a leap of faith. Send me some trophosome tissue, she said, and I'll prove to you that there are bacteria in it.

Jones agreed.

To make her case, Cavanaugh had to become familiar with some fairly sophisticated laboratory techniques, including the preparation of specimens for the scanning electron microscope and the transmission electron microscope. To show the presence of bacteria, these powerful magnifying tools were the instruments of choice. The scanning electron microscope has the advantage over the conventional light microscope of producing an image in great three-dimensional detail. The transmission electron microscope, on the other hand, is able to show clearly extremely small objects, as small as those on the order of five angstroms, or about one ten-thousandth of an inch.

Cavanaugh, with assistance from Jones and other colleagues, took micrographic photos which showed plainly what was inside the trophosome. At the lowest magnification, she saw a stippled texture under the epithelium of the trophosome. At higher magnification this stippling was revealed to be a mass of spherical and rod-shaped cells, which were quite likely bacterial cells. At the next magnification, such cells were seen within the trophosome proper. The composition of the cells clinched the case; they had no nucleus and their cell walls resembled those of gram-negative bacteria. They were bacteria.

Cavanaugh didn't stop with the evidence from the micrographs, but supported her claim with measurements. These left no doubt about the microbes' presence. The quantity of bacteria was some 37 billion cells per gram of trophosome.

Even so, she didn't prove that the bacteria were not just lodgers who had overwhelmed the trophosome rather than functioning symbionts within the worm. Proof depended on a demonstration that the bacteria were using some energy source from the vents. From 1980 to 1981, the same period when Cavanaugh was doing her studies, Horst Felbeck, a biochemist at Scripps, was applying himself to this question. Were the bacteria the source of energy for the worms?

Felbeck had just arrived from Germany to do postdoctoral work under George Somero, and when he came he did not have a specific project in mind. However, one of Somero's grad students had come back from the 1979 Galapagos expedition with a frozen tube worm, and Somero told Felbeck that Meredith Jones had found sulfur particles in its trophosome. As it turned out, Felbeck was familiar with the metabolism of marine invertebrates which lived in sulfide-rich mud flats, and he immediately supposed that the worms had enzymes for metabolizing sulfide.

In just a few days, Felbeck had prepared extracts of the trophosome and discovered an enzyme associated with bacteria that used sulfide. He did not isolate the bacteria themselves in pure culture and discover the enzymes directly there, but he did show evidence of several enzymes that were typical of bacterial metabolism. This strongly suggested that the worms were indeed living off bacteria that lived inside of them. What the precise mechanism of this relationship was would need to be the subject of other studies by microbiologists.

Meanwhile, those who were studying *Riftia* still had important discoveries to make. The worms might be living off bacteria, but it was still unclear how they were managing to survive at all in the midst of hydrogen sulfide, which should have poisoned them. Sulfide is an even more powerful poison than cyanide, the substance used in gas chambers.

In May 1982, several research groups converged on the East Pacific Rise off the coast of Mexico. Among the scientists working on *Riftia* were George Somero and his grad student Mark Powell, and another pair from the University of California at Santa Barbara, James Childress and Alissa Arp. The groups worked independently on different ships, pursuing different approaches to the problem of how the worms were surviving the sulfide.

Somero and Powell knew that sulfide poisoning occurs when respiration, the ability of an organism to use oxygen, is blocked.

This blockage occurs in two main ways. Either the available places on the hemoglobin molecule which normally carry oxygen are occupied by sulfide, or a key enzyme involved in respiration is inhibited. The enzyme, common to most animals, is known as cytochrome *c* oxidase.

Somero and Powell wondered whether the enzyme in *Riftia* was somehow biochemically different from other cytochrome *c* oxidases, and insensitive to sulfide. They began to try to isolate and purify the enzyme, using the bright-red plume tissue as their starting material. They noticed that the more they purified the enzyme the more sensitive it became to sulfide. At the same time they observed that their experimental extract was becoming less red.

There might well be a connection between the two observations, they realized, so they decided on a test. They added some blood, which gave the plume its red color, to their extract of inhibited enzyme. Almost immediately the enzyme activity returned to normal. Something in the blood was protecting the enzyme from becoming poisoned.

Subsequent experiments by the two groups showed that the something in the blood was in fact hemoglobin. But the worm's hemoglobin showed some fascinating variations from the human variety.

Tube-worm hemoglobin is a very large molecule, about thirty times larger than human hemoglobin. Along with this increased size come separate sites where oxygen and sulfide attach.

So not only could the worm's hemoglobin bind sulfide and keep it from poisoning the worm, it could transport both sulfide and oxygen. It transported them from the plume, where they were absorbed from seawater, to the trophosome, where the bacteria used them in their metabolism. With its unusual hemoglobin the worm had apparently evolved an elegantly simple solution to the problems of both toxicity and nutrition.

By 1982, the anatomy and physiology of *Riftia* appeared to be coming clear. The discovery of the bacteria inside the worms, however, had underscored an enigma that continued to provoke Meredith Jones: How did the bacteria get inside the worms to begin with? None of the adult specimens showed signs of a mouth or any opening that would serve this purpose. At the beginning Jones had only one clue, and it set him off on a ten-year search.

The clue came from the detailed anatomical description of a tube worm done by two European researchers. The researchers had observed a muscle that appeared to extend to the body wall from a perforation in the brain. The mouth and the brain are in close proximity in some worms; the foregut actually passes through the brain-nervecord complex in some species of annelids, such worms as earthworms. Perhaps, Jones surmised, this "muscle" found by the European researchers represented some vestige of a gut in the tube worm.

At first Jones had only adult worm specimens to examine, but gradually, by the early 1980s, the Smithsonian curator gained plenty of samples of baby worms as well. In examining under the microscope a *Riftia* two millimeters long, Jones saw what he considered an unmistakable snout. There was only one best way to prove it. If it was a mouth and it did function in feeding, it should connect to a gut. The challenge would be to show the connection.

The difficulty could be imagined as rather like seeing from an airplane a narrow road twisting through mountain country. The route would be obscured by overhanging cliffs in some places and would apparently double back in others. A flyover wouldn't leave you certain that the road segments in two different places were part of the same road. You would have to travel each step of the way by foot to know.

For Jones, the difficulty was even greater. Extending the comparison to the mountain route, it would be as if the identity of the road could be determined only by the landscape through which it went. Whether it was a supply road—a food channel—or indeed a river—a blood vessel—only the surroundings would reveal.

To follow the path every step of the way, Jones had to cut the worm into razor-thin sections across the body from top to bottom, zeroing in on what he thought was the path and seeing where it led in each successive slide. These thin slices were on the order of five microns thick—200 of them together would have the thickness of a dime. So it wouldn't work to cut a slice, pick it up with one's fingers, and put it on a glass slide. Correctly preparing the thin sections was a crucial part of the process of discovery.

As much art as science was involved in the preparation. A typical worm arrived at the laboratory preserved in a solution of 10 percent formaldehyde. Jones would select a juvenile worm, shorter than an inch, and begin to get it ready for slicing.

The goal of the first stage of the process was to embed the worm in hot paraffin, which would keep it firm enough so that when the thin blade cut through the tissue it would make a distinct cut and not just mangle and mess it up. It would be convenient if the worm could just be dropped into hot paraffin; unfortunately, it couldn't be.

First the formaldehyde-water solution had to be removed, so that the sample would be dry. To accomplish this the worm was transferred to baths containing increasing concentrations of alcohol, which displaced the water. But alcohol and hot paraffin do not mix well, so the alcohol in turn had to be displaced by xylene, a solvent. The same bathing process as before was run, but this time with increasing xylene concentrations.

Finally, the xylene was mixed with hot paraffin. The paraffin was allowed to cool, and the firmed-up worm was cut into the five-micron sections with a mechanical cutter called a microtome. At the end of this first stage, Jones had a ribbon of paraffin and tissue.

The goal of the second stage was to remove the paraffin and get back to a water-based medium for the tissue, so that it could be treated with dyes. The dyes would help reveal the organization of the cells in the tissue. The process was essentially the reverse of the first half. Once the tissues were stained with the dyes, they were laid out on a glass slide and covered with a slip of glass, the slip held in place by a drop of pine pitch or Canada balsam.

"I'm a nineteenth-century biologist," Jones liked to say, for except for a couple of mechanized parts of the process in cutting and washing the specimens, the process was essentially the same as it was a hundred years ago.

When the preparation was all over, with slides in hand, Jones photographed the thin sections under a conventional light microscope. The pictures showed persuasively that in infant form, *Riftia* indeed do have a mouth that connects to a rudimentary gut.

Having made the discovery, and poised on the verge of publishing it in early 1988, the curator betrayed a degree of ambivalence toward it.

"It is quite an extraordinary development," he said. "Or, I suppose, it turns out that it makes the worms not quite so extraordinary."

In possessing a mouth and a gut, the worms get the bacteria inside their bodies and to the gut wall in a straightforward way.

After the worms grow beyond a certain tiny size the mouth atrophies and disappears, and the gut closes off and fills with bacteria. The cells of the gut wall, filled with bacteria, grow to suppress any indication of the former gut.

Despite these trappings of normalcy, Jones decided that *Riftia* are nonetheless clearly different from other animals. So different, the taxonomist classified them in their own phylum, Vestimentifera.

Only the taxonomic rank of kingdom is higher than phylum, and members of different phyla are as different as a bottlenose dolphin is from a cockroach. To call *Riftia* a member of a separate phylum, therefore, signifies just how far removed from other animals is this denizen of seafloor hot springs.

The unusualness of the situation he found himself in—naming, godlike, a new order of life—was not lost on the modest Jones. With only about thirty different phyla of animals classified to date, the Smithsonian scientist appreciated the rarity of naming a phylum himself. As it happened, the chance to name a new phylum seems not to have been lost on other scientists, and the opportunity led to an extraordinary incident.

In August 1985, Jones was visited at the Smithsonian by a scientist from Uruguay, Raoul Montero. Montero had obtained two specimens of worms from his country's fisheries agency; they were unfamiliar to him, and he had published an article in 1982 describing them. Jones told his visitor about his intent to propose a new phylum for such animals, the tube worms. Jones's article proposing the phylum and giving names for the organisms in it was in the process of being published.

Jones's article ultimately was published and available for distribution on December 30, 1985. Some months later the Smithsonian scientist received an article by the Uruguayan which described his visit with Jones and the *"franco y positivo intercambio de ideas"* which had occurred. An "exchange of ideas" was not how Jones would have described it, but he was more surprised by what the article proposed. Montero and a colleague proposed another, different phylum classification system for the worms. The date of their publication was also 1985.

Jones might only have felt exploited and deceived and left it at that, but he also saw a practical problem. Since the article by the Uruguayans bore the same year as his publication, but indicated no month or day, Jones was concerned that specialists in the field might be uncertain about which article was first and therefore unclear about which nomenclature they should use in referring to the worms. Jones set about trying to answer the practical problem; that answer would also, presumably, settle the question of priority.

The farther he got into his inquiry the more suspect the 1985 date on the Uruguayan article appeared. In telephone calls, the Montevideo publishing company that printed the article revealed that the article was printed and available for distribution not in 1985, but in June 1986. The National Library of Uruguay recorded that the article was available to readers in July 1986.

Jones also wrote letters to the Uruguayan biology journal that published the article, and to the scientists as well, asking them about the date of publication. These went unanswered.

After waiting a year, and after reviewing the appropriate professional rules, the International Code of Zoological Nomenclature, Jones concluded that the earliest date of publication of the Uruguayan paper should be considered the last day of the year the authors claimed for it. That was how papers were dated when no exact month or day was indicated. As it happened, December 31, 1985, was one day after the publication of Jones's own paper.

Having still received no reply from the Uruguayan scientists by 1989, Jones considered the affair closed. Although he did not expect further disputes over priority of the animals' names as such, he did expect the phylum classification itself to be scrutinized and perhaps contested by other qualified taxonomists.

Sitting in his crowded Smithsonian lab, surrounded by a lifetime of work, jars of worm specimens, cabinets of glass slides, stacks of dusty professional articles all around, Jones shrugged at the prospect. Intellectual challenges are the life of science. And yet, to hear him discuss the matter, he would clearly be pleased if his identification of the Vestimentifera phylum withstood all challenges.

As he put it, "I don't really expect to identify another one."

The naming of a new phylum was only the extreme example of what became a regular astonishment over the vent organisms in the early 1980s. When William Newman of Scripps assembled that list of vent invertebrates in 1985, he showed that not only were fifty-eight species new but thirty-three of those species belonged to one or another new genus. Of those, fifteen genera belonged to families which had to be created for them.

It was as if no one had ever seen a hawk before, and scientists suddenly discovered that not only were there bald eagles but also red-tailed hawks, goshawks, and golden eagles; and the scientists recognized that each bird was different enough, one to the other, to be part of a separate genus. But they also saw that these diverse animals still resembled each other as a group enough to constitute a family, and a distinctly different one from the family of falcons. That realization had happened fifteen times over with hot springs invertebrates in the six years before 1985.

What did it mean that such a high percentage of organisms were new to science, and that the organisms were new at taxonomic levels higher than the species?

One could be tempted to argue that the reason they were new is that scientists simply hadn't explored their habitat before. And this observation is true, though the important point is that not only was the habitat new, it was different enough from other habitats to host unique organisms. If it hadn't been sufficiently different it might have been colonized completely by organisms from elsewhere.

Part of what was "different" about the vents was that they were what biologists call an ecotone, a transition zone between environments—in this case an extreme transition between the near-freezing desert of the deep sea and the superheated oasis of the vents. As in other ecotones such as estuaries, where sea and freshwater zones merge, few species had succeeded in establishing themselves, and a relatively few species tended to dominate.

But the vent organisms could have been new to science because their habitat had simply been physically isolated for long periods of time. William Newman began to explore this line of reasoning in 1979, when he studied the first barnacles brought back from the Galapagos.

Newman, who is a specialist in barnacles, realized quickly that he was on to something quite unusual as he examined the structure of a particular group of barnacles. His specimens were barnacles that grow on stalks. These stalked barnacles had been studied for some time; Charles Darwin himself had studied fossil forms, and the literature describing them was quite rich and detailed. Newman had only to consult his references showing photographs and drawings of fossil barnacles to identify the closest relative of the one he held in his hand.

It was unmistakable. The arrangement of the barnacle's shell plates and its overall form revealed that this living barnacle's closest relatives were barnacles that had lived and died out during the Jurassic period, about 150 million years ago. It was, as Newman put it, a "missing link" to the past, a relic, a survivor of an ancient lineage and time. The Jurassic was the heyday of the dinosaurs, when long-necked plesiosaurs ruled the seas.

As other hot springs creatures were compared to living and to fossil animals, the same thing happened. Many species were indeed very old. One group of barnacles, snails, mussels, polychaete worms, and tube worms that Newman examined ranged from 135 million years old, for a barnacle, to 600 million years old, for a tube worm. Six hundred million years, apart from being quite a long time, was also an extraordinarily long time for little change to have occurred in a species. The hot springs provided, Newman suggested, an exceedingly rare glimpse of antiquity. This antiquity raised many interesting questions for biologists to pursue.

Meanwhile, as some research on the animals went on in the laboratories, other researchers focused on the animals where they lived. For field biologists and ecologists the discovery of a new environment offered a rare opportunity; the novelty of the hot springs made them irresistible.

The second Galapagos Rift expedition, in 1979, brought fifteen biologists there. It was a little less than two years after the first expedition, which was about the minimum amount of time needed to plan and fund a cruise to the South Pacific. That same year the hot black-smoker chimneys on the East Pacific Rise at 21 degrees north were also explored for the first time; the Oasis Biological Expedition returned there in 1982.

The first Galapagos expedition laid out the territory for the biological cruises that followed. Mussels, clams, crabs, limpets, and the tube worms were the main larger animals found. Given the generally large body sizes and the number of individuals, it was clear that the animals were doing more than surviving in that extreme environment. They were apparently thriving. The obvious question was how.

The answers came from two sources. Zoologists showed how the symbiotic relationships of animals and bacteria solved nutritional problems for the animals. Meanwhile, microbiologists conducted experiments to understand the fundamental role of free-living bacteria in the vent food chain.

Microbiologist Holgar Jannasch had happened to be near that institution's radio room one evening in February 1977, when the daily report from the first Galapagos cruise was received, and he listened to Jack Corliss describe "big clams living in milky-bluish" water. The color caught Jannasch's attention immediately; it was an indicator he had learned about in his earliest professional training, in his student days in Germany. It was there that he first encountered the history of Sergei Winogradsky and the clue to the milky water.

In 1884, Sergei Nikolayevich Winogradsky, the son of a wealthy Russian landowner, had just received his master of science degree in St. Petersburg. However, the young scientist felt that the Russia of 1884 was not a very good place to begin his career. Winogradsky was a Jew, and in the aftermath of the assassination of Alexander I, the new czar, Alexander II, had come down hard on liberals, intellectuals, and what he considered foreign elements in Russian society, including native Jews. Finding this intolerance intolerable, Winogradsky moved to Strassburg, Germany. There he began directly to specialize in the study of certain bacteria that lived in some aquatic environments and that appeared to nourish themselves in a way no one quite understood.

Others had suggested that this peculiar type of bacteria, *Beggiatoa*, produced hydrogen sulfide in the course of somehow obtaining its nourishment. But by employing some cleverly designed experiments, Winogradsky showed that *Beggiatoa*, on the contrary, consumed hydrogen sulfide. The discovery that these organisms used sulfide, which was believed to be universally toxic, for their nutrition caused quite a stir in microbiology and launched the young exile's career. (Curiously, it appeared that the scientist-exile was specially attuned to the way organisms make use of apparently foreign substances for their survival and growth.)

The process that Winogradsky discovered became known as chemosynthesis. In chemosynthesis, as in photosynthesis, an organism exploits energy from an external source to produce energy-rich substances—food—for itself. The difference is in the energy source. Sunlight is the ultimate source for all the other life on earth. But Winogradsky's bacteria depended on the energy contained in certain chemical bonds, such as those of hydrogen sulfide.

Jannasch knew that if hydrogen sulfide was exposed to oxygen in seawater it would react, forming elemental sulfur. The reaction would be accompanied by an iridescent blue haze in the water, the signature of sulfur. At the same time, the research that Jannasch and his associate Jon Tuttle were doing led Jannasch to believe that bacteria were likely to be involved in the process.

Could Corliss be observing hydrogen sulfide? he wondered.

He asked him over the radio.

Yes, said Corliss, the water samples smelled bad, like rotten eggs.

Jannasch surmised the rest. His research specialty was bacteria that live off sulfur compounds. He thought bacteria would be found in the vent waters, and he drafted a research proposal to test the hypothesis soon after the 1977 Galapagos cruise was over. In January 1979 at the Galapagos Rift he ran the experiment.

He placed six syringes containing radioactive carbon dioxide into a small carrier, which was put onto the *Alvin*. On the seafloor the carrier was set out next to a hot spring, where the sub's mechanical claw filled the syringes with samples of water from the vent.

Jannasch's hypothesis was that if the vents did contain bacteria and the bacteria used hydrogen sulfide, then they would incorporate radioactively labeled carbon during the experiment. His expectations were based on the reactions involved in chemosynthesis.

In chemosynthesis, an organism synthesizes molecules of organic carbon from inorganic carbon compounds, such as carbon dioxide. To do this requires energy, chemical energy, from energy-rich molecules, such as hydrogen sulfide. (Hydrogen sulfide releases energy when it yields electrons to another substance, such as oxygen.) Jannasch reasoned that if bacteria were able to use hydrogen sulfide in the vent fluids, they would assimilate the radioactive carbon into their cells.

He left the syringes at the vent site to incubate for up to two days. When they were retrieved, his expectations were confirmed: radioactively labeled organic carbon was detected. The truth was that the first results of the syringe experiment were disappointing; little radioactive carbon was taken up, probably because the syringes were incubated at the cold seawater temperatures present outside the vents, rather than at vent temperatures. Still, there was enough radioactivity to show that chemosynthesis was occurring.

Later, laboratory tests were done on pure cultures of the micro-organisms in the samples, and they were found to be members of the bacterial genus *Thiomicrospira*. A new species, *T. crunogena*, meaning "spring-born," was named. Held at warmer temperatures of 25 degrees C., *Thiomicrospira* assimilated considerably more carbon dioxide than had occurred in the experiment outside the vent. When a sulfur source, thiosulfate, was added, the carbon dioxide uptake increased.

The 1979 Galapagos expedition gave other strong indications of the importance of chemosynthetic bacteria to the vent ecosystem. Two hundred different strains of bacteria were collected. The bacteria grew prodigiously in the subsurface spaces of the seafloor, as densely as a million cells per cubic centimeter. They grew in great colored mats, and when dislodged by a jet of water or a probe from the *Alvin*, they would drift up into the water in thick blobs. Clams, tube worms, and mussels all lived in close proximity to the bacteria and appeared to be dependent upon them.

The details weren't by any means all in place, but after the 1979 Galapagos expedition, a startling hypothesis was becoming widely accepted. Seafloor hot springs apparently were a unique ecosystem on earth. In the absence of sunlight, organisms were getting their energy from chemicals derived primarily from molten rock in contact with seawater. True, the oxygen that oxidized the sulfur and other compounds was ultimately derived from the splitting of water molecules into the component parts during photosynthesis. But the vent ecosystem would not have existed without the presence of an energy source other than the sun. That primal source was the radioactive decay of the earth, which melted the rock. The versatile chemosynthetic bacteria of the vents exploited this extraordinary energy. Like green plants on land they were the primary producers, the foundation of the food web.

As it turned out, Jannasch and the other fourteen biologists on the 1979 expedition should have been reasonably confident of observing chemosynthesis, as it had already been proposed from studies on the collections from the 1977 expedition. John Baross of Oregon State demonstrated that organisms collected from the hot springs were capable of chemosynthesis. Baross showed that certain cultures of bacteria were able to use sulfur in their metabolism, growing in culture on thiosulfate. And Baross also anticipated another of the discoveries of the second Galapagos cruise in his laboratory. Under the microscope, he observed bacteria in quantities greater than 100 million per milliliter. For such a high concentration of bacteria to have gone through the vents suggested that a very large population of bacteria was living within the seafloor rock mass.

The confirmation that hot springs bacteria were chemosynthesizers served to remind the broad scientific community how extremely versatile bacteria are. To most humans, bacteria—technically prokaryotes, or cells without nuclei—are generally unappreciated, being associated for the most part with their roles in infection and disease. But as their happier roles in the fermentation of wine and the digestion of food attest, bacteria also unwittingly produce benefits for humans as they go about their own business.

As Holger Jannasch continued to work with bacteria from the Galapagos and then from the hot springs at 21 degrees north it became clear to him that hot springs bacteria were able to exploit a variety of chemical energy sources, not only sulfur compounds, but also hydrogen, methane, iron, and manganese. Given this metabolic versatility, Jannasch began to consider the potential usefulness of these organisms.

He decided to try growing the sulfur-oxidizing bacteria in the laboratory. He knew that vent mussels fed on the bacteria, and in laboratory tests he determined that mussels grew almost as well on the sulfur-oxidizing bacteria as on algae. This result suggested to him a use for the hydrogen sulfide that was a by-product of mining and coal burning. Industrial societies blow hydrogen sulfide as a waste material into the atmosphere, and it causes acid rain. But it could also be mixed in seawater to grow bacteria to feed mussels.

Jannasch grew edible mussels himself in his lab following this procedure. Although he recognized that there were few incentives for this sort of waste recovery in recent years, he held out the hope that someday the double benefits of reducing acid rain and growing food might make sense on some economic agenda.

It was also in this spirit that Jack Dymond of Oregon State proposed in 1987 that the Gorda Ridge be given legal protection from mining. The potential long-term societal benefits that might derive from the hot springs bacteria, for industry and medicine, were likely to be worth more than the short-term revenues from mining.

Compelling as such hopes were of practical advantage from the bacteria, there was another value in the bacteria, impractical though it might seem, that drew others to study the hot springs microbes. John Baross had a feeling for this value, this potential, when he was working in the lab at Oregon State with the bacteria from the first Galapagos cruise.

Baross is a specialist in bacteria that inhabit extreme environments; during this period, for instance, he had written one professional article on microorganisms that thrive on salt, and another article on the ecological aspects of life at low temperatures. The hot springs "bugs," as he called them, fascinated him, for he knew that such resilient, unusual creatures might be very primitive.

During the 1970s, trailblazing investigations of primitive bacteria were conducted by Carl Woese of the University of Illinois. Woese had analyzed the genetic material of certain simple bacterial cells and discovered that it was as different from that of other bacterial cells as those cells were from the nucleated, eukaryotic, cells of higher organisms. "Archaebacteria," Woese called these particular bacteria. He conjectured, from the analysis of their genetic makeup, that they were at least as ancient in their origin on earth as the other major groups of bacteria.

Among Woese's archaebacteria were the salt-loving halophiles, which Baross specialized in, and the methanogens, methane-producing chemosynthesizers. Baross suspected that his microorganisms from the Galapagos might offer some additional insights about the nature of primitive bacteria. But he wasn't interested in the bacteria only for themselves. If these bacteria were indeed replicas of very ancient organisms, he might be able to glean some understanding about one of the deepest-shrouded mysteries of life itself: How it began.

As it happened, Jack Corliss was engrossed in the same subject.

CHAPTER NINE

THE EDGE OF CREATION

The way Jack Corliss tells it, the more he thought about that first moment, the more significant it seemed to him. He had been staring out the *Alvin*'s port at the shimmering warm water coming out of the rocky floor. The water was like a veil. And as he stared at it, through it he saw the strange animals.

That moment was a revelation.

"I was *convinced* that the animals were very important—that they were fundamentally powerful in some way." His gaze becomes intense as he says this.

After the Galapagos expedition, he got to thinking about a phrase of Jean Cocteau's: "First I find, then I seek." The saying had never made sense to him before, but now it did. He was convinced that what he saw was a replica of the earth when life began. Astonishing though it was, he was convinced that hot springs created living organisms. Now he wanted to know how they did it.

His curiosity set him off on perhaps the highest intellectual quest in the life sciences today, the search for the origin of life.

Among those on the Galapagos expedition, it was by no means a unique idea. As if intuitively, and in any event without the sort of background that would allow William Newman to make the case later, other geologists and geophysicists on the cruise also recognized that hot springs might be a window into an ancient world. After all, here were animals living in the dark, in warm and chemical-laden water streaming out of the earth. It was as if these organisms had been left behind as the rest of the planet evolved toward the sun.

Corliss was talking about the idea when he arrived back from the expedition. The first story written about the cruise by the news bureau at Oregon State quoted him saying, "What we found there may even have implications for the origin of primitive life in the oceans."

Two months later, in June 1977, Corliss gave a talk at a symposium about the Galapagos in which he presented his first, tentative thoughts about the origin of life at the hot springs. "An interesting question for further speculation regarding these submarine hydrothermal systems," he said, "concerns their possible role, early in the earth's history, in providing a site . . . for the origin of life."

Meanwhile, because of the findings John Baross had made on the Galapagos bacterial specimens, Baross was asked along on the November 1979 cruise to 21 degrees north on the East Pacific Rise. The cruise was mainly devoted to geochemical and geophysical studies, but Baross had a chance to dive in the *Alvin*, see some hot springs firsthand, and collect some bacterial samples. Something extraordinary occurred. Twenty-one degrees north was the site of the discovery of the first hot black smokers, and Baross collected some bacteria in water temperatures greater than 300 degrees C.

If life was really surviving those temperatures, he wondered, what did it mean? Life was only supposed to exist between the freezing and boiling points of water, 0 degrees and 100 degrees C. at normal atmospheric pressure. But here organisms, apparently ancient in their mode of operation, lived in fluids which were superheated yet not boiling. Baross returned to the university with his new samples, full of new thoughts about the origin of life.

He and Corliss began talking about the topic in earnest. They agreed that the idea of life beginning at the hot springs had enough substance that it ought to be developed and written up into a scientific article. A brief article by some California researchers had appeared in May in the journal *Nature* suggesting that there might be a connection between the evolution of the earth's crust at spreading centers and the origin of life. This *Nature* article was on the scent, too, though its focus was on chemical precursors for life and was quite tentative. Nonetheless, it underscored the point that the idea was ripe.

Sarah Hoffman came to feel that way, too.

In 1979, Hoffman was a first-year oceanography graduate student at Oregon State. An older student, she had come to Oregon after graduating from San Francisco State University with two majors, one in geology, the other in physical science with an emphasis on astronomy. In one of her last classes at San Francisco, she had also become deeply interested in the puzzle of the origin of life, and coincidentally, during this time, she had attended a guest lecture by Bill Normark of the Geological Survey, who showed slides of the animals from the Galapagos Rift. Sitting in the darkness of the lecture hall, she thought about the perpetual darkness of the rift zone, and it occurred to her, too, with a strange mixture of gloom and exhilaration, that the animals had *always* been there.

In April, she visited Oregon State, one of the graduate schools she was considering, and she met Jack Corliss. She thought that he was "wonderful."

"He was charming, engaging, loved to talk about all sorts of stuff," she said later. "So, I came up to work with him." With Corliss as her adviser, the emphasis of her graduate program at Oregon State was in the geology and geophysics of the early earth. She was intrigued when she learned that her interest in the origin of life was shared by him and Baross.

Early in 1980, she heard Baross lecture about his recent dives and research. Later, after a long talk with him at a party, she borrowed a book from him which discussed the conditions that would be necessary for life to begin. It excited her and focused her interest, and she decided to write a term paper on the subject.

Doing background reading, she read about some laboratory experiments conducted at the University of Miami by Sidney Fox. These experiments showed that not only proteins but primitive "protocells" could be produced from simple gases. The reactions had two requirements: an environment where the temperature was above the boiling point of water, and the introduction of liquid water.

When she read that, "everything clicked," said Hoffman. She sat down and wrote.

Charlie Miller was the professor for the course.

"Coincidentally," he remembered, "I had read all the other term papers first. It was eleven o'clock on a Sunday night, and I was getting pretty tired of reading. Then I picked up her paper."

He shook his head. "It just lifted me right out of my chair."

Miller offered an ironic smile.

"Here it was. A student in my class had hit upon—and documented in a very thorough and convincing way—a response to one of the fundamental problems that has been with us since Darwin: If life evolved, then how did it get started?"

Since the 1950s the prevailing scientific opinion is that life began in the sea. Two researchers at the University of Chicago, Stanley Miller and Harold Urey, had done famous experiments in which they made some of the building blocks of life from inorganic chemicals in the laboratory. They heated a closed flask filled with water, methane, ammonia, and hydrogen gases; these were believed to be the primary components of the sea and atmosphere when life began.

They boiled the water in the flask and shot an electric spark, imitating a lightning bolt, through the vapor. The reaction produced among other things two amino acids, the constituents of protein. The assumption was widely made that given enough time, this "primordial soup" would cook up increasingly more complex molecules. Ultimately, living organisms would appear. The experimental results were reasonably easy to duplicate, and the general idea that life began in the early ocean gained currency. However, many detailed questions remained. Two of the main ones were exactly where and exactly how this origin at sea occurred. Hoffman's paper had given some answers.

The morning after he read her term paper, Charlie Miller remembers rushing into work and going to find Corliss. He told him that an article for a professional journal should be done, and quickly. The ideas Hoffman presented were so plausible, Miller felt, that other scientists were liable to have those ideas as well and write them down first. Corliss and Baross agreed. They promptly met with Hoffman, and together they planned an article. Hoffman would have the responsibility for pulling their contributions together and writing the final version. Working feverishly, drafting thirty pages in twelve days, she was done.

Submarine Hydrothermal Systems: A Probable Site for the Origin of Life is a rather unusual paper for scientists. It is of a kind rarely tried, let alone accomplished well. In it, the authors attempted two tasks. First, they synthesized information from numerous scientific fields, including geology, oceanography, biochemistry, and microbiology. Then, using this material as background, they presented a unified view of an elusive subject, one which went beyond any of these fields. Academic writing for scientific journals is usually more limited in its aims, and more cautious.

The paper is nonetheless familiar as a professional science article. It proposes how nature works, supports its arguments with available facts, and suggests further tests.

To support their proposal that the hot springs were the site where life began, the Oregon State scientists needed to address two apparent questions. They needed to make a case that hot springs were not only ancient but fecund—that they could provide the conditions to generate the earliest forms of life.

Their argument that seafloor hot springs existed on the early earth depended on two well-established scientific notions about the planet of 4 billion years ago.

It was hot. And it was wet.

Earth had formed when space dust and gas were drawn together by gravity, and the planet grew as huge meteors smashed into the spinning ball. While the meteors heated the surface, the center of the young planet pulsed in a turmoil of heat. The impact of the bombardments and the force of gravity compacted the hot matter there; the heat was so great that the core began to melt. In the melting, gases that had been trapped in the internal rocks were released toward the surface, where volcanoes belched them out in enormous quantities. Water vapor was among the gases, and as the earth cooled, some of the water vapor condensed in the atmosphere and rained back on the planet. Before long, the planet was covered by a warm ocean. The now-submerged volcanic vents became the first submarine hot springs.

The researchers supported their proposal that submarine hot springs were ancient by interpreting other scientists' evaluations of earth's oldest rocks known at that time. These rocks, the Isua Series, were from the coast of Greenland and approximately 3.75 billion years old. The Oregon State authors argued that the chemical composition and the pattern of layering of the rocks indicated that they were produced by submarine volcanism and the hydrothermal activity accompanying it.

As an argument they were halfway there. However, seafloor hot springs might have been present without providing the conditions in which life could begin. That was another, more difficult, argument.

To know whether they had met the challenge, the researchers needed to know what they were looking for. Ever since the discovery of DNA as the molecule of heredity, that self-replicating molecule has been considered the foundation of life as we know it. So, scientists know where they want the origin of life process to end up—with a nucleic acid, DNA or perhaps RNA, its cousin, replicating itself. However, many scientists have argued that some version of a protein was more likely to have been the first replicator, since it was believed that the nucleic acids couldn't do the necessary cutting and splicing of themselves without outside help. This view changed by the mid-1980s when Thomas Cech of the University of Colorado conducted the first experiments showing that RNA could replicate itself. By the end of the eighties the scientific consensus was that the earth of earliest life was dominated by RNA.

However, these discoveries about RNA were years away in 1980, and given the uncertainties in the field, the Oregon State collaborators didn't address the question of priority between nucleic acids and proteins directly. They did describe a system in which proteins could be made. From them the first replicating biomolecules would follow.

The crux of their 1980 description is simple and compelling. The chemical elements needed for life are present in the hot springs fluids, and earth's geothermal energy that heats these fluids can make complex molecules out of those building blocks. The process didn't happen all at once, but rather occurred over time and over the interior space of the hot springs system.

In outline, the process worked like this. From Clive Lister's work they argued that the presence of hot rock below the seafloor caused cracks to form in the floor. Seawater trickled down through these cracks, cracking the rock at deeper layers as it descended. At the cracking front, above a chamber of hot rock, the water might be heated to 1,000 degrees F. At such extremely high temperatures, the water would react with the rock, extracting basic ingredients needed to make organic molecules. These ingredients are carbon, nitrogen, oxygen, hydrogen, and sulfur.

This chemically enriched, superheated seawater would become transformed in successive steps as it returned to the surface through channels in the rock. First, amino acids would be formed at the highest temperatures. Then, as the water became comparatively cooler as it rose farther away from the magma chamber, other organic molecules would form, ultimately sheathing the amino acids in a "protocell"—an encapsulated structure.

Here the laboratory work of Sidney Fox, which had captured Hoffman's imagination, was brought in to show that such transformations were possible. They described the method Fox and his colleagues used for creating the protocell in the lab.

> . . . [T]hey heated the amino acids above the boiling point of water and created polymers with high molecular weights. When the polymers came into contact with liquid water, they spontaneously formed structurally organized units which had "a cellular type of ultrastructure, double layers, abilities to metabolize, to grow in size, to proliferate, to undergo selection, to bind polynucleotides, and to retain some macromolecules selectively."

A "parallel" process happened in the vents, Hoffman, Baross, and Corliss said. A primordial cell would be formed, something not too elaborate, but rather simple. It would be like a bacterium, an archaebacterium most likely, an organism "which could utilize the hydrothermally delivered gases." Like Fox's protocell, it would grow in size, proliferate, and undergo natural selection. In short, it would live and evolve. There would be life in the ancient vents.

Completed, the thirty-page essay appeared to offer potential solutions to the key questions of "where" and "how" which stymied origin-of-life researchers. The Oregon State researchers sent their paper off to the influential journal *Nature*, in hopes of seeing it published there.

About this time a dispute arose over the exact contributions of Corliss and Hoffman to the paper. Corliss was listed as the first author, Hoffman the third. His first place "fairly represented my contribution to the paper," Corliss said, reflecting on the dispute in 1988. Though he admitted to not writing much of the actual paper, he said he had "outlined the whole origin-of-life model as I saw it" to Hoffman in conversation, as she was preparing her term paper for Charlie Miller's course.

Hoffman did not deny that Corliss talked with her about the origin of life. Both said they were on friendly terms before the dispute over the paper. But Hoffman slighted his role as originator of the overall working concept or "model," and she angrily claimed that his "contributions to the paper were so negligible as to not be significant." Nonetheless, as the first author, Corliss has tended to be identified most closely with the paper by colleagues.

Disputes among academic scientists may seem to sully a high-minded profession, and the genteel might prefer that history ignore them. But the modern profession of science is intimately concerned with priority. As historian of science Derek de Solla Price has written, since about 1850 the dominating motive for publication of journal articles, "beyond a doubt," has been "the establishment and maintenance of intellectual property." The motive, Price asserts, "was the need which scientists felt to lay claim to newly won knowledge as their own, the never-gentle art of establishing priority claims."

Just as priority of publication is important, so is order of credit. It would have brought Corliss more respect, Corliss's critics charge, to have put the name of the graduate student, Hoffman, first, especially since she actually composed the paper, rather than putting his own name first. It's not at all uncommon for senior, supporting authors to put themselves in a secondary position.

A dispute in this case might not have arisen if the subject had been less significant, or if the personalities had been less powerful. Ultimately, it's probably impossible from the outside to judge how important each one's role was. John Baross may not be impartial, but his comment about Hoffman's role seemed revealing. She "synthesized the origin-of-life model," he said. "Synthesized" seemed like a carefully chosen word.

Synthesizing, putting together and making sense of material from diverse sources, is a special kind of creation. But to say that someone synthesizes material also acknowledges that science doesn't occur in an intellectual vacuum. The three scientists, each of them described by other scientists as "brilliant," no doubt influenced each other. The three were a chemical reaction waiting to happen.

Mitchell Lyle, an oceanographer who knew all three and who

listened to discussions about the dispute for several years, came to take a philosophical outlook on the matter. He acknowledged that many people were talking in a general way about the possibility of life beginning in the hot springs. But the paper was important because "the hard part is marshaling enough facts so that other people actually think the idea is reasonable."

Lyle pointed out that in the years following the paper all three continued working at marshaling the facts, for which he gave them credit.

Nature rejected the original paper. Concerned that the concept was then in circulation in the academic world, the OSU School of Oceanography published it as a special report in June 1980. Later, in 1981, an oceanographic journal published it in a slightly revised form.

Corliss, Hoffman, and Baross hardly waited around for acceptance letters; each plunged ahead refining the hypothesis from their various points of view. These are exceptional, driven people, for whom the origin of life seems an irresistible challenge. For a certain kind of scientist, the topic takes on a kind of otherworldly shine, like a Holy Grail.

In 1986, Baross joined the faculty at the University of Washington. On occasion he could be found out of his lab, sitting in his office in front of journals and papers piled up on his desk. If it was afternoon, the one cup of good coffee he allowed himself after lunch might be in hand. If you engaged him in conversation, he would talk candidly. But he often sounded bemused, quizzical, as if he had certain standards for reality and he was not sure they were being met.

For him, the question of how life on earth began took hold when he was a teenager attending Jesuit schools. He remembered listening to the Catholic defense of the Creation, and not believing it, not at all. He was interested in Darwin, but the Jesuits "didn't really want to talk about evolution at all. It wasn't something they wanted to mess with."

Just the same, the strict, zealous teachers of the Society of Jesus taught him something else.

"The Jesuits invite you to question everything, even the dogma. One good thing about being raised a Catholic is that you get exposed to a lot of arguments." The doubting was more valuable to the budding scientist than any particular subject matter.

He maintained his interest in the problem of the Creation—or, as he came to think of it, the origin of life—through undergraduate school and his master's degree at San Francisco State in the 1960s and through his doctoral work at the University of Washington. By the time he began postdoctoral research at Oregon State, in 1973, he had collected a good number of books and articles on the subject, and knew them well.

"But I never thought I would get involved in it, writing about it," he reflected. "It always seemed like something you get involved in when you're old and gray. Then you've earned your chance, and you can write your one paper."

He laughed softly, acknowledging with the laugh how deeply involved he was as a participant in the quest. He tried to explain.

"There's a group of scientists, myself included, that consider this the biggest mountain to go for, right now. It's where we want to go with our science."

He paused, then waved a hand at the size of the next thought, and said, "The implications are so far-reaching.

"For us, this is a totally existential effort. It's our only creative outlet. We don't play the piano, compose music or write novels.

"This is it."

What questions are bigger, deeper, more fundamental? his expression asked. For him, the quest is not a matter of credit. Although it was his understanding of microbial life that provided the foundation of the 1980 joint paper, he never advanced himself as the principal contributor. You worked at these things because you wanted to be capable of them: "a totally existential effort."

And then there were the "implications" which were "so far-reaching." One only had to appreciate what has resulted since 1953 from the discovery of the structure of DNA by James Watson and Francis Crick. What might not come from the discovery of how life itself began? The discovery would surely initiate a revolution in understanding.

For Baross, the avenue to understanding the origin has continued in his laboratory. There he dedicated a good deal of effort since 1979 to growing samples of hot springs bacteria. This work resulted in some of the most exciting, and controversial, findings in microbiology in the 1980s.

On the afternoon he showed me around, he singled out boxes in one laboratory room which held flasks of bacterial specimens. The flasks were specially designed and filled, and sealed with airlocks. Inside, inert argon gas lay on top of a liquid containing the bacteria. The argon shielded the microbes from atmospheric oxygen, because oxygen, which is essential to most life on earth, killed these organisms.

For his experiments, Baross used a specially made titanium syringe to transfer bacteria from the flasks into a metal sphere known as a "pressure bomb." The sphere was designed to withstand pressures 500 times normal and temperatures of 500 degrees C. In the controlled environment of the bomb, he tried to grow thermophilic deep-sea bacteria.

Baross's initial studies of these bacteria were done while he was at Oregon State, before he had this new laboratory and equipment. Right after the cruise, he began examining the microorganisms he had collected at 21 degrees north. There were two groups: bacteria in vent water samples, collected in gold-plated stainless-steel samplers to prevent contamination or reaction; and bacteria embedded in pieces of chimney. The bacteria in the chimney pieces provided the first intriguing findings.

Baross, assisted by a group of colleagues, found and took electron micrographs of odd "tube-forming" microorganisms on the chimney pieces. Minerals from the springs encrusted the tubes, making the microorganisms look like living fossils. But even more "remarkable," Baross wrote, was that their form resembled fossil organisms known from the Precambrian era, more than 3 billion years ago. Moreover, these Precambrian fossils were found in environments that the researchers believed to be hydrothermal in origin. The implication was clear; further study of contemporary vent communities, Baross and his coauthors wrote, might be a key to understanding the distant past.

This paper on the tube-forming organisms appeared directly after publication of the origin-of-life essay, and then Baross turned his attention to bacteria in the water samples. In 1980, the microbiologist grew some bacteria at 120 degrees C. Later, in collaboration with Jody Deming of Johns Hopkins University, he published a paper in *Nature*, saying they had grown other bacteria at 250 degrees C. Life had never been detected before above about 95 degrees C., so when the Baross-Deming article was published, in 1983, the world of biological research went into an uproar.

"Quite a number of people thought that our results just couldn't have happened," Baross mused later. "People said it was a ridiculous experiment—that the bacteria just wouldn't survive above one hundred degrees Celsius. It'd be like frying an egg in a pan, they said. The protein would just break down."

A group of researchers at Scripps, in whose lab Baross and Deming had done their experiment, published a letter in *Nature* arguing that the Baross-Deming results may have been caused by faulty laboratory techniques.

Baross and Deming rebutted the letter in a reply also printed in *Nature*, but the controversy did not go away. Still, despite the skepticism of other biologists, Baross said that the evidence for his and Deming's claims was clear and that the explanation for the bacteria's remarkable ability was straightforward. The microbiologists could tell that their cultures grew at 250 degrees C. for a number of reasons, one of them being that the amount of protein in the cultures increased in a way characteristic of bacterial growth.

More important than doubts about the evidence, Baross suggested, scientists disbelieved the Baross-Deming results because they challenged a long-held assumption. Life is not *supposed* to be able to exist above the boiling point of water. But of course, as Baross pointed out, the 250-degree-C. water wasn't boiling. Instead, in his experimental setup, he placed the cultures in the pressure bomb and reproduced the pressure of seawater at the hot springs.

At this pressure, 265 times normal atmospheric pressure, "you compensate for temperature effects," Baross said. "You can prevent water from boiling. You can stabilize nucleic acids and proteins by equivalent pressures to increases in temperatures.

"I still don't understand," he said, "what all the commotion was about."

Deming and Baross's data, which argue that hot springs bacteria live and grow at high temperatures, support Baross's belief that the bacteria are of a very ancient lineage. That the bacteria also live in environments which are at least similar to those common on the early earth suggests that they may possess genetic information that gives a signature of that time.

The proof of the argument will ultimately depend on sophisticated molecular analysis. A biochemist at Oregon State, Robert Becker, is working with bacterial samples he and Baross collected. The idea behind his analysis is that the ancestry of the bacteria can be determined by sequencing some of its RNA. RNA is a "master molecule," common to all organisms. Where the sequence of molecules in an unknown organism diverges from the sequence of RNA from other known organisms provides an indication of the lineage and relative age of the organisms.

As part of this effort, a protein biochemist at Oregon State, Robert Becker, is working with protein samples from bacteria Baross collected.

If hot-smoker microbes turn out to be as ancient as his evidence to date suggests that they are, Baross believes that they may offer insights into the biochemical terms and conditions under which life developed.

Sarah Hoffman continued her graduate studies at the University of Washington and, later, at the University of Alberta in Edmonton. She became a specialist in the earliest phases of the earth's development, from the accretion of the planet 4.5 billion years ago to about 3.5 billion years ago. Knowing as much as possible about the conditions on earth during this period is essential, Hoffman believed, if hypotheses about the origin of life are to be grounded in geologic reality.

"You cannot build a reasonable 'how,' " she argued, "until you know a reasonable 'where.' "

The difficulty of Hoffman's research field is that the information about the solid earth of around 4 billion years ago is difficult to arrive at, at best. As in Baross's work, making sense of ancient time requires a suitable clock. While the timepiece for organisms is the sequence of molecules in RNA, the clock for rocks is, if anything, trickier to see. The fleeting hands of the clock are the radioactive elements which decay over time.

To begin, Hoffman had to become familiar with the various methods of radioisotopic dating. Then for her own work she turned to stable isotopes, variants of an atom that have the same number of protons but a different number of neutrons. The ratio of stable isotopic forms in a common element like oxygen can be a clue to the nature of the environment in which the oxygen-bearing substance formed. Hoffman used this oxygen ratio in determining whether the water which altered rocks of 3.5 billion years ago had come from the sea or from meteors.

Combining isotopic data with interpretations of how the earth loses heat over time, Hoffman and colleague Dallas Abbott developed a description of the earth after the formation of the planet. Hoffman contributed this perspective to a paper written with Baross, in which they reconsidered and expanded their thoughts on the first paper. Published in 1985, this new article combined the results of Baross's research into the hot springs bacteria and his ideas about their evolutionary significance with Hoffman's view of earth's first ocean.

She argued that the ocean formed during the Archean era, about 4.2 billion years ago. It was probably warm or hot, with temperatures in the range of 30 degrees to possibly greater than 100 degrees C. It was reasonably deep, with a maximum depth between about a half-mile and a mile and a quarter. And it was considerably more active hydrothermally than the seafloor is today. Perhaps five times as many seafloor hydrothermal systems vented their burden of heat and metals and other chemicals into the ocean during that time.

If the hot springs are plausible as the site for the origin of life, the researchers wrote, the chances of life beginning in them would have been greatly increased by the number of them present during the Archean.

The task of imagining in detail the origin of life is pursued in different ways. While Baross and Hoffman extracted insights from experimental work in their areas of specialization, Jack Corliss pressed ahead on another tack. The insights of laboratory and field work he assimilated from other scientists. His role became that of theoretician synthesizing a system which best fits the known facts and the best guesses.

Corliss left Oregon State in 1982, under circumstances that, perhaps remarkably, are rather unusual for a college professor. By his own admission he became obsessed by the riddle of the origin of life, and he spent much of his time thinking and reading on the topic. His other academic obligations—teaching, finding grants, and writing articles—slipped to levels below what the university expected of him.

"Jack just 'got religion,' " said George Keller, university vice president. "Nobody could fault him when he got that devoted to an issue. But the reality was that if he had done it in some moderation, he could have continued here."

Corliss apparently couldn't, or wouldn't, moderate his interest in the problem, and he was gone from the university. He traveled to Europe. There he led the life of the itinerant scholar, visiting, meeting with, and being influenced by some of the world leaders in theoretical physics and chemistry. Among them was Nobel Prize–winning physicist Ilya Prigogine. Prigogine is a guru of nonlinear thermodynamics, of chaos studies, a field which only five years earlier was as radical to trained physicists as it still sounds to the layman today. What Corliss learned about from Prigogine was how natural systems can achieve order out of chaos. The necessary ingredient is a flux of energy. In his thinking and writing in the late 1980s, Corliss tried to apply this new physics in describing the precise steps that would occur in the hot springs in order to turn nonliving matter into life.

In the original paper, the trio of Oregon State researchers characterized the hot springs primarily as a kind of flow-through system. Seawater goes in at one end, chemical reactions take place, and a series of products, from complex organic compounds to—eventually—living organisms, comes out at the other. Baross and Hoffman, in their 1985 paper, emphasized the role of gradients, of different complementary gradations of temperature and chemical components within the hot springs, in this production process.

Corliss took the outline of the original paper and refined it, specifying the steps of the process. He also reconceived the original flow-through system as something a good deal more elaborate, a thermodynamically complex flow-reactor system.

Essentially his model has five steps. To visualize them, it helps to imagine the hot springs as an upside-down funnel with the front cut away, exposing the flow of events. The entrance to the inverted funnel is in touch with the top of the magma chamber below the seafloor. The exit of the funnel is just above the seafloor. Corliss's five steps follow the seawater as its components go through a remarkable transformation.

In the first step, the seawater percolates down through the seafloor to the cracking front at the top of the magma chamber, where at very high temperatures, about 600 degrees C., it literally cracks the molecular bonds of the rock molecules and releases carbon and simple carbon compounds like methane into the solution.

In the second step, which follows rapidly, simple organic molecules form out of the rich mixture of chemical elements at the cracking front. The heat of the hot springs provides the energy to build the molecules. What happens, Corliss believes, is that the heat energy available at the cracking front becomes "frozen," or fixed, in the high-energy bonds of the new molecules. The bonds are set as the high-temperature fluids are rapidly quenched in the cooler spaces immediately adjacent to the cracking front.

The seawater, along with these organic building blocks, begins to rise up the funnel. Not all components, however, will rise together or at the same time. Some of the simple organic molecules get stuck in rock fractures in the funnel, and there another transformation takes place. This one depends on a substance with special physical properties—not to mention Biblical overtones. The substance is clay.

Clay minerals form crystalline lattices, and like the lattices of common salt, clay lattices "grow" as the elements which make them up come out of solution and attach themselves to the appropriate place in the latticework. In Corliss's hypothesis, clays perform two crucial functions. They provide a surface that the simple organic molecules can accumulate on, just as if the clays were providing a surface for their own growth. And the clays offer a relatively safe haven out of the direct hot springs flow. The simple organic molecules, accumulating on the clays, have the opportunity to form longer and more complex organic molecules.

Out of the jumble of such molecules, the primary building blocks of life on earth can arise in step four. This transformation from organic molecules to "biopolymers"—such species as fragmentary nucleic acids and amino acids—can happen because enough energy is moving through the system to move the system away from equilibrium. In conditions far from equilibrium, the elements of a system can organize themselves into new forms.

How convection currents arise in a pot of water brought to boiling offers a commonplace example. Heat applied to the bottom of the pot establishes a simple pattern of heat flow from bottom to top, hotter to cooler. As heating continues, gradually a little curlicue, a vortex of heated fluid, arises in the water. At first these vortices are cooled and dissipate, but at some point the thermal stress on the system leads to a persistent vortex. It rises to the top and draws in cooler water around it, establishing a new flow in the water, a convection loop of cold to hot. Since the water is all being heated the same way, all poised on the edge of instability, the whole system abruptly jumps to this new structure, and many convection loops are formed.

What's important about convection loops arising is that they are unpredictable from the initial conditions. Self-organization within the system has taken place.

In such a way, as thermal energy flows through the hot springs, new biochemical forms arise. Energy first causes an instability in the components of the system and then, as it dissipates, it leaves behind a "dissipative structure." In the beginning, Corliss would argue, life was not "created," nor did it "just" happen. It arose spontaneously and *necessarily* under certain fluxes of energy working within constraints of matter.

Step five puts the fragmentary biopolymers into a cell which could become capable of self-replication. Corliss acknowledges that laboratory experiments have produced several candidates for the first self-replicating unit, including collections of proteins and nucleic acid fragments, Sidney Fox's "proteinoid protocell," and lipid vesicles.

Corliss makes a case for lipid vesicles. "Since a lipid membrane is the universal boundary of living cells, [its] appearance at some point is required; I choose to make it at the beginning," he wrote.

The structure of a lipid vesicle enables further development. It "is a prime example of a classic reaction-diffusion system," Corliss explained. "The essential function of the boundary of a reaction-diffusion system," the membrane in this case, "may be thought of as filtering or selecting information." The membrane provides "the necessary combination of freedom and constraint required for creativity"—here creation of a cell.

With a selective membrane in place, Corliss finds it easy to imagine small, appropriately charged molecules getting into the cell, forming large molecules which can't get back out. As the cell grows, the membrane becomes unstable and the cell divides. Among these protocells, the ones that divide most rapidly and efficiently will become favored for continuation. This is the beginning of natural selection of species, the beginning of evolution.

Revolutions in scientific thought rarely happen quickly. As Corliss himself admits, reaction to all the hot-springs-origin hypotheses has been mixed. Some scientists have been generally friendly, like

Robert Shapiro, a nucleic-acid chemist at New York University and author of a popular book on the origin of life. But even Shapiro appears impatient for more detail about the primeval chemical reactions. "The problem is, you can set up the reactor," Shapiro says, "but what chemicals do you pump in and what do you look for?

"Anyone who has ever tried making a nucleic acid in the test tube," Shapiro continues, "knows that it just doesn't want to do that at all. Ever."

The odds of spontaneous assembly happening are insignificant, the chemist argues, "even if you have the whole ocean.

"That is," he adds, "unless you want to invoke a deity."

Other scientists have challenged that the very conditions of the hot springs would subvert the chemical assembly processes. In August 1988, Stanley Miller (of the 1950s "primordial soup" experiments) and Jeffrey L. Bada wrote a paper contending that the "high temperatures in the vents would not allow synthesis of organic compounds, but would decompose them, unless the exposure time at vent temperatures was short."

This argument overlooked, however, the essence of the hypothesis that Corliss, Baross, and Hoffman have held since the beginning of their work. The organic molecules would not be exposed continually to the high temperatures of the cracking front, but would move rapidly into higher and cooler parts of the vents system.

Low-temperature springs are found commonly at seafloor ridges, Corliss wrote in response to Miller and Bada, and they in turn conceded that if "lukewarm water came in contact with minerals that catalyzed critical prebiotic reactions," they might change their views. But the discussion couldn't go forward, they added, "until the minerals and reactions are named."

What the molecules in contact with high heat actually are and whether the time of contact would be too great to allow synthesis to occur are likely to be matters of lively debate for some time.

A more common criticism is that the hypotheses have not been "tested" or may, indeed, not be testable. Corliss smiles when he hears such criticism.

All three researchers are well aware that untestable hypotheses are not worthwhile. Hoffman and Baross specifically included a list of tests in their 1985 article. Corliss himself considers the growing understanding of the evolution of bacteria as one successful test of the hot springs argument.

If life originated in the hot springs, he reasons, there should be some evidence in the earliest surviving life forms from that environment. Since the 1970s, Corliss points out, microbiologists, led by Carl Woese, have been developing an evolutionary tree for bacteria, and it has consistently pointed to the primacy of sulfur-using and heat-loving bacteria. In 1988, a computer model of the evolutionary tree developed by James Lake, a molecular biologist at UCLA, predicted that all living things evolved from a single-celled organism that probably lived in boiling sulfur springs.

Beginning in 1989, Corliss was advancing his own test of his hypothesis at a very sophisticated computer array, the 16,000-processor Massively Parallel Processor at NASA's Goddard Space Flight Center in Maryland. With a grant from NASA, Corliss hoped to make a model of evolution on the computer system. He believed he could write a program in which the 16,000 processors would act like his evolutionary entities. Operating simultaneously and playing off each other, they would show that his sense of the sequence in the hot springs was plausible.

If the hot springs hypothesis is ultimately verified, Hoffman, Baross, and Corliss realize, the implications are profound. It used to be thought that only a planet with a temperate surface and with liquid water below the normal boiling point could support life. But if hot springs promote life, the range of possibilities opens up.

"Consider other planets with the critical conditions of the earth— hot on the inside, as earth is with radioactive decay, and cool on the outside," said Corliss.

"Underneath the ice on the moons of Jupiter, if there's a hot core, there will be a place with liquid water.

"It's interesting to imagine what we could do five hundred years from now," he continues, "landing on one of these moons, drilling down through the ice, putting a submarine below the ice, and seeing what's there."

If exotic life forms like the sulfide-eating bacteria and the tube worms can thrive in earth's dark, noxious, and hot seafloor hot springs, what is to prevent local variations on other planets?

For Corliss, the attraction of the subject appears to go beyond even this sort of heady speculation. Rather, it seems to be a case of difficult scientific inquiry as a path to the sublime. He says that it seems to him now that the emergence of life on earth was inevitable.

He lets out a hearty laugh. "Imagine it," he says, "the natural evolution of the universe led very clearly to the production of these highly ordered structures.

"Within our universe, matter condenses from radiation, and once accreted into large bodies, like the earth and the sun, the energy flows out of them again, in the form of radioactive decay. And those energy flows create self-organizing systems, like the hot springs. And the subsystems that appear in the hot springs in this focused flow of energy are also self-organizing systems. This is how we end up with cells."

Life.

It is almost a litany, and for a moment, he looks starry-eyed. Then he flashes a smile. "Of course, we shouldn't be surprised to find that our universe is perfectly designed to create us. That's the only kind of universe we could observe anyway."

Such are the kinds of thoughts a scientist may well enjoy. The possibilities open out, like the tip of the water curlicue heating up, reaching out.

CHAPTER TEN

WORK AT SEA

They were alone.

A plane flying overhead at the right time of the month might have seen an oil tanker pass in the vicinity, on its way to Puget Sound or Portland. But few jets came this way, and not many tankers. From the deck of the ship, it was rare to see either. Most days, there was only the sea and the sky, one great bowl of blue and gray, sometimes like porcelain, sometimes more like lead. The *Discoverer* was a spot, a speck, an irregularity in this huge retort of nature. Except for radio contact with shore, 250 miles away, they were by themselves.

On an early morning in August 1988, the crew of the NOAA ship awoke to a calmer sea than had jostled them at bedtime. The swell still rose a quick five feet, but the thirty-knot wind that had driven the waves the night before had slackened. The *Disco*, as the crew called her, made headway without much struggle. The 300-

foot ship was on its way toward the other ship of this research expedition, the *Atlantis II*.

Morning's first business was a transfer of personnel between ships, a regular event of a research cruise. Five men, dressed in bulky orange float suits, clambered one at a time down the rope ladder from the deck of the *Disco* and stepped into the twenty-foot launch lurching alongside the ship. They moved awkwardly in the suits, like Pillsbury doughboys. The survival suits would keep the body inside bobbing at the surface if the launch capsized. The men tried not to think too hard about such things.

The launch sped away toward the *Atlantis II*, a dark gray outline against the horizon, backlit by the first light of morning.

The aft deck of the *A-II* had been a flurry of activity since before dawn, as the *Alvin* was being readied for launch. As the scientists and observers arrived from the *Disco*, the pilot in charge was nearing the end of the fourteen-page checklist on his clipboard. He spoke by walkie-talkie with the pilot inside the sub and with the *Alvin*'s other pilot in the communications room on the top deck upstairs.

All the bustle around the submersible had the air of a scaled-down space launch, with equally scaled-down dramatics. As if obeying a script, attendants finished their scurrying about and gradually moved into the wings out of view. Then the second, and last, of the scientists who were to dive that day mounted the scaffolding leading to the submersible's open hatch.

Melvin Peterson did not rush. A handsome, florid man in his sixties, with a look of authority, for him this day's dive to 4,800 feet was the fulfillment of something he had begun twenty-two years before. In 1988, Peterson was the federal government's top civilian oceanographer, the chief scientist of NOAA. But in 1966, Peterson was a professor of oceanography at Scripps who had co-written a rather interesting research article. It made the case that high concentrations of certain metals in sediments of the East Pacific Rise indicated the existence of "hydrothermal exhalations."

He had not predicted the actual form of submarine hot springs, but his essay was one of the first to suggest their possibility. Yet, despite the passage of time and his own growing stature in oceanography, he had never seen what he cheerfully called "the real thing," the hot springs themselves, with his own eyes. This day's dive, therefore, held special meaning for Peterson.

Now, waving down to the others watching from the deck, Peterson paused for a last, optimistic look about. Then he lowered himself into the sub.

Time seemed to creep by as the winch hoisted the *Alvin* off the deck and lowered it toward the ocean. Everyone continued to watch the sub, as if it were truly a door that would open into another world. When it splashed into the frigid ocean, two divers in wet suits, riding the sub like cowboys, released the *Alvin* from its cables. The sub lingered at the surface for a moment, then slipped from beneath its riders and was gone. Without waiting for the divers to return to ship, the scientists and most of the crew turned away and set to their own work.

More than two dozen scientists voyaged on board the *Disco* and *A-II* on this leg of the cruise. Many of them had been developing their research for some years, and the results they hoped to get from this cruise would move them forward, keep them occupied for another year, perhaps more. Assuming, that was, that everything went well, that the ocean and their instruments did not foil their plans.

They were geologists, geophysicists, geochemists, biologists. They came from different institutions, from universities with a history in this work like Oregon State, Washington, Hawaii, Scripps, and Lamont, and from U.S. and Canadian government agencies. They were more than a loose assemblage, though. The NOAA Vents Program was leading the three legs of the expedition, and for months before it began, Steve Hammond and the others had been discussing a cooperative research plan.

At the beginning of this leg, they had reconnoitered a section of the Juan de Fuca Ridge adjoining Axial Volcano. From there they had moved up over Axial's caldera, where they were on the day of this dive. They were trying to fill in their picture of the venting system, trying to understand the system in three dimensions and probe its operations over time.

Verena Tunnicliffe, for one, was thinking a lot about time. This morning she sat at her desk in the small laboratory she was sharing during the cruise. It was wedged into the corner of the upper deck behind the soft-drink machine and the freezer chest. She kept some of her samples in the freezer. At the moment, though, she wasn't working with her collections. The biologist from the University of Victoria had more than a few projects going.

"You think you know where you're going to and what you want," she said. "But probably along the way you'll find seven more interesting projects.

"I don't know where it ends."

She was, in fact, working on about seven separate biological investigations, all of them related in some way to how the vent's animals change over time.

In the aftermath of the 1983 Canadian-American expedition, Tunnicliffe had observed that of the sixteen species first identified on Axial, only one had been found elsewhere along the global ridge system. Among the sixteen were limpets and snails and tiny "palm" worms with little frondlike fingers that waved in the water current. Also represented was a new species of the large tube worms, dubbed *Ridgeia piscesae* after the *Pisces*, the Canadian submersible.

As she collected more animal specimens and looked more closely into the differences between the Juan de Fuca animals and those from the East Pacific Rise, two observations stood out. The species of organisms at the two ridges were clearly different. Of forty-nine species collected on the Juan de Fuca, only eight were known species from the southern ridge. But as Tunnicliffe evaluated the organisms at higher levels of biological resemblance—at the ascending taxonomic levels of genus, subfamily, and order—she found something interesting. Of the forty-nine different organisms, thirteen were members of some genus that was also present on the East Pacific Rise.

What did this mean? To Tunnicliffe, it implied the passage of a certain amount of time, enough time so that evolution could produce its distinctive changes, so that an original parent organism, represented by the genus, could evolve into two distinct species. And it also suggested the physical separation of the two populations, so that they could maintain their distinctiveness. Her working hypothesis proposed populations that had once been together but had been forcibly separated.

The Juan de Fuca and the East Pacific Rise were certainly separate today, but when Tunnicliffe delved into the geologic history of the Pacific ridges she learned that until about 35 million years ago what is now the Juan de Fuca Ridge was directly linked to what is now the East Pacific Rise. Since that time the ends of the original ridge were gradually separated as the ridge was overridden by the North American continent. Today the western edge of California lies between the two ridge parts. The San Andreas Fault is their hidden link.

The separation of the original ridge could explain the resemblances and the differences between the animals of the Juan de Fuca Ridge and the East Pacific Rise, she reasoned, and she wrote a scholarly article establishing this argument.

Still, there was much to learn about both the biological and geographical history of the vent organisms from looking closely into the organisms themselves, so Tunnicliffe was happy to be out at sea, making her collections.

One of the questions that intrigued her concerned the tube worms. Based on their physical structure and form it appeared that several different species inhabited the ridges of the eastern Pacific. But how were they related to each other? What were their evolutionary relationships? How could one learn?

What couldn't be deduced from their external appearance might be learned from their biochemical makeup. So Tunnicliffe was collecting worms, so that she could compare the structure of certain proteins in the worms to try to map their evolutionary relationships over millions of years.

She was also interested in the survival of animal communities over much shorter periods of time. The odds for individual survival, she saw, weren't reassuring.

"Vents are messy, dirty places to live," she said unequivocally. Tunnicliffe has a soft expression, with wavy blond hair and gentle features. She seemed to enjoy pricking any preconception one might have of daintiness.

"The animals get encrusted with heavy metals, which we know is nasty stuff. How do they cope—not so much as individuals, but as a species?"

To see how the animals fared over a year, she and a University of Washington colleague had placed a camera in the caldera in front of a vent the previous summer and set it to take a picture once every thirty hours. She was looking forward to recovering the camera system. In the meantime, she had some idea of what to expect from observations of the same vent mound over the course of two previous summers. Worms had lived on the front of the mound in

1986, but spires grew up in 1987, and then the worms died in avalanches as the spires collapsed. The new time-lapse system might well show another grim scenario such as this.

But what was the use of knowing how these strange animals endure such harsh conditions, generation after generation?

"In the long run, we may come up with something *wonderful*," she said. Her voice was serious.

"Maybe chemosynthesis will show us a way of synthesizing sugars. Maybe some of these species will show a wonderful mechanism for coping with metal poisoning, and so on.

"But right now, you can't argue that sort of thing. Basic science doesn't deliver economic gains on a schedule."

She looked mock-inquisitorial. "But looking into the animals of hot vents, *really*, is that something important to be doing?

"I think it is," she answered herself.

"*Why?*

"Because we don't know anything about them."

The behavior of the vents over time also brought Tunnicliffe's Canadian colleague, Ian Jonasson, back to Axial. The previous year's discovery of gold begged following up, and Jonasson, who worked with Jim Franklin, hoped to learn more about the genesis of the precious metal.

In practice this meant collecting more water and rock samples, labeling them, and lugging them into storage. This isn't glamorous work but takes instead the sort of patience and thoroughness that seems to come with the territory of the geologist. Jonasson, a former rugby player and a field geologist who has had to deal with meddlesome grizzly bears in his expeditions to the Yukon, seemed ideally tenacious in a good-humored way. He knew that he and his colleagues may well be on to something of lasting importance.

Relaxing after breakfast for a moment in the small quarters he shared with another man, Jonasson reflected that this was the first time scientists have been able to see gold deposits forming.

"It's profoundly important," he said. "We probably have the best model laboratory that one could have for understanding volcanogenic gold right here."

Mining of Axial continued to be extremely unlikely, he felt, partly because the mining techniques did not really exist, and partly because, if they did, the quantity of minerals would hardly be worth the effort. But what had been discovered of the process so far was already applicable to land. That was his opinion and Jim Franklin's as well.

The Canadian researchers were already convinced that they could give the mining industry some valuable prospecting clues from their seafloor studies. The clues would help identify geologic settings where gold-enriched massive sulfide deposits should be expected.

Although there were certainly other factors, boiling was one key factor that would lead to gold enrichment, as Axial showed. Since boiling will occur in relatively shallower water settings, what's wanted on land is the geological evidence for a former shallow water environment. That can come from studying volcanic rocks. Signs of shallow water origins are recognized by working geologists; they include such features as vesicles, numerous bubbles in the rocks.

The Axial research was showing that another requirement for a hydrothermal gold deposit was oxygen; at the time of deposition the seawater must contain oxygen to precipitate the gold. That effectively would limit the age of the rock formations that would be worth examining. Seafloor rocks that formed before oxygen became abundant on earth would not be likely rocks for gold. But that event occurred about 2 billion years ago, so it wasn't a tremendous limitation.

Jonasson was optimistic that the gold research would not have to justify itself on scientific merit alone. With the insights of the Axial research supporting them, miners would be examining massive sulfide deposits, and he felt it was a good bet, given the stakes, that sometime in the next decade a large sulfide deposit containing gold would be found on land.

The imaginative reconstruction of a hidden process was also one key goal of the NOAA researchers on this cruise. They wanted to know the cause of the megaplume they had first discovered in 1986 and had detected again the next year.

From the outset, the NOAA group recognized that if megaplume events were at all common, their heat and chemistry might have significant effects on the ocean. For starters, it wasn't too difficult to imagine effects on ocean water circulation, or on the dispersal or survival of fish larvae, perhaps even on the migration routes of such animals as salmon, tuna, and whales. And if there was truly a significant pulse of heat, and it happened at all regularly, perhaps climate might be affected in some way. But such intuitions would be no more than speculation without a better understanding of the phenomenon.

The physical evidence of the plume suggested it was the result of some recent, catastrophic release of heated water from the seabed. Perhaps a volcanic eruption had occurred on the ridge, or perhaps the seafloor had spread. To try to find out what had occurred they decided to go to the seafloor and take a look.

On the first leg of the *Discoverer* cruise before arriving over Axial, they took deep-tow photographs of sites on the megaplume segment of the ridge. The pictures they took complemented another set of photographs taken the year before. After they identified places worth exploring in a submersible, the scientists made ten dives onto the megaplume section of the ridge.

Descending one and a half miles in *Alvin*, they saw an eerie landscape. Over about seven miles of seafloor in the megaplume area, the sub's searchlights showed abundant flows of recently extruded lava. Interspersed among the lava flows were many large, deep holes and low-temperature hot springs. The holes made it a fascinatingly different terrain, but what they saw did not add up to a simple explanation for the megaplume.

Now enjoying a late breakfast in the scientists' mess on the *A-II*, Steve Hammond gave his interpretation of what he had seen on the ridge floor.

"First of all, there was no obvious volcanic maw," he said between bites. No gigantic hole in the ground. No new volcanic crater.

Curiously, high-temperature hot springs, of the kind that might have released the 1986 megaplume, also were not evident. But Hammond was intrigued by the deep pits in the seafloor at the megaplume site, where fresh lava flows had fallen in. The broken flows were quite thin, a matter of inches in some places. From the submersible he examined what was underneath the broken flows.

"When you are down inside a collapse pit," he said, "the entire area seems to be underlain by caverns."

He began to sketch as he talked, drawing rudimentary caverns in pencil on a napkin.

The caverns were created, he theorized, when molten lava

drained away after an eruption. The lava drained because it was kept liquid by a thin veneer of chilled lava that solidified between it and the cold seawater. Large reservoirs of heated water might then be introduced into these caverns by the venting of hot water, which could accompany a large eruption. After that, all that would be needed for a megaplume would be a way to collapse the roof.

Hammond saw two ways.

For one, the kind of lava that makes up the cavern roofs cracks extensively as it cools and shrinks. As the underlying support of molten rock was removed, the roofs would be prone to collapse.

For the other, the megaplume region was located, after all, along a ridge which was subject to frequent tremors as it spread. These tremors could also collapse the roofs of the cavern.

"So, after either of these events—blamo!" said Hammond. "There you go—a catastrophic release of heated water."

He made a jagged scrawl on the napkin and put down the pencil.

Release of a megaplume, then, would be associated with movement in the seafloor rocks. But this begged another question: Why so much shaking in the vicinity of the megaplume? Hammond described the theory that Chris Fox had talked to him about just a couple of days before.

Fox had studied sonar data for the megaplume ridge section, and he believed that the fabric of the ridge's spreading zone was being ripped there in an unusual way. Normally, spreading on a ridge is visualized as occurring out to each side along a single axis. This sort of spreading did occur along the Juan de Fuca. Lava welling up along the ridge creates the Pacific crustal plate on the west side of the ridge and the Juan de Fuca crustal plate on the east side.

In particular places along ridges, however, nature isn't so tidy. Two axes of spreading may exist simultaneously, approaching each other from opposite directions. Both will continue to spread independently, until the spreading tip of one "propagating rift" bangs into the body that lies behind the tip of the other. When that happens, the active tip takes over the spreading axis of the other rift and becomes the single, dominant spreading rift. This behavior of two such propagating rifts is called "dueling." In a duel, the rifts crack the crust of the ridge in numerous places roughly parallel to their line of advance.

Fox had been studying sonar data of the Juan de Fuca, and he detected what looked like such "dueling propagators" in the process of passing each other. The sidescan sonar imagery revealed traces of numerous fractures in the ocean floor. They were right in the megaplume area. If these really were dueling propagators, he believed, they could cause the cracking of the reservoirs of heated water that Hammond proposed.

Megaplume was on Bob Embley's mind that morning, too, as he pored over maps in a room on the lower deck of the *A-II*. Embley realized there might be a reservoir of heated water, and there might be a way to crack it, but where did the heat for the water come from? The geology of the megaplume region, at first glance, was not what geologists have come to expect for heated regions.

Hot spring vent fields, according to the model of Ballard and Francheteau, are typically found at the high elevations of a ridge segment, where the ridge is buoyed by an infusion of magma. But the megaplume vents were topographically low on their ridge segment. This raised doubts that magma was present in the megaplume section. But if magma wasn't present, where would the heat for megaplume be coming from?

The answer might be found, Embley thought, in imagining ridge segments as long and narrow volcanoes. Comparisons could be made then with comparable and well-studied volcanoes such as Kilauea, on Hawaii. The Kilauea caldera lies at the summit of a large volcano, and eruptions there are often followed by others at lower elevations. The plumbing of the Juan de Fuca might be similar, Embley thought. Magma might migrate subsurface down the rift. The low-temperature springs and the young lava flows along the megaplume segment of the ridge might be evidence of this migration.

Embley had the idea that the scientists actually might be seeing a key phase of seafloor spreading taking place: They might be witnessing the creation of new ocean crust.

That would be something worth talking about.

While progress for the scientists on the *Atlantis II* revolved around the dives of the *Alvin*, the success of the Vents cruise depended equally on the work conducted from the ocean surface aboard the *Discoverer*. The activities on the two ships were intended to complement and inform each other.

Part of what it took to get research done well on both ships did not involve the scientists, and most never saw it. "It" was down in the bowels of the ship, and on the *Disco* its lair was a labyrinth of pipes, shafts, rods, and gears. "The beast," the engineers called it: four diesel electric engines capable of 5,000 horsepower. Surrounding the beast, feeding it, were thirty-four tanks holding 320,000 gallons of diesel fuel. With the engines' power at full, the ship could make sixteen knots when it needed to. When it did it consumed a hefty 200 gallons per mile. Geared down, it also had the power to stay on track while towing an instrument at two knots against a contrary ocean.

The ship could do much more than go forward and backward. A powerful bow thruster could also move it sideways or, if the situation required, even around in a circle. The bow thruster was invaluable in research. With 10,000 pounds of thrust, this engine allowed the ship to stay in one place, which was an ability critical for some scientific experiments.

Mechanical muscle was part of what was needed, then, to get work done. But a little drama whose last act was unfolding that morning on the *Disco* underscored the value of some particular human qualities as well. The drama had begun two nights before, at about eleven o'clock.

Chris Fox, the chief scientist on board, had been lying in bed when the phone rang. It was the voice of one of the graduate students. She had been guiding the towing of a scientific instrument behind the ship.

"I think we've crashed the gear," came the anxious voice.

"Don't panic," Fox said. And he climbed out of bed, pulled on his clothes, and went belowdecks to the scientific lab.

Fox saw that the grad student had apparently made a critical, though understandable, misjudgment. With just a minute to react when an undersea cliff appeared on her sonar screen, she had been unable to give the crew the proper instructions to avoid a collision.

The student was in despair, the crew was flustered, but when Fox checked the monitors in the lab, he wasn't convinced that the $50,000 magnetometer was damaged. Perhaps it was only the torpedo-shaped "depressor" weight that preceded it on the line, holding it underwater, that had crashed into the cliff. He decided that the crew should continue towing the magnetometer and the weight, on the assumption that the instrument was okay. They would gain nothing if they brought it up on deck and found it was not okay. Better not to endanger their schedule and pay twice over with an unnecessary delay.

He had gone back to bed. Early the next morning, when the tow was hauled on deck, the grad student was relieved to find that the magnetometer was apparently fine. The depressor weight, however, was not; its dorsal fin, made of acrylic, had been ripped off. It needed to be repaired before the towing could resume.

So, the night after the mishap, the ship's machinist had made the repair, and now everything was ready, just after breakfast, for the towing experiment to continue. Fox went down to the fantail to watch.

The machinist had had no acrylic to make a new fin for the depressor weight, but he had found a sturdy piece of wood that would work, and he had bolted it to the torpedo-shaped weight. He hadn't stopped with making the new rudder merely functional. He had cut the wood in the shape of a fish and had added some scales, eyes, and a smiling mouth. As four crew members were preparing to muscle the deadweight out onto the fantail and hook it to the cable, someone added red plastic streamers to the tail of the fish.

The streamers fluttered in the breeze, and for a moment there were compliments and grins all around. A few quick photographs were taken.

Chris Fox was laughing. They hadn't lost equipment; they had gained something that he thought was—well—*beautiful*. With the right kind of spirit, all this work at sea did seem manageable.

The magnetometer research was important to the cruise because it was one of the two new approaches being tried in an attempt to locate the volcano's magma source. All the scientists presumed that the source was somewhere beneath the volcano fueling the springs. But all the earlier seismic studies had failed to detect it.

Both new techniques depended on the fact that magma behaves differently from unheated rock. Because seafloor rocks heated to high temperature are not magnetized, while cooled ones are, the contrast could help show the magma zone. The magnetometer towed behind the *Disco* was designed to reveal such a contrast.

Earlier in the cruise, Fox had been involved in the other experiment, which depended on hot rock being less dense than cool rock. Dense rock would have a stronger gravitational field. Theory was that this difference would cause local variations in the volcano's gravity field, and the presence of magma might be shown by lower gravity readings.

Getting accurate readings was the demanding part. Measuring gravity means measuring the pull down toward the center of the earth. On the sea surface the *Disco* was considered always the same distance from this center, so at least no adjustment had to be made for a change in this distance. The gravity would be the combination of two pulls on the ship, that of the ocean and that of the rock below it.

Fox calculated the water depth and also the variations in seafloor elevation from point to point from the Sea Beam bathymetry. Theoretically, all that had to be done was subtract these effects of local contour and water mass, and any remaining difference from place to place would be due to differences in the density of the rock itself.

The researchers did two kinds of gravity surveys over the volcano. On the first leg of the cruise, Fox measured the gravity from the surface along 400 miles of trackline. Working with John Hilderbrand of Scripps, he also tried something new. There on Axial, for the first time in seafloor ridge studies, they placed a gravimeter, a portable gravity measurer, on the ocean floor. The electronic device, about the size of a washing machine, was lowered gingerly from the *Disco* onto fifty-five different locales.

The researchers were delighted to find that the bottom readings were a couple of orders of magnitude more accurate than those taken from the surface, though they weren't that surprised. The difference between a surface and a deep survey is 2,000 meters, 6,400 feet of water. The water is just an additional source of error in the measurements.

During the cruise, it was already apparent that both the magnetic and the gravity survey revealed regions of the volcano where measurements differed from normal values. But whether those anomalies would provide the intended geological insights—that was something that cruises didn't provide. Fox knew that it would take days of computing in his office, distilling and comparing data, before he would know if they were closer to finding the magma source of the hot springs.

The routine of a cruise day may be filled with activities such as examining samples and data, studying research literature, and preparing, often feverishly, for the next experiment. But a research vessel is not only a little floating think tank; it is also a floating hotel, albeit one with special activities for the guests. One of the activities on the *Atlantis II* this particular afternoon was participation in the weekly Fire and Abandon Ship Drill.

During a real abandoning of ship, one would want to have a hat, for its consolation against the weather. So a hat is required in a drill. This could be a serious business, and this afternoon everyone dutifully showed up on the appointed landing amidship, wearing a life preserver. And a hat.

But no Government Issue here. Most of the scientists wore base-ball caps, expressing their allegiance to the Chicago Cubs, the Pitts-burgh Pirates, or, in several cases, Woods Hole Oceanographic. One wore a pith helmet. Another drew some admiring glances and sev-eral wisecracks with his sombrero, gaudy with sequins and deedle balls hanging from the brim. And then there was the joker with the towel held in place by a bandanna, for the threadbare-sheik look.

Sure, the sea is dangerous, all of this seemed to acknowledge. All the more reason not to become a humorless cipher.

There may be moments of comic relief, but late in the afternoon or early in the evening comes the moment of truth of a day at sea on the *A-II*. The *Alvin* is recovered then, and the scientists who have stayed behind learn whether their colleagues in the sub have been successful in activities on their behalf. The crew also has its main challenge of the day in bringing the sub on deck safely.

An hour and a half before the sub was to be back on deck that August afternoon, the *Alvin*'s pilot had radioed to the communica-tions room on the *Atlantis*, seeking clearance to rise. Getting it, the sub had dropped about 500 pounds of steel plate into the caldera, making the craft buoyant.

The ascent went without a ripple until the sub broke the sea surface; then six-foot waves began to bob the eighteen-ton *Alvin* around like a rubber duckie. For Melvin Peterson and William Powell inside the sub, looking out the port was like looking through the window of a washing machine.

What may have felt like hours but was only minutes later, the launch pulled alongside and the wet-suited divers mounted the sub, securing it with some lines. The *A-II*'s winch began hauling, and before long the sub was easing up out of the water toward the rear deck.

On the deck, many of the scientists had come out to watch the recovery. Nearly all had cameras with them, and as the sub swung over the deck they broke off their conversations and inched toward it, taking pictures. The gray steel A-frame drew a sharp border around the glistening white sub; the deep blue sky of the late afternoon offered a backdrop.

As the sub came on deck, Verena Tunnicliffe let out a little whoop of satisfaction. She had been eyeing the array of sampling baskets, and as the winch brought the sub closer, she saw tube worms crowding one of the baskets as thick as spaghetti in a box. She strode up toward the sub to take a closer look.

A perfunctory voice came from across the deck, telling her to please stand back until the submersible was fully docked.

"Oh, bother!" said Tunnicliffe. "They are my worms." And she made a face of mock disdain. She could take care of herself, thank you. She wanted to get busy sorting and cataloguing her samples. And besides, there was the barbecue coming up.

Attention of the people remaining on deck shifted to the *Alvin*'s hatch, as, moments later, it was pushed open. A dramatic pause, and then, looking a bit rumpled and tired but immensely glad to be standing upright, Melvin Peterson emerged onto the catwalk. He was followed quickly by his colleague, Powell; the two of them waved happily and were soon on deck. Now the barbecue could begin in earnest.

A barbecue out on deck was roughly a weekly affair on the *A-II*, as long as the weather was good. This was a special event, however, as it was at least in part a celebration for the NOAA top brass, Peterson and Powell. The cuisine was beyond any reasonable expectation. There were steaks done to order, fresh mahi-mahi, California and French wines, a variety of fresh vegetables and fruits. A few scientists and their assistants were obliged to work on the day's *Alvin* samples right away, but everyone else was there, comfortably crowded onto the side deck, sitting on it, or on one of the benches, or leaning against one of the lifeboats. The wine, the mild breeze, the sun, the company, the limitless expanse of sea—this was a moment to savor.

Some of the conversation turned to an astonishing discovery made just a couple of weeks before on the *Alvin* by scientists who were colleagues of many of those on board. Cindy Van Dover, a biologist from Woods Hole, had been studying a species of shrimp that is common around hot springs on the Mid-Atlantic Ridge. She had noticed a bright, reflective spot on the back of the shrimp, and using biochemical analysis and electron microscopy, she had discovered that the spots were eyes. These eyes had no lenses, however, and Van Dover concluded that they must be adapted to detecting low levels of light.

But where would the light be coming from? They all knew, or thought they knew, that there was no light at the deep-sea vents. Or at least no sunlight. Van Dover developed the rather iconoclastic idea that perhaps hot smoker vents, the kind that the shrimp were found at, were hot enough to glow. She figured they could be like a heating element in an electric stove.

Van Dover had had the chance to test whether hot springs could emit such "black body" radiation on a cruise to the Endeavor segment of the Juan de Fuca Ridge in July. On the last dive of the cruise, John Delaney and a colleague from the University of Washington had selected a hot smoker for the experiment. Using a specialized videocamera mounted on the bow of the sub, the scientists prepared to take time-exposure photographs to see if they could detect a radiative glow. The digital camera system was extremely sensitive, being able to shoot at a film speed equivalent to 50,000–100,000 ASA. (Most photographers rarely get beyond 400 ASA.)

The researchers encountered two difficulties. To make the experiment valid, they needed to have all lights on the sub turned off, even the ports covered over. Having done that, a strong bottom current made it difficult to hold the *Alvin* steady enough to take twenty-second exposures. Pilot Dudley Foster did what needed to be done; he held the sub firm against a rock by running the engines at full throttle, more or less blind.

As the video images appeared on the screen inside the sub, the three men had a difficult time believing what they saw. The smoker glowed dimly.

Van Dover's hunch had been right, and at the barbecue her colleagues speculated about what the discovery meant. There certainly wasn't enough light so that the photosynthesis would be a factor in the vent ecosystem. But what kind of light was it, and why did the shrimp have eyes?

Van Dover had found that the shrimp lived on bacteria that grew in the sulfides. The shrimp she dissected had lumps of sulfide in their guts. Did the adaptation have something to do with the way the shrimp found their way to food?

*   *   *

"Hey, you want a nice rare one? I could put one on the grill now. Who wants another steak?"

The chef was still holding forth over the charcoal and waving his long-handled fork like a baton. But for the twenty or so scientists and technicians who didn't have to get back to their labs, other business was at hand. Each evening, the scientists who had dived that day would tell their colleagues about what had happened in the sub and what they had observed outside on the seafloor.

Everyone moved inside to the scientists' mess. It was homey, with wood dining tables arranged around the room, covered with red-checked tablecloths. Outside the perimeter of tables a couple of sofas, a TV set, and a convenience kitchen constituted a lounge. All the scientists, men and women of different ages, different fields of specialization, different degrees of professional status, sat around in the smallish room, at the dining tables, on the sofas in the corner, on the floor. The atmosphere was relaxed, but the scientists sat with their notebooks, many of them the old hardbound lab-style, on their laps, taking notes.

Each morning a couple of them would put themselves into the seven-foot pressure sphere of the sub and dive below the surface of the ocean. No one had to be reminded of the potential danger, of the murderous external pressure, the cold and remoteness of their destination. They were always likely to be interested in what those returning from a dive said. And this night they were especially curious about Mel Peterson.

Peterson had a feel for the occasion, too.

"To see firsthand what one imagines for a lifetime is something I'll never forget," he began.

He paused and looked over the rim of his glasses to the faces around the room. "You know," he said, "it was simply magnificent down there."

He paused again, as if considering whether that was enough. He looked at the intelligent faces, watching him calmly. They knew in their different ways what it was to go down and ascend again from the hot springs. It wasn't something you talked up: the risking death, the glimpsing of another world, the coming back. Outside, through the round windows with their brass fittings, Peterson could see the ocean rolling lightly.

He looked back to his notes.

He described how he and Powell had cruised a section of the eight-square-mile caldera floor, observing several active hot springs. They had collected samples of worms and limpets for Verena and also performed other experiments. He gave some details.

In the questions which followed, people wanted to know more about how gear performed, about features the divers had observed, about their perceptions. The questions were thoughtful and well-considered, as were the answers. The tone, though, wasn't ponderous. Paul Tibbetts saw to that.

With his hair tied back and a bandanna neatly folded around his brow, Tibbetts, one of the younger *Alvin* pilots, still looked like a freewheeling spirit from the late 1960s. His wisecracking was as well known as his competence as a pilot, and when one of the scientists, explaining the plan for the next day's dive, referred to Tibbetts as the "number-two" pilot, Tibbetts, with a tone of mock umbrage, spoke up, "Is that number *two*, as in caca?" A ripple of laughter slipped around the room.

Gradually, the debriefing concluded, and some of the scientists went back to their labs, to work. Others went to stand on deck and watch the last rays of sun and talk. While they spoke together the lights on the radar tower and on the bridge of the *Atlantis* were turned on against the darkening sky.

From about a mile away, the running lights of the *Discoverer* began to grow slowly larger as it approached to pick up some people and take them back to the ship for the night. Finally the two ships were opposite each other about 200 yards apart, and scientists on board the ships brought out their binoculars to have a look and wave at one another in the dusk.

In the growing darkness of sky and sea, this gathering of individuals seemed a small shining. They were a tiny node of intelligence, a terribly tiny speck in the mute, indifferent world of the ocean. And yet somehow they were not so insignificant. To their task they brought some of humankind's finest qualities, qualities like inquisitiveness and dedication, civility and cooperation.

They were that thing much talked about, but rarely seen: a community of scientists, embarked on discoveries.

BROADER VIEWS

"Thirty seconds to go."

All the lights were up on the television cameras. A technician finished taping the microphone cord out of sight to the host's shirt while the host twisted his headset into place, microphone in front of his mouth.

"Ten seconds to go," said the director. "Bob's mike up.

"Stand by, please, Open. Cue Bob.

"*Go* Bob."

The cameras rolled, and halfway around the world, eighth-graders sitting in a museum auditorium in Dallas saw a tall, smiling man in a blue jumpsuit say, "Hello, I'm Bob Ballard. We're in a very special control room aboard the research vessel *Star Hercules* in the middle of the Mediterranean Sea.

"During the next forty minutes we're going to show you—live—the floor of this sea and some active hydrothermal vents there. I think you're going to see a very exciting amount of team-work going on."

The camera cut to a bank of video monitors behind Ballard, and the picture dissolved immediately to the image in one of them.

As they watched the clear jet of water bubbling out of the rock, the students and teachers in the auditorium couldn't see Ballard's smile anymore, but they could hear it.

"You're seeing this now just as we're seeing it here on the *Star Hercules*," he said.

"Now, if I could just get the 'telestrator' over there . . ."

Seemingly from a magic pen, a circle appeared on the screen highlighting a vent.

In the Dallas auditorium and in one in Vancouver, British Columbia, and in about a dozen others across North America, kids' eyes grew bright with recognition.

"We're mapping all of these 'vents.' They're along a north-south fissure," Ballard confided in his young audience.

"You're looking at images of our planet that no one's ever seen before."

Bob Ballard might well have sounded pleased. The Jason Project, in April 1989, was realizing his vision for the kind of work he wanted to do. Exploration shouldn't be something that's done by only a few lucky people, he was fond of saying. It should be something that everybody can participate in. Now he was doing this sort of exploration and incidentally making some kind of first in documentaries; he was taking more than 200,000 kids along with him to the bottom of the sea.

He liked to talk about it as a much-needed effort to excite youngsters about science, and it might well have done that. But the Jason Project was fundamentally something else, too. It was visible proof of a new era in seafloor exploration, the era of remote sensing. Being there without going there yourself. "Telepresence" was what Ballard liked to call his version of remote sensing.

He had seen the handwriting on the wall ten years before. For the return expedition to the Galapagos Rift in 1979 the *Alvin* had been outfitted with a TV camera outside and a color monitor inside. Ballard participated in a number of the dives, and he watched bemused as the biologists that dove with him turned away from looking outside in order to watch the TV monitor.

"I was sitting there thinking, Wait a minute, we went through a tremendous amount of trouble to bring these people halfway around the earth, get them all the way down here in a submarine—and they turn their backs to the windows!"

"Clearly, they thought they could do a better job looking through a robot's eyes, rather than through their own."

That moment was the inspiration for the idea of telepresence; that was the beginning of the Argo-Jason system.

As in the Greek myth, in which the ship *Argo* carried the adventurer Jason, so in the design by the Deep Submergence Laboratory of Woods Hole, Argo brings Jason to the place where the adventure begins. Ballard and his group worked on the system for eight years, and the unit that was prepared for deployment in the Mediterranean in April 1989 represented the state of the art of seafloor exploration technology.

Argo and Jason were designed as deep-ocean "search-survey-and-sampling robots" that could be operated from a surface ship. The ancestry of the Argo could be traced to the gorilla cages used for seafloor research since the mid-1970s. A steel frame about the size of a minivan, Argo carried sonar and cameras and was attached to the surface ship by an umbilical cable. Jason was a little smaller and sported advanced instruments, including two sonar ears for navigation, seven thruster motors to muscle it in any direction, a manipulator arm and hand of nearly human dexterity, and four color video cameras to see through the ocean.

But the nervous system of the Argo-Jason unit was what made it special. A fiber-optic cable united the remotely operated vehicles and their operators on deck. Through this thin, tough transmission route the operators sent the instructions that moved the craft and told them what to do. Also through the cable came the information from the ROVs to prompt the next instructions. The entire fiber-optic system was based, as Ballard liked to say, "on passing signals by light." In essence, electrical energy, such as digital computer data, was transferred into light energy and transmitted through a bundle of hair-thin glass fibers.

As it turned out, an accident at sea incapacitated the Argo in its maiden voyage in the Mediterranean, and Ballard and his crew aboard the *Star Hercules* had to improvise a backup unit for the live broadcasts to the museums in North America. But the backup, which Ballard dubbed Medea (after Jason's wife, who helps him to obtain the Golden Fleece), performed well enough with Jason that many others besides Ballard became believers in the ascendancy of ROVs.

Ballard's advocacy for remotely operated underwater vehicles over manned submersibles might seem a departure for the man who once risked the censure of all the big shots in his field by arguing for use of a submersible. But nearly two decades of exploration after the FAMOUS expedition, and after more than 200 submersible dives, Ballard was clear in his conviction that ROVs are a logical choice for many deep-sea uses.

He made his case by talking about perhaps his greatest public success to date, the discovery of the *Titanic* in 1985. Ballard used a prototype of the Argo along with the *Alvin* in searching for the *Titanic*. The juxtaposition of those two craft on that expedition only confirmed his belief in the value of remotely operated vehicles.

Each time Ballard dove, he was reminded of how long the diving to and from the seafloor took—in the case of the *Titanic* site, two and a half hours each way. Ballard described it as "five hours in a freezing elevator to get three hours of productive labor." It was simply not good use of his time. ROVs, by comparison, were less costly to operate, could be operated around the clock, didn't expose humans to the risks of diving, and could be made to do nearly anything humans do from a sub.

Even so, there was that hallowed argument that humans need to go to the seafloor personally, to observe, to make decisions. Ballard replied that the argument is founded on an illusion; humans aren't actually *outside* in the underwater environment.

"You were never 'manned' in a submersible," Ballard said. "You were always remote there. You could never reach out, or walk around, so you really weren't *there* anyway.

"You were always looking through a window.

"We simply moved the window."

Submersibles will continue to be used for seafloor exploration, and manned craft will continue to be refined. But Ballard and the Deep Submergence Lab are clearly among the leaders of what will be the dominant development in deep-sea exploration and research in the 1990s. New technology is increasingly dedicated to understanding ever more about the seafloor without the need for humans to go there physically. This new technology promises to accelerate the rate of exploration and, perhaps, the rate of understanding.

As the decade began, research on seafloor hydrothermal systems was being conducted by academic institutions and government agencies of a number of nations, not only the United States and Canada, but also Great Britain, France, Germany, Japan, Iceland, and the Soviet Union, to name just the most active. The sites for their research were found throughout the oceans, but most of them were still along the East Pacific Rise and the Gorda–Juan de Fuca Ridge system in the Pacific, and the Mid-Atlantic Ridge. Seafloor hot springs were being explored in other settings besides the characteristic midocean ridges, places such as the Guaymas Basin in the Gulf of California and the Lau Basin in the western Pacific.

Along Valu Fa, a spreading center located in back of the Tonga-Kermadec trench in the Lau Basin, a team of French, German, and Tonga scientists in fact discovered one of the most active hydrothermal vent areas in the ocean. Black smokers with temperatures as high as 400 degrees C. and white smokers as high as 320 degrees C. were measured; so pronounced was the venting that near-bottom seawater was measured at up to 30 degrees C. rather than at the more normal temperature of a few degrees.

Continuing innovations in technology supported research in all the diverse elements of these hot springs systems, including the biological and chemical elements. Some examples of new technology applied to understanding just one part of these systems—the geological and geophysical elements—may suggest some trends.

Since the early 1980s the primary reconnaissance tools to map and image seafloor areas have been multibeam bathymetric instruments like Sea Beam and sidescan sonar systems like the first-generation SeaMARC. A number of scientists appreciated the value of these tools when used in combination, and by the mid-1980s researchers at the University of Hawaii's Institute of Geophysics, led by Donald Hussong, had pioneered the use of a single surveying instrument which collected both depth data and sidescan sonar images of the seafloor topography.

This SeaMARC II has attributes that make it uniquely valuable. Towed behind a ship at a depth of 100 meters, the torpedo-shaped "fish" angles beams of sound downward over an area up to ten kilometers wide at a time. Since it can be operated around the clock at relatively fast ship speeds, the SeaMARC II can cover a lot of ground in a day, up to about 3,500 square kilometers, or an area the size of the state of Rhode Island. By comparison, Sea Beam systems could generally cover only about one-third as much territory.

Such quickness is a preferred feature of the new seafloor technology. So is high image quality—"high-resolution" images. Images generated by the second-generation SeaMARC are, like those of the first version, comparable to aerial photographs. Tones from black to white represent the acoustic return off seafloor features from predominantly rough (black) to smooth (white). The trained viewer can interpret a fair amount of the geology and the geophysical forces operating in a particular area by examining the sidescan sonar images.

Chris Fox of NOAA was one scientist who spent a fair amount of his working time examining seafloor imagery, and the mode of image analysis that he had evolved in Newport by 1988 was well advanced. Fox uses imagery to understand the geological and geophysical constraints on venting, so for him, the ability to "massage" the data, to look at it from various points of view, is very important.

Fox used sidescan data collected by the SeaMARC I, which, since it is towed close to the ocean floor, produces more detailed "pictures" than the SeaMARC II. (Typically, the digital picture areas, or pixels, for the model I are about one by five meters, while the pixels for the model II are five by forty meters.) The pictorial character of sidescan made it ideal for checking depth contours determined by Sea Beam.

Valuable as this function was, by 1988 Fox had acquired a new computer system which could make the sidescan data even more helpful in his investigations.

The key unit was an image processor, which connected to a powerful minicomputer. With the image processor and a keyboard "mouse," Fox could select any image from his sidescan data base, view it from any angle, stretch it, contract it, color it any way he wanted, and do all of this right on the screen. The image processor let him sidestep the need to print a paper copy of an area in order to be able to view and work with it.

Not only did the image processor offer the technical ability to see more and faster, it also offered opportunities for insight through the application of advanced mathematical techniques. For example, Fox generated and compared images of Axial Volcano from data collected in 1981 with images from 1985 data to try to see if they showed an eruption during this period. No eruption was apparent, and he came to consider it unlikely there was such an eruption.

Investigators like Fox typically worked with individual images of a relatively limited area of seafloor. By the late eighties, however, a few research groups were exploring the advantages to be had from larger-scale video animation.

One of these groups in the United States was the Ocean Mapping Development Center at the University of Rhode Island. *Cruise Without Water*, produced there in 1989, gives the viewer the experience of flying through complex seafloor topography as if the ocean weren't there. In watching the video it's immediately apparent that a three-dimensional color display of Sea Beam bathymetry allows insights beyond those offered by a standard two-dimensional "aerial" view. And the video illusion of actually moving around through the environment and viewing it from different vantage points offers another potentially valuable perspective.

Developments of new technology in geology and geophysics were not limited, by any means, to new systems for viewing and analyzing only the surface of the seafloor. Perhaps the most significant new technique with implications for ridge studies to emerge in the 1980s was seismic tomography.

Seismic tomography does for an earth scientist what a CAT— Computerized Axial Tomography—scan does for a physician. They both give pictures of the hidden interior of a body, and as their names suggest, they are generated by similar means. CAT scanning combines information from a large number of crisscrossing X-rays to produce an image of the body parts the rays have gone through. In the case of seismic tomography, the crisscrossing rays are seismic waves, generated by earthquakes.

By the mid-1980s, specialists were producing the first three-dimensional views of the earth's interior using seismic tomography. Seismic waves travel through the earth at different rates depending on the chemistry and temperature of the rock at different points. So by measuring the arrival time of earthquake tremors at a broad network of receiving stations, it's possible to draw three-dimensional views of the distribution of heat in the interior of the earth. Moreover, the wave data can be analyzed to show the direction of flow of this internal heat.

Seismic tomography therefore seemed the perfect tool to develop a three-dimensional picture of the convection of the mantle. Understanding this convection, the supposed driving force in the movement of the crustal plates, is clearly a fundamental element to any comprehensive description of plate tectonics. Yet discussions of mantle convection had previously been dominated by laboratory and theoretical research, since field research had lacked the tools.

To appreciate the significance of what tomography specialists like Don L. Anderson of Cal Tech and Adam Dziewonski of Harvard observed in their examinations of the mantle, it helps to put the elements of the earth's interior into perspective. Much of the attention of those who study seafloor hot springs is focused on the top few kilometers of the crust. The crust itself, however, is thinner relative to the body of the earth than an eggshell is to an egg. The crust descends to thirty-five kilometers, where it meets the upper mantle, which extends to about 670 kilometers. From there the lower mantle continues to a depth of 2,900 kilometers, where the molten outer core begins. The solid inner core begins a little deeper than 5,000 kilometers, and finally, the hard dead center of the earth is about 6,300 kilometers below the surface. That's about 3,700 miles, slightly more than the distance from Vancouver, British Columbia, to Key West, Florida.

As Anderson and Dziewonski noted in 1984, the results of their initial seismic tomography studies confirmed the expectations of plate tectonic theory, "to a certain extent."

They expected, for instance, to find slow seismic areas under ridges, where molten material slows the waves down, and indeed, they did observe slow seismic velocities under there as well as under other tectonic and volcanic areas. However, as they looked deeper into the earth they found a more complicated picture of internal heat.

At 350 kilometers below the surface, in the middle of the upper mantle, where they might have expected a continued presence of hot material under ridges, the researchers often found fast velocities, suggesting cooler material.

At 550 kilometers down, they found "even less relation" between mantle and surface features. This led them to conclude that mid-ocean ridges were "not simply the surface expression of vertical upwelling currents." This was a provocative idea.

In the years following, debate about mantle convection intensified, with one of the key arguments being whether all the mantle or only some layer of it is involved in convection. A brief summary of the field written by an insider in the spring of 1990 reveals the ferment. "The controversy of layered versus whole mantle convection (or some combination) remains," wrote D. L. Turcotte. "Many workers are convinced, but not consistently on one side. Do slabs penetrate into the lower mantle? Can the mantle have a homogeneous composition? Geochemistry has provided constraints, but they are subject to interpretation. Laboratory studies have provided constraints, but they are also subject to interpretation. Progress on these subjects requires a broad range of studies from observations to laboratory studies to models."

Despite the uncertainties, seismic tomography promised to eventually provide new insights into the driving force of plate motion. Meanwhile, the technique was proving useful on studies of smaller scope. One of the long-standing questions that seismic tomography was applied to successfully in the late eighties was the location and configuration of a magma chamber under a ridge crest. In 1989, researchers at Scripps published a tomographic image of a chamber beneath the East Pacific Rise southwest of Acapulco, Mexico.

The Scripps researchers used a sophisticated net of 2,500 receivers to collect wave travel times produced by a series of explosions generated for the experiment. By mapping the region where the sound velocities slowed, the researchers were able to define a principal chamber of mostly molten rock surrounded by a reservoir of very hot or partially molten rock which fed it. The molten chamber was 1.4 kilometers beneath the seafloor at the axis of the ridge, and was quite small, about four kilometers wide. The reservoir of slightly molten rock, which carried a temperature of more than 1,000 degrees C., was at least six kilometers wide. The depth of the chamber was not determined in the study.

As seismic tomography exemplifies well, the technology of the nineties will serve a broader understanding of earth dynamics—and not only broader but also more finely detailed in both space and time. Indeed, as the decade began, seafloor venting itself was being considered from much larger perspectives than had been associated with it before.

One of the most intriguing studies published at the end of the eighties was prompted in part by some research that James Moore of the U.S. Geological Survey had been doing off the Hawaiian Islands. In mapping the seafloor around the islands, Moore, a senior geologist, was startled to discover huge lava flows. One group of flows east of the Big Island was as deep as 5,000 meters; another group north of Oahu covered 150,000 square kilometers. The flows were about a million years old and had accumulated over a relatively short time span, and Moore began to wonder about the effects of lava flowing onto the ocean floor and releasing its heat.

Moore and Herbert Shaw, also of the Survey, wrote up a paper that put some initial calculations to this question. They estimated that the global volume of both seafloor-erupted lava and magma that stays just beneath the seafloor is about thirty cubic kilometers per year; they proposed two cubic kilometers as the annual erupted volume in the central Pacific. They then calculated that cooling one cubic kilometer of lava from its liquid state would be roughly equal to heating 1,000 cubic kilometers of water by one degree.

One thousand *cubic* kilometers heated one degree had the sort of scale that one might think could have a noticeable effect on the ocean. Indeed, Moore and Shaw then examined the data about the oceanic event known as El Niño, and discovered something quite interesting. El Niño is a warming of the eastern equatorial Pacific Ocean which recurs about every three to seven years; the warming of the ocean is coupled to changes in oceanic and atmospheric circulation patterns, which, in turn, affect climate, and life, over broad areas of the globe. The major El Niño of 1982–83, for instance, caused severe damage in many places. The heaviest floods in a century hit Ecuador; in Louisiana, Mississippi, and Alabama, floods forced evacuation of 60,000 people. Australia, by contrast, saw its worst drought in two centuries, culminating in firestorms that left 8,000 people homeless.

The increase in sea-surface temperature associated with an El Niño is also about one degree, Moore and Shaw noted, and the volume of ocean water associated with the event is about 100,000 cubic kilometers. So the cooling of magma could account for about one percent of the El Niño temperature rise.

Moore and Shaw were on to something, and they extended their analysis. Since seafloor lava eruptions probably occur irregularly, the scientists suggested that if the calculated central Pacific supply of lava, two cubic kilometers per year, in fact erupted only once every five years, ten cubic kilometers of lava would be cooled. This quantity of lava would generate an effect equal to 10 percent of the El Niño rise in sea-surface temperature. Ten percent of the total temperature rise might be enough to trigger an El Niño, Moore and Shaw reasoned. The onset of the phenomenon depends on a shift in the balances between large water masses, and these masses are like bodies on a seesaw. A little extra push on one side can reverse the balance.

A 10 percent estimate was conservative, in light of other calculations Moore and Shaw produced. Estimates for one of the great lava flows on land, a flow of 100 cubic kilometers, placed the minimum time it might have taken at one week. Such rates have been calculated for some of the basalt flows that built the giant Columbia River plateau in Oregon and Washington. If a similar flow occurred on the seafloor, Moore and Shaw saw, the heat released to the ocean would be equal to 100 percent of an El Niño temperature rise.

Although Shaw and Moore's paper didn't document a coupling of seafloor "magmatic processes" to El Niños, it suggested that such a coupling was reasonable. This was a conceptual breakthrough. The idea that seafloor volcanism might affect climate thrust ridge studies immediately into the arena of the most important environmental issue of the 1990s, global climate change.

As the decade began, scientific organizations all over the world were establishing plans for coordinated studies of the causes and consequences of global climate change. Much of the research focused on understanding whether, when, and where a predicted global warming, brought on by an enhanced greenhouse effect, would occur. To be confident about matters of such significance to the well-being of human society required that earth scientists devote new attention to understanding how the earth works as a "system." The pursuit of a comprehensive, holistic "earth system science" suddenly became a new imperative not only for formerly insular scientists, but for environmentalists, planners, and politicians.

In the United States, the Global Change Research Program was established as the multiagency lead organization for scientific studies. The organization's 1990 research plan recognized volcanism as one of "six geologic processes determined to be the most important" for the understanding of global change. The plan suggested an awareness of the arguments advanced by Moore and Shaw. An estimated 80 percent of the earth's volcanic activity takes place underwater, the plan declared. "A major improvement in our knowledge of the geographic distribution, magnitude, and frequency of submarine volcanic activity is needed." To address these issues, the plan identified a new research initiative, the RIDGE program, which had just recently been developed.

At the time that Shaw and Moore were working on their paper, many of the principal U.S. researchers involved with seafloor ridges were contributing their expertise to the development of this new research program. Under the auspices of the National Science Foundation, the program considered venting as part of the broader relationship between the mantle and the crust that occurs at mid-ocean ridges.

The proponents of the program argued for the importance of the ridges in the largest terms, calling them "a dynamic manifestation of internal convective processes that control the shape of the ocean basins, the interaction of continents over time, and the physical and chemical evolution of the planet." And again, "The global spreading center network may be viewed as a single, dynamic system of focused energy flow from the earth's interior to the lithosphere, hydrosphere and biosphere."

RIDGE (an acronym for Ridge Inter-Disciplinary Global Experiments) gave ridge-crest studies a new identity and tied them into a larger scientific context. It didn't hurt that the context happened to be the hottest issue in earth studies, an issue which was generating great interest and attention far beyond the scientific community.

The initial science plan for the program, outlined in 1989, called for exploration as well as experimental and theoretical work to understand the "dynamic system" of the ridge crest. It actually called for more than a mere combination; the word of choice was "integration." The RIDGE effort was to be "comprehensive," "interdisciplinary," "hierarchical," and "coordinated." The overall strategy of the program was stated as nothing less than "to achieve sufficient spatial and temporal definition of the global ridge-crest system to allow development and extensive testing of numerical models." These numerical models would "investigate major aspects of energy flow through the system." At the end of it all, the goal was "to understand the causes and to predict the consequences of mantle-driven physical, chemical, and biological fluxes within the global spreading center system."

RIDGE planners were led by John Delaney of the University of Washington. For the first year of projects, beginning in fall 1990, they identified several priority areas for funding. The relationship between the dynamic behavior of the mantle and the growth of oceanic crust, not surprisingly, was one priority. The plan designated a section of the southern East Pacific Rise as a laboratory for an early phase of field studies designed to provide more information about upper mantle flow and magma generation. Seismic tomography and electromagnetic studies were planned for following years.

Baseline reconnaissance of previously neglected parts of the global ridge system was another priority; during 1991–92, RIDGE planners proposed to begin mapping and sampling the huge unexplored territory of the 9,000-kilometer Pacific-Antarctic Ridge.

Among the other components of the first year's science plan was a concerted effort both to start developing new technology and to adapt existing technology that could accomplish RIDGE objectives. The plan envisioned the use of a number of tools to gain perspective on both short- and long-term variability in ridge-crest-system behavior. One of the suggested approaches to detecting short-term, transient events, like earthquakes and volcanic activity on ridges, was use of the network of hydrophones positioned throughout the world's oceans. Acoustic signals received by hydrophones could distinguish between volcanic and seismic events, and they were fairly sensitive. Under certain conditions hydrophones in the central Pacific, for example, could pick up the sound of two pounds of TNT being detonated underwater along the U.S. West Coast.

To understand longer-term behavior of the ridge system, the plan looked ahead to the mid to late nineties, when one or more observatories would be in operation on the seafloor. Then observing systems would provide measurements of how the physical, chemical, and biological components of ridge-crest systems varied over time. And not only varied—"co-varied"; the measurements would give insights into relationships among these components.

One of the pieces of equipment RIDGE planners discussed for possible use was being developed at Woods Hole. Known as Sentry, the device was designed to perform the sort of recurring study of a site that could be accomplished by the Argo-Jason system, or by *Alvin*—if they were available. But these systems were greatly overbooked and not available for regular, routine studies.

Sentry was designed as a self-propelled, unmanned, untethered vehicle that would go to a site and make measurements. It would carry a digital videocamera and 35mm camera along with other vent-monitoring instruments, and it would be able to navigate with centimeter-scale accuracy within a network of transponders. Sentry would be launched from either a research ship or from a "ship of opportunity" that happened to pass over some desired area. The ROV could then either go through a programmed survey and be immediately recovered, or be left on site in a dormant mode and timed to conduct a survey at certain specified intervals. It could also be programmed to respond to a particular event, such as a sudden increase in water temperature. That way it might be able to capture on film something that had never been seen occurring on the seafloor, such as an active volcanic eruption.

Taken as a whole, the RIDGE science plan made a strong case that seafloor hot springs studies had arrived at a new stage of maturity. The Vents Program, by contrast, had always been conscious of the bigger picture, but wasn't equipped to undertake the broader, global studies envisioned under the RIDGE plan. The new plan, of course, would also require substantially more money than that devoted annually to Vents, if it was to accomplish its mission.

Even so, even without major programmatic money, a number of the key RIDGE researchers, again led by John Delaney, had worked on what they termed a "prototype" RIDGE experiment on the Endeavor segment of the Juan de Fuca Ridge in summer 1988. To try to gain better information on the relationship between earthquake activity and the flow of fluid through the vents, they deployed a group of sixteen instruments during a six-week period around a well-known vent site. The list of instruments illustrated the "integrated," "comprehensive" research plan in action. Among other instruments were six ocean-bottom seismometers to record microearthquakes around the vents, three newly designed video flow meters to take time-lapse images of three active black smokers, and a new electromagnetic flow meter to measure temperature and diffuse flow through a sulfide deposit.

The instrument array allowed the researchers to obtain concurrent data about events occurring during the six-week period, perhaps the most interesting of which was an eighteen-hour swarm of small earthquakes. The video flow meter revealed a rather wide variation in the velocity of smoker plumes during this same period.

Biological studies at the leading edge of vent science were also conducted as part of the six-week project. John Baross and Jody Deming developed new information regarding their highly controversial 1983 finding that microorganisms had grown at 250 degrees C.

From the *Alvin* the researchers deployed specially designed instruments to collect samples directly from the smoker environments. One instrument was a large syringe, which they used to collect samples of fluids from fourteen black smokers.

In the shipboard laboratory and later in their university labs, Deming and her associates took measurements to determine the quantity of microscopic life contained in the fluids coming out of the springs. The researchers measured the particulate DNA, or genetic material, contained in the sample. This is the definitive method for intact microorganisms; it measures DNA bound in bacterial cells. Most of the smoker samples showed significantly more DNA than would be expected in the deep sea, and one smoker showed fifty-six times as much DNA as would be expected. Even more interesting was that the highest counts of DNA came from the hottest smokers.

Deming noted that critics have charged that bacteria found in smoker fluids are not " 'real' smoker bacteria," but instead bacteria carried along, or entrained, in seawater. While she acknowledged that some seawater—and therefore, potentially, some non-smoker bacteria—would get into the syringe, she had devised a method to distinguish between smoker bacteria and seawater bacteria.

At first glance this measurement might seem impossible, since the "seawater" is completely mixed with the "smoker water" in the syringe. But because the element magnesium is present in seawater in known percentages but is absent from undiluted smoker fluids, the researchers only needed to measure the magnesium to infer the quantity of seawater present in the sample. Then they measured the quantities of particulate DNA in normal seawater near the hot springs. Combining the two measurements, Deming was able to estimate the amount of non-hot-springs bacteria in her samples.

The measurements involved extremely small units, billionths of a gram, or nanograms, per milliliter, a volume equal to about one-fifth of a teaspoon. In the surrounding seawater, the researchers measured particulate DNA concentrations from .21 to .32 nanograms per milliliter, while in the thirty-four syringe samples, the DNA concentrations ranged from .05 to 3.1 nanograms per milliliter. Given the numbers, Deming was convinced that at least some of the samples contained DNA that could not be explained by entrainment of seawater.

For a second experiment, Deming employed a titanium incubator. It was designed to test whether microorganisms contained in the hot smoker fluids were capable of growth or survival at the elevated temperatures and pressures found at the seafloor smokers. From the outside the incubator looked like a polished can slipped over a pipe whose ends protruded at top and bottom. In operation, the six-inch intake pipe at the bottom was inserted into the "throat" of a smoking chimney, in order to obtain the best sample of organisms coming from inside the hot spring.

Fluid from the hot spring entered into the chamber inside the "can" and passed out through the top, until the fluid melted a pin inside the device and closed the valves, thereby sealing the chamber with some fluid inside. At the same time, a glass vial inside the chamber broke and released a food source for bacteria. The incubator was then left in the smoker for a known period of time.

Deming and her colleagues at sea conducted such an experiment thirty-nine times, at ten vents. It worked according to plan only four times, but these successes provided her with what she considered compelling results.

In two cases, samples were collected and incubated at a smoker for 40 and 105 minutes and then measured for particulate DNA content. The temperature of the smoker samples was at least 250 degrees C. and probably quite a bit higher, she believed. She measured particulate DNA at 1.2 nanograms per milliliter in both samples—levels more than twice as high as those of unincubated samples. To her way of thinking, this finding contradicted the conventional wisdom that microorganisms should be destroyed under smoker temperatures. An additional finding from the experiment was that the food source in the incubator decreased during incubations while the DNA counts increased.

In a published summary of the research, Deming argued that the incubation test results "suggest that intact microorganisms at least survive superheated smoker temperatures at the Endeavor vent pressure of 220 atmospheres." Deming did not initially identify the species of microorganisms contained in the samples, but she hoped to do so by sequencing their DNA.

Analysis of unusual microorganisms, on the other hand, was the key element of research conducted by John Baross. Baross also collected his samples at the Endeavor hot springs in the summer of 1988, but rather than studying organisms in the hot spring fluids, he focused his attention on organisms found in a unique and previously unstudied hot spring environment there.

Some of the hot springs on the Endeavor segment form massive, steep-sided rock structures as tall as sixty feet. At several places around these structures, ledges, or "flanges," jut out. Some of the flanges, sited above hot spring vents, collect very hot fluids on their bottom surfaces. Since the flanges are somewhat porous to the fluids, the fluids move up through them, becoming cooled and changing their chemical composition as they rise.

In their passage through the flange the fluids appear to establish different microenvironments in porous rock. Baross and his colleagues studied the microorganisms inhabiting these flange environments, seeking to identify them by examining their makeup.

The key to their analysis was the recognition that the three kingdoms of life—the eubacteria, or common bacteria, the archaebacteria, or exotic bacteria, and the eukaryotes, which include everything else—can be differentiated by the chemical composition of their lipids. Only archaebacterial lipids contain a molecule of ether at a place in their structure where the others contain a molecule of ester.

When the researchers examined the lipids they discovered something quite in line with Baross's hopes. They found lipids from archaebacteria in the bottom through middle zones of flanges, and extremely high levels of archaebacterial lipids in the upper middle area of the flanges.

Since lipids compose only about 1 percent of the total carbon of a bacterial cell, the quantity of lipids the researchers found translated into 100 million to 1 billion bacteria per gram of solid flange. This is a huge population of bacteria.

Baross also grew bacteria in the laboratory at temperatures above the normal boiling point of water. Among the organisms collected from the flange, he said that one grew at 114 degrees C. This is about 15 degrees higher than had been previously reported for archaebacteria. They were lively "bugs." When grown under optimal conditions, these bacteria doubled in population every hour and reached densities of a billion cells per milliliter.

Baross planned to continue studying the flanges, because they appeared to offer the best opportunity to probe the relationship between life and very high temperatures.

While some research on the ridge system probed its effects on the conditions life can tolerate, another research project was exploring yet another new dimension of ridge effects—on the conditions life can't tolerate. Roman Schmitt, a cosmologist and professor of chemistry, geology, and oceanography at Oregon State University, hadn't started out interested in the hot springs at all. What he was interested in was a hypothesis which seemed to explain the death of the dinosaurs.

In Walt Disney's *Fantasia* the dinosaurs meet their end staggering across a parched landscape toward a blood-red sun. Not a bad interpretation, contemporary scientists would say, just not violent enough. Many scientists now believe that the earth was struck by an asteroid or by comets with such force that an environmental catastrophe resulted. This hypothesis originated with Nobel Prize winner Luis Alvarez and his coworkers at Berkeley in 1980 and was gradually refined through the eighties. By the end of the decade, most scientists appeared to accept it.

Schmitt, however, had some problems with certain parts of the hypothesis. A wiry, energetic man with eclectic scientific interests, Schmitt became perplexed as he analyzed a large group of ancient sediments from the western Pacific Ocean. In these sediments from the Shatsky Rise, Schmitt found that more than twenty-five different chemical elements were enriched in certain layers. Some enrichments were in the layer from 66 million years ago, the time that the main comet was supposed to have hit. But other enrichments dated from 200,000 years before this time and 1.2 million years after. On Schmitt's graph of enrichments were three peaks, not the one peak he had been expecting.

Schmitt's logical conclusion was that not one comet but many comets must have bombarded earth off and on for quite a long time. Still, he wanted more proof if he was going to diverge from a well-documented argument.

The "one-asteroid theory" argued that when an asteroid, about eight kilometers in diameter, hit the earth, it excavated a crater some 100 kilometers across, vaporizing both itself and a significant amount of the earth's crust in the crater. The particles in this vapor ultimately settled back down to earth and were preserved in deep-sea sediments, where one would expect to find an increased quantity of elements that had been present in both the comet and the crust.

So, for example, Schmitt expected to see quantities of iron at 66 million years ago that were ten to twenty times greater than he did. He saw no such enrichment for iron, nor for a group of other elements he examined. These results confirmed his belief that more than one comet impact must have occurred—and that some comets exploded in the atmosphere.

But where did these comets come from and how did they get here? Other scientists have proposed that comets come from the Oort Cloud, a region of our solar system where there are thousands of billions of them. The comets are ejected toward the earth when the solar system comes in contact with this region, an event which occurs roughly every 32 million years. This cycle agrees well with the history of mass biological extinctions, which have occurred at this same frequency during the last 250 million years.

Like many other scientists who have contributed to the research, Roman Schmitt believes that the comets are deflected toward the earth by a companion star to our sun, which is invisible on earth, but which has considerable mass. It has been dubbed the Nemesis star. Schmitt goes somewhat farther than other scientists, however, in portraying the effects of the comet impacts.

During the period around 66 million years ago, the boundary between the Cretaceous and Tertiary geological periods, several effects were felt. Although some of the individual comets exploded in the atmosphere, Schmitt believes, others hit the earth with the force of a million atomic bombs, fracturing the earth's crust and putting the planet's innards into a turmoil. Great lava flows occurred, notably in India. Huge volumes of carbon dioxide and sulfur dioxide came spewing out of these flows and out of volcanoes, polluting the atmosphere, altering the climate, and ultimately killing off the dinosaurs. At the same time, half the creatures in the ocean died off. On the oceanic effects, Schmitt becomes particularly animated.

"What's really happening," he says, "is that at that time hydrothermal venting went wild. The smokers *poisoned* the ocean."

The fracturing of ocean crust would have led to increased emissions from very hot seafloor hot springs. Following impact events, the ocean would have become both more acidic and also highly enriched in such elements as cobalt, copper, zinc, silver, gold, cadmium, mercury, and lead. The combination of the two effects would have easily proved too stressful for much of marine life, Schmitt argues. Entire marine families and genera did in fact die out. On the other hand, most species of freshwater organisms apparently survived this period.

Schmitt believes that his view of what happened 66 million years ago may fit all the known facts better than any other version. It rests upon his initial chemical analysis, in which he tried to come up with a consistent interpretation for his seafloor data of thirty-two chemical elements in the sixty-four Shatsky Rise samples.

"Measure one or two elements and you can weave any scenario you want," he says. "Measure thirty-two elements, of different properties, which behave differently in oceanic and terrestrial regimes, and you can probably only find one or two scenarios which fit all the data."

Finally, after considering the work of people like Schmitt, Deming, Baross, and Moore, one might well ask what the ingredients of scientific creativity are.

Some might say this begs the question. Are scientists really "creative" at all?

One commonplace of popular culture doubts that they are. This is the "absentminded professor" stereotype, the darling of caricaturists; and indeed, casual observation of the behavior of scientists often seems to support the caricature. Albert Einstein, for example, reportedly couldn't remember his home telephone number. Harold Urey, an eminent chemist, a Nobel Prize winner, and one of the collaborators in the 1953 origin-of-life experiments, must get some sort of prize in this category if a certain anecdote told about him is true.

According to the story, Urey met a colleague at lunchtime as they were passing through the grounds of the University of Chicago. They chatted about research. As he was taking his leave, Urey asked the colleague if he had noticed the direction from which he had come as they met. Asked why, he replied, "Well, if I was coming from that direction, it means I was going to lunch, and if from the other direction, it means I have had it."

Amusing as such anecdotes and observations are, the stereotype of the absentminded professor is surely a distortion, a kind of funhouse-mirror exaggeration of one feature of a character. And like many other caricatures it seems to show a lack of sympathy, and probably a lack of understanding, of what exactly it is that scientists do.

Nonetheless, views that tend to doubt the role of creative imagination in scientific activity are not limited to popular stereotypes. In his *Structure of Scientific Revolutions*, Thomas Kuhn suggested that what motivates a scientist "is the conviction that, if only he is skillful enough, he will succeed in solving a puzzle that no one before has solved or solved so well. Many of the greatest scientific minds have devoted all of their professional attention to demanding puzzles of this sort.

"On most occasions any particular field of specialization offers nothing else to do," Kuhn asserted, "a fact that makes it no less fascinating to the proper sort of addict."

Scientific activity, then, is normally puzzle-solving and a kind of addiction, according to Kuhn. (He is not solely a deflator of scientific activity, of course; Kuhn also argues that at revolutionary moments, scientists rise above this normal mode.)

Nevertheless, as ingenious and revealing as this argument about "normal" scientific activity is, it also seems too simple. To say that dedication to solving a particular question is only a sort of game or, worse, a symptom of an addiction probably goes too far. Listening to innovative scientists talk about how they actually do their work reveals something rather different. You hear, for example, about such absorption in a project, such bearing down on it, that the seeker ultimately passes right through it and comes out the other side where the problem has been solved.

Donald Hussong's efforts to make his prototype SeaMARC II perform correctly during sea trials offers one example. In 1980, Hussong realized that his efforts to persuade funding agencies to give the University of Hawaii a Sea Beam system were not going to pan out. So he began devoting more attention to altering the less expensive, and available, sidescan sonar technology so that it would also generate depth soundings. The strategy that Hussong and his colleagues hit on was to use two rows of transducers rather than one. The principle was that echoes from the seafloor would arrive at the two different transducer rows at slightly different times; the time difference depends on the angle of the returning echo, which could be interpreted to yield depth information.

The first time they put the instrument through a test at sea, nothing worked. The ability to interpret depths depends on stability of the transducers, but the torpedo-shaped instrument wobbled erratically through the water as it was pulled behind the ship. Hussong was desperate, and he turned to the Navy for help. Not surprisingly, they had a multimillion-dollar research project to study designs which could provide just this sort of stability.

Later, after working unsuccessfully with the Navy on a new fin design for the torpedo and setting out to sea to try it out, Hussong suddenly saw the solution. He grabbed some rope on the dock and fashioned it into a yoke, which was slipped around the torpedo and extended behind it into a tail. Just as a kite will be more stable in the air with a tail, so the SeaMARC abruptly calmed down in the water with its new tail.

Although the solution came to him suddenly, Hussong believes that its arrival was not just some serendipitous event. "You're thinking about it all the time," he says. "You're thinking about making it work while you're in the shower, while you're eating, you wake up in the middle of the night worrying about it, and you wind up trying a lot of things." Then it comes.

It seems safe to say that single-minded absorption in a problem enhances the likelihood of creative success in science, as in many other things. But even if a scientist exercises great attention as well as appropriate skill and knowledge, these are no guarantee of a significant contribution to understanding. Part of what's needed is imagination, the talent for seeing novel connections. But another part is discrimination, the ability to choose a suitable problem.

In order to create, a creator, whether that person is a poet, a painter, or a scientist, must believe that he or she is offering something new, something that goes beyond what already exists, beyond the history, the tradition, of the field. But here a paradox arises. The creator must both have absorbed the "tradition" and yet not be stifled by it. This individual must find space beyond or outside the existing territory of knowledge.

There are a number of ways in which this can be accomplished. Harold Bloom, the literary critic, has described six basic strategies that poets use, as revealed in their poems; all involve a maneuver that essentially devalues the work of their powerful predecessors, thereby making enough psychological space in which to work. That this sort of psychological maneuvering is characteristic of creative scientists as well as poets is attested to by the experience of Clive Lister, one of the hot springs pioneers.

Lister recalls a formative moment for his understanding of how science is done when he was a graduate student in the late 1950s at Cambridge. At the time Lister was wondering whether there might be other sources of heat at the ridges besides conduction through the crust. He broached an idea to the professor with whom he was working, the famous and influential Sir Edward Bullard.

Iceland is on the Mid-Atlantic Ridge and is well known for its hot springs and geysers, Lister remarked. Why shouldn't there be something similar on the part of the ridge that was underwater?

But Bullard turned away without even answering the question, Lister remembers.

Reflecting on the event some years later, Lister believed he knew the reason for the snub. Bullard "was a past master of getting funds for some rather way-out projects, and one thing you didn't tell prospective fund givers is that there are problems with interpreting the measurements. You have to pretend that what you're doing is absolutely definitive."

Perhaps the snub especially strengthened Lister's own beliefs. In any event it seemed to confirm a habit of outlook that came to serve Lister well. His particular mode of dealing with the constraints of the tradition is what he calls "hyperskepticism."

"Conventional wisdom," he remarks, "says that older people are less creative, and only younger scientists can be creative." But this may be less a function of creative insight than of the lack of the burden imposed by other creators. Older scientists, Lister suggests, "know about so much that has been done already, so they throw up their hands and say it's not possible to do anything more."

But he sidesteps this psychological block by refusing to accept results published in the literature in his field unless he can himself duplicate them. "If you're sufficiently skeptical," he says, "it is possible to maintain enough space to maneuver."

So, a healthy, functioning skepticism in the face of received opinion seems to be another important ingredient of scientific creativity.

And yet, even if one has a certain mental intensity which promotes insights, and a certain unfazed skepticism which permits one not to be overawed by predecessors and colleagues, the scientist will still need one other key quality if his energy and analytic ability are likely to result in real creative achievement. The scientist will want an aptitude, an instinct perhaps, for new synthesis.

Such an aptitude is shown by the work of Tuzo Wilson in the late 1980s. As he approached eighty years old, Wilson set out to reexamine the entire edifice of plate tectonics that he had been instrumental in constructing.

"If only 25 years ago a study of the ocean basins increased our knowledge of the Earth's surface so greatly and altered our views of its behavior so profoundly, might not a study of the whole interior of the Earth today change ideas as much again?"

Pointing out that until recently most of the direct knowledge of the earth has been limited to the outer 1 percent of the planet's sphere, he asked, "Why should anyone suppose that so thin a shell should provide all the information necessary to explain the behaviour of the whole Earth?"

Then Wilson launched into an essay whose "aim," he declared, was "to suggest ways in which the scope of the earth sciences should be broadened." He brought to bear the insights of seismic tomography and other current techniques to propose ways in which flows from the mantle, the formerly unknown interior of the earth, may have affected the surface of the planet.

"Convection tectonics," is what Wilson called his new synthesis of ideas, his proposed next step in the evolution of plate tectonic theory.

As Wilson's new synthesis suggests again, evolution, expansion, and integration of ideas will be the hallmarks of research related to seafloor hot springs in the 1990s. Scientists who study the springs and their related environments will extend the knowledge gained in their specific research to enlarge the understanding of such major scientific questions as the origin of life, the adaptation of species, the driving forces of climate change, and the evolution of the planet.

The coming years promise new insights, some of which may well be as unexpected, exciting, and fruitful as those that have occurred in the field already.

NOTES

These notes are listed by chapter, page, and key words, which are usually the first words in the sentence to which the note refers. Except where an interview is mentioned, references are to texts in "Works Cited."

Chapter 1

18 *Just a bit nervous:* Interviews with Steve Hammond are the primary source for material about him in this chapter.

21 *Navy rated the* Alvin: Woods Hole, p. 3.

21 *Deepest-diving submersible:* The *Sea Cliff*, operated by the Navy and used occasionally in the later 1980s by researchers, could go deeper. But in 1984, only the *Alvin* was in use for science.

25 *Leaped into civilian life:* Hollis, interview.

25 *When, in 1493, Columbus returned:* Boorstin, p. 631.

Chapter 2

30 *Feats of scientific imagination:* In developing this chapter and the next I found three books especially valuable: *The Road to Jaramillo*, by William Glen; *The Dark Side of the Earth*, by Robert Muir Wood; and *Continents in Motion*, by Walter Sullivan. For material in Chapter 2, I am particularly indebted also to Brent Dalrymple and Fred Vine, who were generous with their time in interviews and reviews.

31 *Fomenting a "revolution":* A succinct statement of this interpretation is by one of its main advocates, J. Tuzo Wilson, in "Preface," n.p.

32 *Lodged in his neck:* Alfred Wegener's brother, Kurt, notes this in his biographical sketch. Wegener, p. iv.

32 *"Congruence of coastlines":* Wegener, p. 1.

32 *The creation and its mysteries unveiled:* Concise critiques of Snider-Pellegrini are offered by Wood, pp. 37–38, and LeGrand, p. 29.

33 *Prominent in Snider-Pellegrini's:* Snider-Pellegrini had also argued for continental connection based on fossils, plants found in both Europe and North America. Glen, interview.

33 *"A former land bridge":* Wegener, p. 13.

33 *"The water displacement":* Wegener, p. 13.

34 *The mesosaur population:* Wegener, p. 98.

34 *Influential scientists were arguing:* Woods's *Dark Side of the Earth* offers many insights into the evolution of the continental-drift debate. LeGrand's *Drifting Continents and Shifting Theories* is a virtually seismographic study of the twitches, tremors, and jolts that moved the scientific community on this subject.

35 *"It did not":* Menard, p. 28.

35 *"Vexing geologists":* Menard, p. 29.

35 *"Is this revolutionary?":* Hallam, pp. 15–16.

35 *Argand observed:* Wood, p. 71.

36 *Enemy submarine:* Menard, p. 110, notes, "Despite the existence of Japanese submarines, and the detectability of 12kHz echo-sounding pulses, he [Hess] interpreted the fleet standing orders to maintain silence rather liberally. The result was the discovery of deeply submerged, flat-topped, extinct volcanoes, which he called 'guyots.' "

36 *It was not the sort of place:* Kennett, p. 5.

37 *"The chief interest":* Sverdrup et al., p. 14.

37 *On the day after Pearl Harbor:* Merritt, p. 10.

37 *"U-boat captains":* McVay, p. 16.

37 *One apocryphal story:* Cited by McVay, p. 16.

38 *The most direct:* E. M. Moores, interview.

38 *The rift valley descended:* Wilford, p. 289.

38 *Navy had slapped a security classification:* Wood, p. 139.

39 *Heezen spoke about his theory:* Wood, 1985, p. 140.

40 *Finally published in 1962:* In the intervening year, Robert Dietz published "Continent and Ocean Basin Evolution by Spreading of the Sea Floor," *Nature* 190 (1961), pp. 854–57. This paper coined the term "seafloor spreading" and was similar in many points to Hess's as yet unpublished essay. Later, Dietz acknowledged that Hess was the originator of the seafloor-spreading concept.

40 *"The birth of the oceans":* Hess, p. 599.

41 *"Continents do not plow":* Hess, p. 609.

41 *"The ocean basins are impermanent"*: Hess, p. 618.

42 *They had two problems:* Glen, p. 186. *The Road to Jaramillo* is the definitive intellectual history of the geomagnetists and the development of the time scale.

43 *The drill system:* Glen, p. 187.

43 *One evening sitting around:* Dalrymple, interview.

43 *"The world as seen"*: Roberts, p. 38.

45 *The other problem:* Glen, p. 66.

46 *"I think he thought"*: Vine, interview.

46 *Inside plywood geodesic domes:* E. Shor, p. 101.

47 *Theory has it:* Press and Siever, p. 422. "This description (of the 'self-exciting' dynamo) sounds vague because it is," they write.

47 *British chemist Robert Boyle:* Fisher, p. 71.

47 *"A single glance"*: Sullivan, p. 94.

48 *"The theory," he wrote:* Vine and Matthews, p. 947.

48 *"If spreading of the ocean floor"*: Vine and Matthews, p. 948.

48 *But the concept drew little attention:* Indeed, another scientist had separately developed a hypothesis virtually identical to that of Vine and Matthews. Lawrence Morley, then with the Geological Survey of Canada and a former student of J. Tuzo Wilson, had submitted a paper outlining the idea to two journals before Vine and Matthews submitted theirs. Morley's paper was rejected as "speculation," and his work never had the influence their paper and Vine's subsequent work had. Nevertheless, Morley was later acknowledged to have been right all along. For a full discussion of the Morley affair, see Glen, pp. 297–302.

48 *"One day"*: Vine, interview.

50 *"Well," he said, "if"*: Vine, interview.

50 *"At the time"*: Vine and Wilson, p. 485.

51 *This new reversal was a revelation:* Vine, interview.

Chapter 3

55 *"One of the reasons"*: Kuhn, p. 37.

55 *"The new theory"*: Kuhn, p. 155.

56 *"Like the choice between"*: Kuhn, p. 94.

57 *Those who thrived:* As H. W. Menard reflected after it was all over, "In this revolution, the winners were the fastest starters." Menard, p. 297.

57 *"Any loose statement"*: S. W. Carey, p. 9.

57 *Coined the phrase:* Wilson, "The Movement of Continents," n.p.

57 *Wilson had read Kuhn:* J. T. Wilson, letter to author, 16 Nov. 1986. Also J. T. Wilson, letter to author, 11 Sept. 1987: "I agreed with Kuhn, but I don't recall whether he changed my views and if so by how much."

58 *"We really should hire"*: Franklin, interview.

58 *"Most people don't like it"*: J. T. Wilson, letter to author, 11 Sept. 1987.

58 *An essay he wrote*: Wilson, "Consequences."

59 *"The traditional"*: Wilson, "Continental Drift," p. 41.

59 *"I believe that"*: Wilson, "Movement," n.p.

59 *For many scientists*: Wood, p. 167.

60 *"It's so good"*: Glen, p. 339.

60 *"I hadn't really believed"*: Sullivan, p. 103.

60 *Four whole sessions*: Wood, p. 168.

60 *"This is the most exciting"*: Cited in Sullivan, p. 121.

61 *In 1965 he had been*: Wilson, 1965.

61 *A stint*: Wood, p. 126.

62 *"We're paying for this"*: Schlee, p. 153.

62 *Explosives would be detonated*: Schlee, p. 158.

63 *Suddenly Sykes*: Wertenbaker, p. 211.

64 *The answers were found*: McKenzie and Parker; Morgan.

65 *"Formerly, most scientists"*: Wilson, "Preface," n.p.

67 *"The result of"*: Lemke et al., p. 614.

67 *"Just as the aftermaths"*: Wilson, "Conclusion," p. 160.

67 *Bikini plaza*: E. Shor, p. 464.

68 *Students were pretty much*: Noted in interviews with both Normark and Corliss.

68 *"Marine geology"*: Menard, p. 278.

69 *"We're on the threshold"*: E. Shor, p. 472.

69 *One morning he and van Andel*: Corliss, interview.

71 *The existence of submarine volcanism*: Skinner.

73 *"Most successful experiment ever done"*: Roberts, p. 44.

73 *Some scientists*: Van Andel, interview.

73 *Drake, who had used*: Ballard, interview.

73 *Submersibles weren't being put to best use*: mentioned by both Keller and Normark in interviews.

74 *Professional skepticism*: Ballard, interview.

75 *"Titanium paper clips"*: Ballard, interview.

75 *Those who were to be*: Keller, interview.

76 *"For the first time"*: Heirtzler and Ballard, p. 586.

76 *"The seafloor is"*: Van Andel, p. 172.

76 *"Was like walking"*: Oregon State University, "OSU Oceanographer."

77 *Over $2 million*: School of Oceanography, 1971.

Chapter 4

78 *They were also persuaded:* Van Andel, interview.

78 *Lister was a specialist:* Lister, interview.

79 *But Von Herzen's concern:* Lister, interview.

79 *The solution:* Lister, "Thermal Balance."

80 *The cold seawater:* Lister, "Penetration of Water."

81 *One of the technicians:* Corliss, interview.

81 *Under the direction of Bob Ballard:* Ballard, "Notes."

82 *A makeshift 100-foot catamaran:* Allyn C. Vine, p. 15.

82 *Right away:* There is some difference of recollection on this point. Corliss remembers (interview) that this first dive (with Corliss and van Andel) was conducted without benefit of the ANGUS bottom photographs, which were coordinated by Ballard. Van Andel (letter to author, 21 Nov. 1989) concurs. Ballard (interview and "Notes") remembers that this dive was conducted with benefit of the ANGUS bottom photographs. Ship's logs for *Alvin* and *Knorr* (which carried ANGUS) tend to confirm Ballard's depiction of events. No one questions that photographs were available for the third dive, with Corliss and Edmond.

84 *They studied in detail:* Corliss et al., 1979.

86 *Six lengthy news stories:* The articles by David Perlman in the *Chronicle* were "Probing Underwater Mysteries" (7 March 1977), "Astounding Undersea Discoveries" (9 March), "Exploring the Ocean's Young Volcanoes" (12 March), "Scientists' Fantastic Underwater Voyage" (16 March), "Sea Research—Ceaseless but Exciting" (18 March), and "Deep Questions from the Sea" (25 March).

86 *One of them quoted Corliss:* David Perlman, "Astounding Undersea Discoveries."

87 *Perlman remembered:* Perlman, interview.

87 *It was apparent to Perlman:* David Perlman, "Exploring the Ocean's Young Volcanoes."

87 *Perlman's account of a dive:* David Perlman, "Scientists' Fantastic Underwater Voyage."

88 *The magazine showcased:* Corliss and Ballard, "Oases."

89 *Some at Woods Hole:* Corliss, interview.

90 *Spiess and some engineers at Scripps:* Spiess, 1980.

91 *Normark was trying to complete:* Normark, interview.

92 *Navy officials were also impressed:* Normark, interview.

93 *All the dives:* "They seemed to have the attitude that there was no need to do more research on the hydrothermal vents," Normark recalled later. " 'Seen one, seen 'em all,' that kind of attitude." Interview.

99 *The NOAA team discovered:* Malahoff, interview.

99 *Malahoff described:* Untitled news report in *Ocean Science News*, 12

Oct. 1981, p. 6. Refers to a "public statement" by Malahoff of 6 Oct. 1981, and quotes him for the size and composition of the deposit.

Chapter 5

103 *The greatest depth:* Diagram Group, p. 34.

103 *He wasn't:* Dietz, p. 22.

104 *Variations on this technique:* Dietz, p. 25.

104 *Leonardo observed that:* Quotation is from Leonardo's Notebook referred to as MS. B. 6r, dated before about 1488. Hart, p. 247.

104 *Colladon and Sturm announced:* Hersey, p. 9.

105 *"I was not sea sick":* Fessenden, p. 220.

106 *By the 1930's the British:* G. C. Shor, p. 41.

106 *Image production improved again:* G. C. Shor, p. 40.

112 *They elaborated a seacoast:* In 1494, for instance, Christopher Columbus required all his crew to sign a deposition that, in effect, said the coast of Cuba, which they had in fact discovered, was the coast of the Asia of spices and gold the Columbus had been hoping to find. Boorstin, p. 240.

113 *"Before the late sixties":* Clancy, pp. 71–72.

113 *The Navy argued against:* McLaughlin.

114 *No record of its whereabouts:* Boorstin, pp. 268–69.

117 *He had them build:* Boorstin, pp. 163–64.

Chapter 6

126 *Conducted a temperature survey:* Crane, 1985.

126 *A conceptual model:* Ballard, 1984.

128 *The gouge was made up of:* Dimensions were approximately 150 × 75 × 60 feet maximum. Canadian American Seamount Expedition, 1985.

133 *The velocity of the flow:* Converse, Holland, and Edmond, 1984. Quantity cited is 200 cm/sec.

133 *The flux was on the order:* Baker and Massoth, 1987. Also, Converse et al. measured convective heat flux at individual black smokers on the East Pacific Rise and estimated it to be 500,000–2,300,000 × 1,000,000 watts.

133 *The power usage of Seattle:* Curtis, p. 4.

134 *For sub-bottom profiling:* Ryan.

135 *One backpack of TNT:* Kennett, p. 42.

135 *Her 1984 profile:* Morton and Sleep.

136 *One straightforward argument:* Lewis, interview.

137 *They calculated that near the caldera floor:* van Heeswijk.

138 *The gist of the process:* Edmond and Von Damm.

141 *Virtually everywhere Talley sampled the water:* L. Talley, personal communication. Vents Program, p. 7.

143 *One to two parts per billion:* Franklin, interview.

143 *A cube 60 feet:* Boyle, p. 60

143 *"There was general agreement":* Boyle, p. 409.

144 *Gold is found in another:* Franklin, interview.

144 *The researchers proposed:* Delaney and Cosens.

145 *20 to 30 percent of its exports:* Franklin, interview.

146 *The other was Axial Volcano:* Hannington et al.

Chapter 7

149 *A smelter, propped up:* Koski and Derkey, p. 123.

150 *"Mesozoic sedimentary":* legend for color-coded section of Klamath Mountains in Walker and King.

151 *An ophiolite is:* In geologic terms, from the mantle upward, an intact ophiolite suite would include peridotites that make up the upper mantle; gabbro and parallel dikes that have intruded into a slowly spreading fracture in the crust; lavas that flowed from the fracture and make up the top layer of crust; and then overlying sediments on the ocean floor. Massive sulfides can be deposited in the lavas immediately overlying the dike sequence or on top of the lavas and in the sediments. Gass.

152 *The word "copper":* Rona, p. 91.

152 *Ronald Reagan called attention:* Robert Dale Wilson, p. 131.

152 *Sometimes not very friendly or stable countries:* According to a 1985 report of the Minerals Management Service, the United States was more than 80 percent dependent on imports for one-third of the thirty-two important minerals used in the nation's economy, and for two-thirds of the minerals was more than 50 percent dependent. Smith, p. 1.

153 *National Minerals Policy:* Public Law 96-479.

153 *A coalition of major U.S.:* Environmental Policy Center et al., p. iii.

153 *"Many of the innumerable tons":* Environmental Policy Center et al., p. vii.

153 *"The most significant event in the history":* Simon, pp. 118–19.

153 *As James Malone recognized:* Malone, interview conducted by James R. Larison and Linda Weimer, 26 Sept. 1985.

155 *An influential book:* Mero, cited in Robert Barton, "The Ocean's Resources," *The Undersea* (New York: Macmillan, 1977), p. 15.

155 *At the last:* John V. Byrne, administrator of NOAA from 1981 to 1985, noted later that the mining industry exerted influence on this decision. "Clearly the manganese nodule issue became one of the stickiest issues in the United Nations Conference on the Law of the Sea (UNCLOS). It

was the nodules and the direction the conference had gone [on them] that led the mining industry to pressure President Reagan to withdraw from the UNCLOS in 1982, all based on the perceived importance of mining." John V. Byrne, "Ocean Minerals: For Profit or Prophecy?" Address to Ocean Agenda 21, Portland, Ore., 20 Feb. 1989.

155 *While legal scholars:* James Malone commented in 1990: "Even though the treaty has not come into force, the U.S. and other countries generally have agreed that, aside from its deep seabed mining and dispute settlement provisions, the substantive portions of the treaty, including the right of a coastal country to establish up to 200-nautical-mile EEZs . . . are statements of customary international law binding on them apart from the treaty. All coastal countries thus enjoy the internationally recognized exclusive legal right to explore and exploit the seabed mineral resources within their EEZs and on their continental shelf." Malone, letter to author, 7 March 1990.

155 *Assertion of sovereignty:* "The policy statement which accompanied this [the EEZ] proclamation stated that the President had taken this action because *recently discovered deposits of polymetallic sulfides* and cobalt-manganese crusts could be a major future source of strategic and other minerals important to the U.S. economy and national security." Emphasis added. Smith, p. 1.

156 *The agency identified:* Smith, Figure 1.

156 *"At which time":* Minerals Management Service, p. 3.

156 *His detailed maps were classified:* Menard, p. 249.

157 *"Stripmining on the coast":* Oregon Shores Conservation Council.

157 *The processing plant would generate:* Minerals Management Service, Appendix C, p. 494.

162 *Mineral deposits would more likely be found:* A feasibility study prepared for the MMS in July 1983 related these general observations about spreading rate and mineralization to the Gorda and stated, "We therefore conclude that the Gorda Ridge south of 42 degrees N. is not a promising area for sulfide exploration." South of 42 degrees N. is the southern half of the Gorda, and the Escanaba Trough. Halkyard, Haymon, and Felix.

163 *The scientists took thousands:* Holmes and Zierenberg, p. 113.

164 *The precious metal was found:* Rona, "Hydrothermal Mineralization," compares 102 known hydrothermal mineral occurrences at seafloor spreading centers (Table 2). Two samples from the Gorda Ridge are listed as containing on the order of 300–700 parts per million (ppm) of silver; the world ocean basin average is .11 ppm.

164 *Several deposits were reported:* Zierenberg et al.

164 *Peter Rona:* Remarks were made during open session, Gorda Ridge Symposium, Portland, Ore., May 1987.

164 *Jim Franklin of the Geological:* Franklin, interview.

165 *The development in the 1980s:* Byrne.

165 *But the state of knowledge:* The attention of biological research was on identifying seafloor animals in the area of the ridge. Only part of this research was completed, and very little attention was devoted to fisheries in the Gorda area. Albacore are known to migrate through the area, and are fished there. Fish larvae of commercially important species such as Dover sole and rex sole are found offshore in the area of the ridge, but how great a contribution these larvae make to the fishery is unknown. Some salmon runs may pass through the area during the winter, but very little is known about salmon migrations near the Gorda, according to William Pearcy, a biological oceanographer at Oregon State University and a Gorda Ridge task force member in charge of the subgroup on biological research.

In 1987 this task force subgroup made five recommendations for further research to assess the effects of potential mining operations on living resources. Of greatest concern to commercial fishermen would likely be those effects that would occur in shallow coastal waters as part of the ore-processing stage of a mining operation, rather than at the offshore mine site. Despite the call for more biological research, it was unclear, following the termination of the draft environmental impact statement activity, when and under whose auspices such research would be conducted.

166 *"New horizons for deep ocean minerals":* Malahoff, "New Horizons," p. 87.

Chapter 8

167 *The first comprehensive list:* Newman, "Abyssal." The number is for both hydrothermal and "related" environments.

168 *Something from a science fiction story:* In fact, Arthur C. Clarke discusses the worms in his novel *2010.* He has them living on one of the moons of Jupiter, in a vent ecosystem.

169 *He found the body:* Jones, "Giant Tube Worms."

169 *He called it:* Jones translated *pachyptila* as "thick feather."

171 *"Really, it's clear":* Cavanaugh, interview.

172 *They were bacteria:* Cavanaugh et al. was the first article, with an initial set of micrographs. Cavanaugh, "Symbiosis," showed even more persuasive micrographs.

173 *Felbeck . . . did not isolate the bacteria:* Indeed, as of 1990 no one had been successful in this quest, despite much effort.

173 *He did show evidence:* Felbeck.

174 *This blockage occurs in two main ways:* Childress et al., p. 43.

174 *The worm had apparently evolved:* Childress et al., p. 45.

177 *The worms get the bacteria inside their bodies:* However, the mechanism used by the worms to select the specific type or types of bacteria appropriate for symbiosis remains obscure. Not just any bacterium will do, and most marine bacteria are not sulfide-burning chemosynthesizers.

177 *Jones's article:* Jones, "On the Vestimentifera."

178 *Perhaps contested by other qualified taxonomists:* Eve Southward, of the Plymouth Marine Laboratory in England, has since called into question the validity of distinguishing the Vestimentifera from the Pogonophora, a group of worms which have the same body plan. The debate may well continue for some time.

180 *A "missing link" to the past:* Newman, "A New Scalpellid."

181 *Holger Jannasch of Woods Hole:* Jannasch, interview.

181 *There he began directly:* Waksman.

182 *The research that Jannasch and:* Tuttle and Jannasch, 1976. This article is an example of Jannasch's research on bacteria and chemosynthesis. The deep-sea settings in the article were not ridge crest hot springs.

182 *Jannasch reasoned:* Jannasch, "Chemosynthesis."

182 *He left the syringes:* Jannasch, "Microbial Processes."

183 *John Baross of Oregon State:* Corliss et al., 1979. The issue date of the magazine was 16 March 1979. John Baross was credited in the article with performing the microbiological studies, though he is not listed as an author of the paper.

185 *He had written:* John A. Baross, "Halophilic Microorganisms," M. L. Speck, ed., *Compendium of Methods for the Microbiological Examination of Foods* (Washington, D.C.: American Public Health Assoc., 1976), pp. 194–202. And John A. Baross and Richard Y. Morita, "Life at Low Temperatures: Ecological Aspects," in D. Kushner, ed., *Microbial Life in Extreme Environments* (London: Academic Press, 1978), pp. 9–71.

185 *"Archaebacteria":* Woese.

Chapter 9

186 *"First I find":* Corliss said he knew the quote from an advertisement by Rolex, the watch manufacturer.

187 *It was by no means:* According to both Mitchell Lyle and Jack Dymond, who were also on the cruise from Oregon State, the idea that life might have originated somehow in the hot springs was widely shared, and discussed a little, by the scientific party on the cruise. Dymond remembers sitting around on the *Lulu*, the tender for *Alvin*, with Corliss, van Andel, and John Edmond and talking about the origin of life.

Jerry van Andel also says that the notion that life might have begun in the hot springs "occurred to many of them," and he mentions his own "fascination with the biology," which "at first, no one would talk" to him about. He credits reporter Perlman with stimulating interest in the fauna by way of his news story. Van Andel tends to downplay Corliss's initial interest in the animals (Tjeerd van Andel, interview, 10 March 1988).

187 *What we found there:* Oregon State University, "Sea Floor."

187 *"An interesting question":* Corliss, "Thermal Springs," p. 29.

188 *A brief article:* Dowler and Ingmanson. The authors wrote, "We identify here the Atlantis-II Deep brine as a promising site for searching for chemical precursors, report finding thiocyanate in the brine and suggest a relationship between chemical evolution and the evolution of the Earth's crust."

188 *She borrowed a book:* Calvin.

190 *Submarine Hydrothermal Systems:* Corliss, Baross, and Hoffman, *Submarine Hydrothermal Systems.*

191 *By the end of the eighties:* Waldrop, "How Do You Read."

192 *They heated the amino:* Corliss, Baross, and Hoffman, *Submarine Hydrothermal Systems,* p. 9.

193 *He said he had "outlined:* Corliss says that initially he wasn't as much impressed by Hoffman's term paper as Miller was. "I was a little disappointed, actually, because I felt she had not gone beyond what I had talked to her about." Yet he does seem open-minded about the matter, adding, "On the other hand, I really don't know whether independently, and in parallel, she came to the same conclusions." Corliss, interview.

193 *As historian of science:* Price, pp. 58–59.

193 *She "synthesized":* "Sarah Hoffman synthesized the origin-of-life model from present-day vent characteristics, and the panoply of old and new geological, chemical and biological ideas on where, when and how life originated." John A. Baross, letter to author, 14 March 1988.

194 *Later, in 1981:* Corliss, Baross, and Hoffman, "An Hypothesis."

196 *Even more "remarkable":* Baross et al., *Procaryotic "Coelacanths,"* p. 8. The other authors were Sarah E. Hoffman, John B. Corliss, Louis I. Gordon, and Marvin D. Lilley.

196 *He published a paper in* Nature: Baross and Deming, "Growth."

197 *A group of researchers:* Jonathan D. Trent, Roger A. Chastain, and A. Aristides Yayanos, "Possible Artefactual Basis for Apparent Growth at 250 C.," *Nature* 307 (1984), pp. 737–40.

197 *Baross and Deming rebutted:* "Reply from John A. Baross and Jody W. Deming." *Nature* 307 (1984), p. 740.

198 *Where the sequence:* Woese, p. 110.

199 *Published in 1985:* Baross and Hoffman.

199 *"Jack just 'got":* Keller, interview.

200 *He also reconceived:* Corliss, "Dynamics."

202 *"Since a lipid":* Corliss, "Dynamics," p. 11.

202 *Author of a popular book:* Shapiro.

203 *"That is," he adds:* Shapiro, interview.

203 *Miller . . . and Bada wrote:* Miller and Bada, p. 609.

203 *The organic molecules would not be:* Corliss wrote: "The products of rapid heating and quenching at the cracking front . . . follow a highly constrained trajectory, rapidly mixing with cool sea water, flowing upward through a matrix of fractured rocks of enormous surface area, lined with a highly catalytic surface of clay minerals. . . . They began their ascent as hot (350–600 C.), acid (pH 3.6), highly reducing fluids, and approach a low temperature end member which is cold (2–20 C.), slightly alkaline (pH 7.9), and oxidizing."

Ellipses indicate references to figures in text. Corliss, "Dynamics," p. 9.

203 *Corliss wrote in response:* Corliss, "Submarine Hot Springs," was responding to Stanley L. Miller, Jeffrey L. Bada, and Nadav Friedmann, "What Was the Role of Submarine Hot Springs in the Origin of Life?" *Origins of Life* 19 (1989), pp. 536–37.

Chapter 10

207 *A rather interesting research article:* Boström and Peterson.

209 *Tunnicliffe had observed that:* Tunnicliffe et al.

209 *What is now the Juan de Fuca:* Engebretson et al.

210 *She wrote a scholarly article:* Tunnicliffe.

219 *The sub had dropped:* A detailed account of an *Alvin* dive, written by a pilot, is Dudley Foster's "Some Dangers and Many Delights: A Pilot's View," *Oceanus* 31 (1988), pp. 17–21.

221 *Did the adaptation:* A good popular account of this research is Richard C. Hill's "Deep Sea Glowing Detected," *Oregonian*, 18 August 1988, Section C, p. 1. Cindy Lee Van Dover's own account is "Do 'Eyeless' Shrimp See the Light of Glowing Deep-Sea Vents?" *Oceanus* 31 (1988), pp. 47–52.

Epilogue

226 *"I was sitting there":* Ballard, interview.

227 *"Search-survey-and-sampling robots":* Bowen, p. 63.

228 *"Five hours in a freezing elevator":* Weber and Schnall.

228 *"You were never 'manned' ":* Ballard, interview.

229 *Along Valu Fa:* NAUTILAU Group.

229 *SeaMARC II:* SeaMARC II, like SeaMARC I, was developed by International Submarine Technology, Redmond, Wash.

229 *SeaMARC II can cover:* Detrick.

229 *By comparison, Sea Beam:* Detrick, p. 3331.

230 *(Typically, the digital picture areas:* Davis et al., p. 14.

232 *"To a certain extent":* Anderson and Dziewonski, p. 64.

232 *They found "even less:* Anderson and Dziewonski, p. 65.

232 *"The controversy of layered versus:* Turcotte, p. 468.

233 *In 1989, researchers at Scripps published:* Burnett, Caress, and Orcutt.

233 *The reservoir of slightly molten:* MacDonald.

234 *Moore and Herbert Shaw . . . wrote up:* Shaw and Moore.

234 *The major El Niño:* Siwolop.

235 *"Six geologic processes":* Committee on Earth Sciences, p. 79.

235 *An estimated:* Committee on Earth Sciences, p. 81.

236 *"Dynamic manifestation":* Delaney et al., p. 1.

236 *"The global spreading center":* Delaney et al., p. 1.

236 *"Comprehensive" . . . "coordinated":* Delaney et al., p. 2.

236 *"To understand the causes":* Delaney, p. 1.

237 *Hydrophones in the central Pacific:* Lupton and Macdonald, 1989, p. E-4.

237 *Sentry was designed:* Walden and Bradley, p. 71.

238 *Six ocean-bottom seismometers:* LaFlamme et al.

239 *Her associates:* Deming collaborated with Rita Colwell and her students at the University of Maryland.

239 *Most of the smoker:* Deming et al.

240 *In a published summary:* Deming et al.

241 *Baross and his colleagues:* Primarily David White and his colleagues from the University of Tennessee.

241 *A huge population of bacteria:* Baross reported his results at the December 1989 fall meeting of the American Geophysical Union in San Francisco. Baross et al., "Preliminary Geochemical."

242 *By the end of the decade:* One strong indicator of community sentiment is a report on a major conference: Chapman.

243 *Schmitt goes somewhat farther:* Schmitt.

244 *Albert Einstein:* His forgetfulness is cited in Ronald W. Clark's *Einstein: The Life and Times* (New York: World, 1971), p. 512.

244 *"Well, if I was coming":* Menard, p. 13.

245 *Thomas Kuhn suggested:* Kuhn, p. 38.

246 *The literary critic:* Bloom, pp. 14–16.

248 *"If only 25 years ago":* Wilson, "Convection Tectonics," p. 1200.

WORKS CITED

Books, Pamphlets, Films

Andel, Tjeerd van. *Science at Sea: Tales of an Old Ocean*. San Francisco: Freeman, 1981.

Baross, John A., et al. *Procaryotic "Coelacanths": Tube-forming Microorganisms from Submarine Hydrothermal Environments*. Corvallis, Ore.: Oregon State University, 1980. School of Oceanography Special Publication, Ref. 80–8.

Bloom, Harold. *The Anxiety of Influence: A Theory of Poetry*. New York: Oxford UP, 1973.

Boorstin, Daniel J. *The Discoverers*. New York: Random-Vintage, 1985.

Boyle, Robert W. *Gold: History and Genesis of Deposits*. New York: Van Nostrand Reinhold, 1987.

Calvin, Melvin. *Chemical Evolution*. Oxford: Oxford UP, 1969.

Carey, S. W. *The Expanding Earth*. Vol. 10 of *Developments in Geotectonics*. New York: Elsevier, 1976.

Clancy, Tom. *The Hunt for Red October*. New York: Berkley, 1986.

Committee on Earth Sciences. *Our Changing Planet: The FY 1990 Research Plan*. U.S. Office of Science and Technology Policy, 1989.

Corliss, John B., John A. Baross, and Sarah E. Hoffman. *Submarine Hydrothermal Systems: A Probable Site for the Origin of Life*. Corvallis, Ore.: Oregon State University, 1980. School of Oceanography Special Publication, Ref. 80–7.

Delaney, John R., et al. *RIDGE: Initial Science Plan*. Seattle: University of Washington, School of Oceanography, 1989.

Diagram Group. *Comparisons*. New York: St. Martin's, 1980.

Environmental Policy Center et al. *Minerals and the Public Lands: An Analysis of Strategic Minerals Issues and Public Lands Policy.* Washington, D.C.: Environmental Policy Center, 1981.

Fessenden, Helen M. *Fessenden: Builder of Tomorrows.* New York: Coward-McCann, 1940.

Glen, William. *The Road to Jaramillo: Critical Years of the Revolution in Earth Science.* Stanford, Calif.: Stanford UP, 1982.

Hart, Ivor B. *The World of Leonardo da Vinci.* New York: Viking, 1961.

Heeswijk, Marijke van. "Shallow Crustal Structure of the Caldera of Axial Seamount, Juan de Fuca Ridge." Master's thesis. Corvallis, Ore.: Oregon State University, 1986.

Jones, Meredith L., ed. *Hydrothermal Vents of the Eastern Pacific: An Overview.* Vol. 6 of Bulletin of the Biological Society of Washington, 1985.

Kennett, James P. *Marine Geology.* Englewood Cliffs, N.J.: Prentice-Hall, 1982.

Kuhn, Thomas S. *The Structure of Scientific Revolutions.* 2nd ed. Chicago: U of Chicago, 1970.

LeGrand, H. E. *Drifting Continents and Shifting Theories.* Cambridge: Cambridge UP, 1988.

McMurray, Gregory R., ed. *Gorda Ridge: A Seafloor Spreading Center in the United States' Exclusive Economic Zone: Proceedings of the Gorda Ridge Symposium, May 11–13, 1987. Portland, Oregon.* New York: Springer-Verlag, 1990.

Menard, H. W. *The Ocean of Truth: A Personal History of Global Tectonics.* Princeton: Princeton UP, 1986.

Mero, John L. *The Mineral Resources of the Sea.* London: Elsevier, 1965.

Minerals Management Service, U. S. Department of the Interior. *Proposed Polymetallic Sulfide Minerals Lease Offering, Gorda Ridge Area: Draft Environmental Impact Statement.* Reston, Va.: Minerals Management Serv., 1983.

Oregon Shores Conservation Council. *Stripmining on the Coast.* Rockaway, Ore., 1977.

Press, Frank, and Raymond Siever. *Earth.* 3rd ed. San Francisco: Freeman, 1982.

Price, Derek J. de Solla. *Little Science, Big Science . . . and Beyond.* New York: Columbia UP, 1986.

Schlee, Susan. *On Almost Any Wind: The Saga of the Oceanographic Research Vessel "Atlantis."* Ithaca: Cornell UP, 1978.

School of Oceanography, Oregon State University. *Annual Report, 1970–71.* Corvallis, Ore.: Oregon State U, 1971.

Shapiro, Robert. *Origins: A Skeptic's Guide to the Creation of Life on Earth.* New York: Bantam, 1987.

Shor, Elizabeth Noble. *Scripps Institution of Oceanography: Probing the Ocean, 1936 to 1976.* San Diego: Tofua, 1978.

Simon, Anne W. *Neptune's Revenge.* New York: Franklin Watts, 1984.

Sullivan, Walter. *Continents in Motion: The New Earth Debate.* New York: McGraw Hill, 1974.

Sverdrup, H. U., N. W. Johnson, and R. H. Fleming. *The Oceans.* Englewood Cliffs, N.J.: Prentice-Hall, 1942.

Vents Program, National Oceanic and Atmospheric Administration. *FY 87 and FY 88 Implementation Plan.* Seattle: 1987.

Waksman, Selman A. *Sergei N. Winogradsky: His Life and Work.* New Brunswick, N.J.: Rutgers UP, 1953.

Weber, Christine, and Peter Schnall, producers. *The Jason Project.* National Geographic Society, 1990. Television documentary.

Wegener, Alfred L. *The Origin of Continents and Oceans.* Trans. John Biram of fourth revised German ed. (1929). New York: Dutton, 1966.

Weiner, Jonathan. *Planet Earth.* New York: Bantam, 1986.

Wertenbaker, William. *The Floor of the Sea: Maurice Ewing and the Search to Understand the Earth.* Boston: Little, Brown, 1974.

Wilford, John Noble. *The Mapmakers.* New York: Knopf, 1981.

Wood, Robert Muir. *The Dark Side of the Earth.* London: Allen, 1985.

Woods Hole Oceanographic Institution. *Briefs of Alvin History from June 1964 to the Present.* Woods Hole, Mass.: Woods Hole Oceanographic Institution, 1984.

Zierenberg, R. A., et al. *Proposal for Drilling in the Escanaba Trough, Southern Gorda Ridge, on behalf of the U.S. Geological Survey, Oregon State University, and the Geological Survey of Canada.* Menlo Park, Calif.: U.S. Geological Survey, 1987.

Articles

Anderson, Don L., and Adam M. Dziewonski. "Seismic Tomography." *Scientific American,* Oct. 1984: 60–68.

Baker, E. T., and G. J. Massoth. "The Along-Strike Distribution of Hydrothermal Activity on a Spreading Segment of the Juan de Fuca Ridge." *EOS* 67 (1986): 1027.

Baker, E. T., and G. J. Massoth. "Characteristics of Hydrothermal Plumes from Two Vent Fields on the Juan de Fuca Ridge, Northeast Pacific Ocean." *Earth and Planetary Science Letters* 85 (1987): 59–73.

Baker, E. T., et al. "Episodic Venting of Hydrothermal Fluids from the Juan de Fuca Ridge." *Journal of Geophysical Research* 94: 9237–50.

Ballard, Robert D. "The Exploits of *Alvin* and ANGUS: Exploring the East Pacific Rise." *Oceanus* 27 (1984): 7–14.

Ballard, Robert D. "Notes on a Major Oceanographic Find." *Oceanus* 20 (1977): 35–44.

Ballard, Robert D., et al. "East Pacific Rise at 21 N.: The Volcanic, Tectonic, and Hydrothermal Processes of the Central Axis." *Earth and Planetary Science Letters* 55 (1981): 1–10.

Baross, John A., and Jody W. Deming. "Growth of 'Black Smoker' Bacteria at Temperatures of at Least 250 C." *Nature* 303 (1983): 423–26.

Baross, John A., and Jody W. Deming. "The Role of Bacteria in the Ecology of Black Smoker Environments." Jones, *Hydrothermal Vents*: 355–72.

Baross, John A., and Sarah E. Hoffman. "Submarine Hydrothermal Vents and Associated Gradient Environments as Sites for the Origin and Evolution of Life." *Origins of Life* 15 (1985): 327–45.

Baross, John A., et al. "Preliminary Geochemical and Ecological Characteristics of Sulfide Flange Environments on the Endeavour Segment of the Northern Juan de Fuca Ridge." *EOS* 70 (1989): 1163.

Boström, K., and M. N. A. Peterson. "Precipitates from Hydrothermal Exhalations on the East Pacific Rise." *Economic Geology* 61 (1966): 1258–65.

Bowen, Martin F. "Jason's Med Adventure." *Oceanus* 33 (1990): 61–69.

Burnett, M. S., D. W. Caress, and J. A. Orcutt. "Tomographic Image of the Magma Chamber at 12°50′N on the East Pacific Rise." *Nature* 339 (1989): 206–8.

Byrne, John V. "Minerals: Opportunities for Profit?" *Ocean Agenda 21: Passages to the Pacific Century.* Corvallis, Ore.: Oregon Sea Grant, 1990. Pp. 5–9.

Canadian American Seamount Expedition. "Hydrothermal Vents on an Axis Seamount of the Juan de Fuca Ridge." *Nature* 313 (1985): 212–14.

Cavanaugh, Colleen M. "Symbiosis of Chemoautotrophic Bacteria and Marine Invertebrates from Hydrothermal Vents and Reducing Sediments." Jones, *Hydrothermal Vents*: 373–88.

Cavanaugh, Colleen M., et al. "Prokaryotic Cells in the Hydrothermal Vent Tube Worm *Riftia pachyptila* Jones." *Science* 213 (1981): 340–42.

Chapman, Clark. "Snowbird II: Global Catastrophes." *EOS* 70 (1989): 217–18.

Childress, James J., Horst Felbeck, and George N. Somero. "Symbiosis in the Deep Sea." *Scientific American*, May 1987: 39–48.

Clague, D., and M. Holmes. "Geology, Petrology, and Mineral Resources of the Gorda Ridge." *Geology and Resource Potential of the Continental Margin of Western North America and Adjacent Ocean Basins*, ed. D. Scholl, A. Grantz, and J. Vedder. Circum-Pacific Council for Energy and Mineral Resources Earth Science Series, Vol. 6, 1987. Pp. 563ff.

Converse, D. R., H. D. Holland, and J. M. Edmond. "Flow Rates in the Axial Hot Springs of the East Pacific Rise (21 N): Implications for the Heat Budget and the Formation of Massive Sulfide Deposits." *Earth and Planetary Science Letters* 69 (1984): 159–75.

Corliss, John B. "The Dynamics of Creation: The Emergence of Living Systems in Archean Submarine Hot Springs." Unpublished monograph, 1988.

Corliss, John B. "The Origin of Metal-Bearing Submarine Hydrothermal Solutions." *Journal of Geophysical Research* 76 (1971): 8128–38.

Corliss, John B. "Submarine Hot Springs Again." *Origins of Life* 19 (1989): 534–35.

Corliss, John B. "The Thermal Springs of the Galapagos Rift: Their Implications for Biology and the Chemistry of Sea Water." *Patterns of Evolution in Galapagos Organisms*, ed. R. I. Bowman, M. Berson, and A. E. Leviton. San Francisco: AAAS, Pacific Division, 1983. Pp. 25–31.

Corliss, John B., and Robert D. Ballard. "Oases of Life in the Cold Abyss." *National Geographic* (1977): 441–53.

Corliss, John B., John A. Baross, and Sarah E. Hoffman. "An Hypothesis Concerning the Relationship Between Submarine Hot Springs and the Origin of Life on Earth." *Oceanologica Acta* 4 supplement (1981): 59–69.

Corliss, John B., et al. "Submarine Thermal Springs on the Galapagos Rift." *Science* 203 (1979): 1073–83.

Cox, Allan. Introduction to "Geomagnetic Magnetic Reversals: The Story on Land." *Plate Tectonics and Geomagnetic Reversals*, ed. Allan Cox. San Francisco: Freeman, 1973.

Cox, Allan, G. Brent Dalrymple, and Richard Doell. "Reversals of the Earth's Magnetic Field." *Scientific American* 216 (1967): 44–54.

Crane, Kathleen. "The Distribution of Geothermal Fields Along the Mid-Ocean Ridge: An Overview." Jones, *Hydrothermal Vents*: 3–19.

Curtis, Ruth L. "Sizing the Surplus." *Northwest Energy News*, March/April 1988: 3–6.

Davis, E. E., et al. "A New Look at the Juan de Fuca Ridge: High

Resolution Bathymetry and Side-scan Acoustic Imagery." *GEOS* 14 (1985): 10–15.

Delaney, John R. "The U.S. RIDGE Initiative." *RIDGE Events* 1 (1990): 1–2.

Delaney, John R., and Barbara A. Cosens. "Boiling and Metal Deposition in Submarine Hydrothermal Systems." *Marine Technology Society Journal* 16 (1982): 62–65.

Deming, J. W., et al. "Evidence for Intact Microorganisms in Superheated Smoker Fluids: Particulate DNA and Preliminary Results from a New *in situ* Incubator." *EOS* 70 (1989): 1163–64.

Detrick, R. S. "Introduction to the Seafloor Mapping Section." *Journal of Geophysical Research* 91 (1986): 3331–33.

Dietz, Robert S. "The Underwater Landscape." *Exploring the Ocean World: A History of Oceanography*, ed. C. P. Idyll. New York: Crowell, 1969. Pp. 22–41.

Dowler, M. J., and D. E. Ingmanson. "Thiocyanate in Red Sea Brine and Its Implications." *Nature* 279 (1979): 51–52.

Edmond, John M., and Karen Von Damm. "Hot Springs on the Ocean Floor." *Scientific American* 248 (1983): 78–93.

Edmond, John M., et al. "Ridge Crest Hydrothermal Activity and the Balances of the Major Elements in the Ocean: The Galapagos Data." *Earth and Planetary Science Letters* 46 (1979): 1–18.

Elder, J. W. "Physical Processes in Geothermal Areas." *Terrestrial Heat Flow*, ed. W. H. K. Lee. American Geophysical Union, Geophysical monograph series 8 (1965). Pp. 211–39.

Engebretson, D., A. Cox, and R. Gordon. "Relative Motions Between Ocean and Continental Plates in the Pacific Basin." Geological Society of America, 1985. Spec. Paper 206.

Felbeck, Horst. "Chemoautotrophic Potential of the Hydrothermal Vent Tube Worm, *Riftia pachyptila* Jones (Vestimentifera)." *Science* 213 (1981): 336–38.

Felbeck, Horst, et al. "Metabolic Adaptations of Hydrothermal Vent Animals." Jones, *Hydrothermal Vents*: 261–72.

Fisher, Arthur. "What Flips Earth's Field?" *Popular Science*, January 1988: 71ff.

Gass, Ian G. "Ophiolites." *Scientific American* 247 (1982): 122–31.

Golden, Frederic. "A Man with Titanic Vision." *Discover*, Jan. 1987: 50ff.

Halkyard, John, Rachel Haymon, and David Felix. "Potential Exploration and Development Plans for the Gorda Ridge Area," *Proposed Polymetallic Sulfide Minerals Lease Offering, Gorda Ridge Area: Draft*

Environmental Impact Statement. Reston, Va.: Minerals Management Serv., 1983. Pp. 515ff.

Hallam, Arthur. "Alfred Wegener and the Hypothesis of Continental Drift." *Continents Adrift and Continents Aground*, ed. J. T. Wilson. San Francisco: Freeman, 1976. Pp. 8–17. Reprinted from *Scientific American*, February 1975.

Hannington, M. D., J. M. Peter, and S. D. Scott. "Gold in Seafloor Polymetallic Sulfide Deposits." *Economic Geology* 81 (1986): 1867–83.

Heirtzler, J. R. "Sea-floor Spreading." *Continents Adrift*, ed. J. T. Wilson. San Francisco: Freeman, 1972. Pp. 68–78.

Heirtzler, J. R., and R. D. Ballard. "FAMOUS—Man's First Voyage down to the Mid-Atlantic Ridge." *National Geographic*, May 1975: 586–615.

Hersey, J. B. "A Chronicle of Man's Use of Ocean Acoustics." *Oceanus* 20 (Spring 1977): 9–21.

Hess, Harry H. "History of the Ocean Basins." *Petrologic Studies: A Volume in Honor of A. F. Buddington*, ed. A. E. J. Engel, H. L. James, and B. F. Leonard. New York: Geological Society of America, 1962. Pp. 599–620.

Holmes, Mark L., and Robert A. Zierenberg. "Submersible Observations in Escanaba Trough, Southern Gorda Ridge." McMurray: 93–116.

Jannasch, Holger W. "Microbial Processes at Deep-sea Hydrothermal Vents." *Hydrothermal Processes at Seafloor Spreading Centers*, ed. P. A. Rona et al. New York: Plenum, 1983. Pp. 677–709.

Jannasch, Holger W. "Chemosynthesis: The Nutritional Basis for Life at Deep-sea Vents." *Oceanus* 27 (1984): 73–78.

Johnson, H. Paul, and Verena Tunnicliffe. "Time-Series Measurements of Hydrothermal Activity on Northern Juan de Fuca Ridge." *Geophysical Research Letters* 12 (1985): 685–88.

Jones, Meredith L. "The Giant Tube Worms." *Oceanus* 27 (1984): 47–52.

Jones, Meredith L. "On the Vestimentifera, New Phylum: Six New Species, and Other Taxa, from Hydrothermal Vents and Elsewhere." Jones, *Hydrothermal Vents*: 117–58.

Koski, Randolph A., and Robert E. Derkey. "Massive Sulfide Deposits in Oceanic Crust and Island-Arc Terranes of Southwestern Oregon." *Oregon Geology* 43 (1981): 119–25.

LaFlamme, B., et al. "Observations and Experimental Studies in the Endeavour Hydrothermal Field—Summer 1988." *EOS* 70 (1989): 1160–61.

Lemke, J. L., M. H. Nitecki, and H. Pullman. "Studies of the Acceptance of Plate Tectonics." *Oceanography: The Past*, ed. Mary Sears and Daniel Merriman. New York: Springer-Verlag, 1980. Pp. 614–22.

Lister, C. R. B. "On the Thermal Balance of a Mid-ocean Ridge." *Geophysical Journal of the Royal Astronomical Society* 26 (1972): 515.

Lister, C. R. B. "On the Penetration of Water into Hot Rock." *Geophysical Journal of the Royal Astronomical Society* 39 (1974): 465–509.

Lupton, John E., and Kenneth C. Macdonald. "RIDGE: Event Detection and Response." Seattle: University of Washington, RIDGE Planning Office, 1989. RIDGE Meeting Report.

Macdonald, Ken C. "Anatomy of the Magma Reservoir." *Nature* 339 (1989): 178–79.

McKenzie, D. P., and R. L. Parker. "The North Pacific: An Example of Tectonics on a Sphere." *Nature* 216 (1967): 1276–80.

McLaughlin, Richard. "The Recent 'Confidential' Classification of NOAA Seafloor Maps and Its Effect on U.S. Marine Scientific Research Policy." *Water Log*, July–Sept. 1987: 3–8.

McVay, Scott. "In Appreciation of Harry Hammond Hess." *Princeton Alumni Weekly*, 28 Oct. 1969: 10ff.

Malahoff, Alexander. "Tectonic Setting of Gorda-Juan de Fuca Ridges: An Overview of the NOAA Program." *Marine Polymetallic Sulfides: A National Overview and Future Needs*. College Park, Md.: Maryland Sea Grant College, 1983. Pp. 69–80.

Malahoff, Alexander. "New Horizons for Deep Ocean Minerals." *Sea Technology* July 1983: 19ff.

Malahoff, Alexander. "Hydrothermal Vents and Polymetallic Sulfides of the Galapagos and Gorda/Juan de Fuca Ridge Systems and of Submarine Volcanoes." Jones, *Hydrothermal Vents*: 19–41.

Miller, Stanley L., and Jeffrey L. Bada. "Submarine Hot Springs and the Origin of Life." *Nature* 334 (1988): 609–11.

Merritt, J. I. "Hess's Geological Revolution." *Princeton Alumni Weekly*, 24 Sept. 1979: 10–15, 22.

Monastersky, Richard. "The Whole-Earth Syndrome." *Science News* 133 (1988): 378–80.

Moores, E. M., and F. J. Vine. "Alpine Serpentinites, Ultramafic Magmas, and Ocean-Basin Evolution: The Ideas of H. H. Hess." *Geological Society of America Bulletin* 100: 1205–12.

Morgan, W. J. "Rises, Trenches, Great Faults and Crustal Blocks." *Journal of Geophysical Research* 73 (1968): 1959–82.

Morton, Janet L., and Norman H. Sleep. "Seismic Reflections from a Lau Basin Magma Chamber." *Geology and Offshore Resources of Pacific Island*

Arcs—Tonga Region, ed. D. W. Scholl and T. L. Vallier. Houston: Circum-Pacific Council for Energy and Mineral Resources, 1985. Pp. 441–53.

NAUTILAU Group. "Hydrothermal Activity in the Lau Basin." *EOS* 71 (1990): 678–79.

Newman, William A. "The Abyssal Hydrothermal Vent Invertebrate Fauna: A Glimpse of Antiquity?" Jones, *Hydrothermal Vents*: 373–88.

Newman, William A. "A New Scalpellid (Cirripedia); a Mesozoic Relic Living Near an Abyssal Hydrothermal Spring." *Transactions of the San Diego Society of Natural History* 19 (1989): 153–67.

Normark, William R., et al. "Active Hydrothermal Vents and Sulfide Deposits on the Southern Juan de Fuca Ridge." *Geology* 11 (1983): 158–63.

Oregon State University, Department of Information. "OSU Oceanographer Reports on Trips to Atlantic Floor." News release, 4 Sept. 1975.

Oregon State University, Department of Information. "Sea Floor Hot Water Springs, Animals Found by Expedition." News release, 27 April 1977.

Perlman, David. "Astounding Undersea Discoveries," *San Francisco Chronicle*, 9 March 1977, p. 24; "Exploring the Ocean's Young Volcanoes," *San Francisco Chronicle*, 12 March 1977, p. 10; "Scientists' Fantastic Underwater Voyage," *San Francisco Chronicle*, 16 March 1977, p. 4.

Powell, Mark A., and George N. Somero. "Blood Components Prevent Sulfide Poisoning of Respiration of the Hydrothermal Vent Tube Worm *Riftia pachyptila*." *Science* 219 (1983): 297–99.

Ritchey, Joseph L., et al. "Economic Perspective on Development of Potential Gorda Ridge Sulfide Deposits." McMurray: 143–54.

Roberts, David G. "The Ocean Floor." *The Undersea*, ed. N.C. Flemming. New York: Macmillan, 1977. Pp. 22–45.

Rona, Peter A. "Hydrothermal Mineralization at Oceanic Ridges." *Canadian Mineralogist* 26 (1988): 431–65.

Rona, Peter A. "Mineral Deposits from Sea-Floor Hot Springs." *Scientific American* 254 (1986): 84–92.

Ryan, Paul R. "A Reader's Guide to Underwater Sound." *Oceanus* 20 (1977): 3–7.

Schmitt, Roman A. "A General Theory of Mass Extinctions in the Phanerozoic, II. A Brief Outline." *Lunar and Planetary Science* 21 (1990): 1087–88.

Shaw, Herbert R., and James G. Moore. "Magmatic Heat and the El Niño Cycle." *EOS* 69 (1988): 1553ff.

Shor, George C., Jr. "Underwater Acoustics in Marine Geology." *Oceanus* 20 (1977): 40–49.

Siwolop, Sana. "Flood, Typhoon, Tornado—And Drought." *Discover,* June 1983: 18–24.

Skinner, Brian J. "Submarine Volcanic Exhalations That Form Mineral Deposits: An Old Idea Now Proven Correct." *Hydrothermal Processes at Seafloor Spreading Centers.* New York: Plenum, 1983. Pp. 556–69.

Smith, J. B., B. R. Holt, and R. G. Paul. "Current Status of Leasing Proposals for the U.S. Exclusive Economic Zone." 17th Annual Offshore Technology Conference. Houston, 6–9 May 1985.

Smith, J. B. "Managing Nonenergy Marine Mineral Development—Genesis of a Program." Oceans 85 Conference. San Diego, 12–14 Nov. 1985.

Somero, George N. "Physiology and Biochemistry of the Hydrothermal Vent Animals." *Oceanus* 27 (1984): 67–72.

Spiess, Fred N. "Some Origins and Perspectives in Deep-ocean Instrumentation and Development." *Oceanography: The Past,* ed. Mary Sears and David Merriman. New York: Springer-Verlag, 1980. Pp. 226–39.

Spiess, Fred N., and Robert C. Tyce. "Marine Physical Laboratory Deep Tow Instrumentation System." La Jolla: Scripps Institution of Oceanography, 1973, Ref. 73–4.

Tunnicliffe, Verena. "Biogeography and Evolution of Hydrothermal Vent Fauna in the Eastern Pacific Ocean." *Proceedings of the Royal Society of London* 233B (1988): 347–66.

Tunnicliffe, Verena, S. K. Juniper, and M. E. deBurgh. "The Hydrothermal Vent Community on Axial Seamount, Juan de Fuca Ridge." Jones, *Hydrothermal Vents*: 453–64.

Turcotte, D. L. "Where Do We Stand on Core and Mantle Dynamics?" *EOS* 71 (1990): 468.

Tuttle, Jon H., and Holger W. Jannasch. "Microbial Utilization of Thiosulfate in the Deep Sea." *Limnology and Oceanography* 21 (1976): 607–701.

Vine, Allyn C. "The Birth of *Alvin.*" *Oceanus* 31 (1988): 10–16.

Vine, F. J., and D. H. Matthews. "Magnetic Anomalies over Oceanic Ridges." *Nature* 199 (1963): 947–49.

Vine, F. J., and J. Tuzo Wilson. "Magnetic Anomalies over a Young Ridge off Vancouver Island." *Science* 150 (1965): 485–89.

Walden, Barrie, and Albert Bradley. "Vent Sentry: An Autonomous Benthic Explorer." *RIDGE: Sea-going Experiments Workshop: Final Report.* Seattle: University of Washington, RIDGE Planning Office, 1989(?).

Waldrop, M. Mitchell. "Hot Springs and Marine Chemistry." *Mosaic*, July/August 1980: 8–14.

Waldrop, M. Mitchell. "How Do You Read from the Palimpsest of Life?" *Science* 246 (1989): 578–79.

Walker, George W., and Philip B. King. *Geologic Map of Oregon, U.S. Geological Survey, Misc. Geological Investigations Map I-595*. U.S. Geological Survey, 1969.

Wilson, J. T. "Conclusion." *Continents Adrift*, ed. J. T. Wilson. San Francisco: Freeman, 1972. Pp. 158–60.

Wilson, J. T. "Continental Drift." *Continents Adrift*: 41–56. Reprint of article originally published in *Scientific American* in 1963.

Wilson, J. T. "Convection Tectonics: Some Possible Effects upon the Earth's Surface of Flow from the Deep Mantle." *Canadian Journal of Earth Sciences* 25 (1988): 1199–1208.

Wilson, J. T. "The Movement of Continents." XIII General Assembly of IUGG. Berkeley, 1963.

Wilson, J. T. "A New Class of Faults and Their Bearing on Continental Drift." *Nature* 207 (1965): 343–47.

Wilson, J. T. "Preface." *Continents Adrift and Continents Aground*, ed. J. T. Wilson. San Francisco: Freeman, 1976. N.p.

Wilson, J. T. "Some Consequences of Expansion of the Earth." *Nature* 185 (1960): 880–82.

Wilson, Robert Dale. "Importance of Marine Mineral Development." *Proceedings: The Exclusive Economic Zone Symposium: Exploring the New Ocean Frontier*. U. S. Department of Commerce, 1986. Pp. 131ff.

Woese, Carl R. "Archaebacteria." *Scientific American* 244 (1981): 92–122.

Wolery, T. J., and N. H. Sleep. "Hydrothermal Circulation and Geochemical Flux at Mid-ocean Ridges." *Journal of Geology* 84 (1976): 249–75.

Interviewees

Dallas Abbott

Tjeerd van Andel

Christian Andreason

Robert Bailey

Edward Baker

Robert Ballard

John Baross

Robert Becker

Robert Bowman
Colleen Cavanaugh
David Clague
Robert Collier
John Corliss
John Craven
Herbert Curl
G. Brent Dalrymple
John Delaney
Jody Deming
Robert Duncan
Jack Dymond
Robert Embley
Richard Feeley
James Ferris
Christopher Fox
William Glen
James Franklin
Richard Grigg
Stephen Hammond
G. Ross Heath
Richard Hildreth
Lewis Hogan
Sarah Hoffman
Ralph Hollis
Mark Holmes
Donald Hussong
Holger Jannasch
Ian Jonasson
Meredith Jones
David Karl
George Keller
Paul Komar
LaVerne Kulm
Randall Koski
Brian Lewis
Clive Lister

Carlos Lopez
John Lupton
Mitchell Lyle
Russell McDuff
Gregory McMurray
Alexander Malahoff
Bruce Malfait
James Malone
Hugh Milburn
Charles Miller
James Moore
E. M. Moores
Janet Morton
William Newman
William Normark
David Perlman
Len Ramp
Michael Rampino
Peter Rona
Roman Schmitt
Robert Shapiro
George Somero
Verena Tunnicliffe
Frederick Vine
Robert Yonover

INDEX

The author would like to thank the following copyright holders for the privilege of quoting from their works:

Anderson, Don L., and Adam M. Dziewonski. "Seismic Tomography." *Scientific American*, October 1984. Copyright © by Scientific American, Inc. Used with permission.

Ballard, Robert. "The Jason Project." Copyright © 1990 by the National Geographic Society.

Boyle, Robert W. *Gold: History and Genesis of Deposits*. Copyright © 1987 by Van Nostrand Reinhold. Reprinted by permission.

Carey, S. W. *The Expanding Earth*. Copyright © 1976 by Elsevier Science Publishers.

Clancy, Tom. *The Hunt for Red October*. Copyright © 1984 by Jack Ryan Enterprises, Ltd. Permission granted by the U.S. Naval Institute.

Dewey, John. "Plate Tectonics." *Scientific American*, May 1972. Copyright © by Scientific American, Inc. Used with permission.

Hallam, Arthur. "Alfred Wegener and the Hypothesis of Continental Drift." *Scientific American*, February 1975. Copyright © by Scientific American, Inc. Used with permission.

Heirtzler, J. R., and W. B. Bryan. "The Floor of the Mid-Atlantic Rift." *Scientific American*, August 1975. Copyright © by Scientific American, Inc. Used with permission.

Heirtzler, J. R., and R. D. Ballard. "FAMOUS—Man's First Voyage Down to the Mid-Atlantic Ridge." *National Geographic* 147, pp. 586–615. Copyright © 1975 by the National Geographic Society. Used with permission.

Hess, Harry H. "History of Ocean Basins." In *Petrologic Studies: A volume in honor of A. F. Buddington*. Copyright © 1962 by the Geological Society of America. Used with permission of the Department of Geological and Geophysical Sciences, Princeton University.

Kuhn, Thomas S. *The Structure of Scientific Revolutions*. Copyright © 1970 by the University of Chicago Press.

Lemke, J. L. et al. "Studies in the Acceptance of Plate Tectonics." In *Oceanography: The Past*. Copyright © 1980 by Springer-Verlag. Used with permission of the author.

McVay, Scott. "In Appreciation of Harry Hammond Hess." Copyright © 1969 by Scott McVay.

Mernard, H. W. *The Ocean of Truth*. Copyright © 1986 by Princeton University Press.

Perlman, David. "Astounding Undersea Discoveries." *San Francisco Chronicle*, 9 March 1977. "Exploring the Ocean's Young Volcanos." *San Francisco Chronicle*, 12 March 1977. "Scientists' Fantastic Underwater Voyage." *San Francisco Chronicle*, 16 March 1977. Copyright © 1977 by the *San Francisco Chronicle*. Reprinted by permission.

Roberts, David G. "The Ocean Floor." In *The Undersea*. Copyright © 1977 by Macmillan Publishing Co.

Sullivan, Walter. *Continents in Motion: The New Earth Debate*. Copyright © 1974. Used with permission.

Sverdrup, H. U. et al. *The Oceans*. Copyright © 1942 by Prentice Hall.

Turcotte, D. L. "Where Do We Stand on Core and Mantle Dynamics?" *EOS*, Transactions of the American Geophysical Union, 1990, p. 468. Copyright © 1990 by the American Geophysical Union.

van Andel, Tjeerd. *Science at Sea: Tales of an Old Ocean*. Copyright © 1977, 1981 by Tjeerd van Andel. Reprinted with permission by W. H. Freeman and Co.

Vine, F. J., and D. H. Matthews. "Magnetic Anomalies over Oceanic Ridges." *Nature* 199, pp. 947–949. Copyright © 1963 by Macmillan Publishing Co.

Vine, F. J., and J. T. Wilson. "Magnetic Anomalies over a Young Ridge off Vancouver Island." *Science* 150, 22 October 1965, pp. 485–889. Copyright © 1965 by the American Association for the Advancement of Science.

Wegener, Alfred. *The Origin of Continents and Oceans*. Copyright © 1966 by E. P. Dutton Co. By permission of Jean Richardson, Routledge, London, England.

Wilson, J. T. "Convention Tectonics: Some Possible Effects upon the Earth's Surface of Flow from the Deep Mantle." *Canadian Journal of Earth Sciences* 25, pp. 1199–1208. Copyright © 1989 by the National Research Council Canada.

Wilson, J. T., "Preface" from *Continents Adrift and Continents Aground*. Copyright © 1976 by Scientific American, Inc. Reprinted with permission by W. H. Freeman and Co.

The author thanks the following photographers and sources for their cooperation (the photographs were taken on many separate occasions, and dates, when known, are indicated):

Front jacket: Photograph by R. Holcomb; courtesy of William Normark, U.S. Geological Survey.

Page 1
Top: Photograph by James R. Larison, 1988

A NOTE ABOUT
THE AUTHOR

JOSEPH CONE is a graduate of Yale and the University of Oregon. He has been writing about science and the environment since 1978, and is currently the science writer with Oregon Sea Grant, a marine research and education program based at Oregon State University. His feature articles have appeared in magazines such as *Sierra* and *Oceans*, and he has written film scripts for the National Geographic Society. He lives in Eugene, Oregon.